The New Prophecy & "New Visions"

North American Patristic Society
Patristic Monograph Series
Volume 18

SERIES EDITOR
Philip Rousseau
The Catholic University of America

The New Prophecy & "New Visions"

EVIDENCE OF MONTANISM IN

The Passion of Perpetua and Felicitas

Rex D. Butler

The Catholic University of America Press

Washington, D.C.

The paper used in this publication meets the minimum requirements of American
National Standards for Information Science—Permanence of Paper for Printed
Library materials, ANSI Z 39.48-1984.
∞

LIBRARY OF CONGRESS CATALOGING-IN-PUBLICATION DATA
Butler, Rex D., 1952–
The new prophecy and new visions : evidence of Montanism in
The Passion of Perpetua and Felicitas.
p. cm. — (Patristic monograph series ; v. 18)
Includes bibliographical references (p.   ) and index.
ISBN-13: 978-0-8132-1455-9 (cloth : alk. paper)
ISBN-10: 0-8132-1455-6 (cloth : alk. paper)
1. Passio SS. Perpetuae et Felicitatis.   2. Montanism.   3. Perpetua, Saint, d. 203.
4. Felicity, Saint, d. 203.   5. Christian saints—Tunisia—Biography—
History and criticism.   6. Christian martyrs—Tunisia—
Biography—History and criticism.   I. Title.   II. Series: Patristic
monography series ; no. 18.
BR1720.P42P2733 2006
272′.10922—dc22
2005024499

To all my professors, especially
Paul Sadler
Jim Spivey,
Bob Williams,
and to Bill Tabbernee.

Contents

Preface & Acknowledgments

Out of the early third-century, during a time of persecution of Christians in North Africa, came an account of joyful suffering and victorious martyrdom, *The Passion of Perpetua and Felicitas.* Included in this document were two prison diaries, written by a catechumen Perpetua and her teacher Saturus, as well as the editor's eyewitness report of their execution alongside several comrades. The unnamed editor preserved these accounts, correctly predicting that "in the future, these things also will be ancient and necessary for coming generations" (*The Passion of Perpetua and Felicitas* 1.2).

Eighteen centuries later, the study of the *Passion* is indeed necessary, for it contains both inspiration for Christians today and information about the Christian church in the early centuries. By reading the *Passion*, the contemporary reader gains insight into the theology of martyrdom in the early church; an intimate look into Perpetua's diary, the earliest extant writing known to be by a Christian woman; a sampling of the sacred works considered authoritative and beneficial during that period; a glimpse of the ecclesiastical structure of the early third-century Carthaginian church; not to mention the thrill of an exciting story about Christian martyrs. During my research for this project, I found all of these benefits and more, but the central purpose for my study was to examine the evidence that those who composed the *Passion* and participated in its events were associated with the early Christian movement known as Montanism.

In the fall of 1999, while conducting research for a biographical sketch of Tertullian, I first became aware of his possible connection to the *Passion*. Then, as I studied the *Passion*, I discovered characteristics of Montanism, which further tied these acts to the Carthaginian teacher. When it came time to consider a topic for my dissertation, I realized that the *Passion* included many themes that I enjoy researching, such as persecution of Christians, women in the church, Spirit-based movements, and the patristic period of Christianity. Furthermore, the relationship of the *Passion* to Montanism, although often discussed, has never received exhaustive investigation and has been minimized by recent scholars. Therefore, I chose to examine the *Passion* for evidence of Montanism and to explore its relationship to that movement, to the early church, and to Tertullian.

Following the completion of my dissertation, I had the privilege of meeting Dr. William Tabbernee, President of Phillips Theological Seminary, Tulsa, Oklahoma, and probably the eminent expert on Montanism in the world today. He graciously offered to read my dissertation, and then he recommended it for publication. Furthermore, Dr. Tabbernee made extensive suggestions for the improvement of my work, and I am very grateful for his support and encouragement.

As a student, I must acknowledge the contributions of all my professors, who shared themselves as well as their knowledge with me. I especially want to mention Dr. Paul Sadler of Wayland Baptist University, who first inspired me to pursue the study of Church History; Dr. James T. Spivey, Jr., who was my major professor at Southwestern Baptist Theological Seminary, allowed me to serve as his teaching assistant and supervised my dissertation; and Dr. Robert L. Williams, also of Southwestern Seminary, who has continued to encourage me in my pursuit of scholarship.

Next, I want to pay tribute to my family for their unfailing support through these many years. The most important people in my life are my wife, Margie, and my sons, David and Truett. They make my life sweet, rich, and joyous. They are my daily support and sustenance, without whom I hardly could survive and certainly could not fulfill my call to ministry.

A special word of thanks is due to Dr. Philip Rousseau, editor of the North American Patristics Society Monograph Series, for giving me this opportunity and to his staff for their assistance. Susan Needham Barnes, in particular, improved my work considerably with her keen eye and attention to details. I express my appreciation to all those who read portions or all of the manuscript and made suggestions to improve it, and I retain all the blame for any remaining faults.

I am grateful for the opportunities that I have had to study under godly men and women and now to instruct the next generations concerning our rich heritage in the Christian church. Truly, "God always performs what he promises, for a testimony to non-believers, for a benefit to believers" *(The Passion of Perpetua and Felicitas 1.5)*.

Abbreviations

Ancient texts

Acts Cyp.	*Acts of Cyprian*
Apoc. Pet.	*Apocalypse of Peter*
Asc. Isa.	*Ascensio Isaiae (Ascension of Isaiah)*

Augustine

Exp. Gal.	*Expositionis epistolae ad Galatas (Commentary on the Letter to the Galatians)*
Haer.	*De haeresibus (The Heresies)*
Nat. orig.	*De anima et ejus origine (The Nature and Origin of the Soul)*
Serm.	*Sermo / Sermones (Sermon / Sermons)*

Barn.	*Epistle of Barnabas*

Basil

Ep.	*Epistola (Letter)*

Clement of Alexandria

Strom.	*Stromata (Miscellanies)*

Cyprian

Ep.	*Epistola (Letter)*

Cyril of Jerusalem

Cat.   *Catecheses (Catechetical Lectures)*

Did.   *Didache*

Epiphanius

Haer.   *Panarion/Adversus Haereses*

Eusebius of Caesarea

Hist. Eccl.   *Ecclesiasticae Historiae (History of the Church)*

Gos. Thom.   *Gospel of Thomas*

Herm.   *Shepherd of Hermas*
  Vis.   *Vision*
  Rev.   *Revelation*
  Mand.   *Mandate*
  Sim.   *Similitude*

Hippolytus

Haer.   *Refutatio omnium haeresium (Refutation of All Heresies)*
Trad.   *Traditio apostolica (The Apostolic Tradition)*

Homer

Od.   *Odyssey*

Ignatius

Phld.   *Letter to the Philadelphians*

Irenaeus

Haer.   *Adversus haereses (Against Heresies)*
Frag.   *Fragments from the Lost Writings of Irenaeus*

Jerome

Ep.	*Epistola (Letter)*
Vir. ill.	*De viris illustribus (Lives of Illustrious Men)*
Mart. Lyons	*The Letter of the Churches of Lyons and Vienne*
Mart. Mar. & Jam.	*The Martyrdom of Marian and James*
Mart. Mont. & Luc.	*The Martyrdom of Montanus and Lucius*
Mart. Pol.	*Martyrdom of Polycarp*
Mart. Scill.	*Acts of the Scillitan Martyrs*

Origen

Or.	*De oratione (On Prayer)*

Pontius

Vita Cyp.	*Vita Cypriani (Life of Cyprian)*

Praedestinatus

Haer.	*Praedestinatorum Haeresis*

Pseudo-Tertullian

Haer.	*Adversus omnes haereses (Against All Heresies)*
T. Abr.	*Testament of Abraham*

Tertullian

An.	*De anima (Treatise on the Soul)*
Apol.	*Apologeticum (Apology)*
Bapt.	*De baptismo (On Baptism)*
Cor.	*De corona (The Chaplet)*
Cult. fem.	*De cultu feminarum (On the Apparel of Women)*
Exh. cast.	*De exhortatione castitatis (On Exhortation to Chastity)*
Fug.	*De fuga in persecutione (Flight in Time of Persecution)*
Jejun.	*De jejunio adversus psychicos (On Fasting)*

Marc.	*Adversus Marcionem (Against Marcion)*
Mart.	*Ad martyras (To the Martyrs)*
Mon.	*De monogamia (On Monogamy)*
Or.	*De oratione (On Prayer)*

Tertullian (continued)

Paen.	*De paenitentia (On Repentance)*
Pat.	*De patientia (On Patience)*
Prax.	*Adversus Praxean (Against Praxeas)*
Pud.	*De pudicitia (On Modesty)*
Res.	*De resurrectione carnis (On the Resurrection of the Flesh)*
Scap.	*Ad Scapulam (To Scapula)*
Scorp.	*Scorpiace*
Spect.	*De spectaculis (Spectacles, or The Shows)*
Ux.	*Ad uxorem (To His Wife)*
Virg.	*De virginibus velandis (On the Veiling of the Virgins)*

Theophilus of Antioch

| *Autol.* | *Ad Autolycum (To Autolycus)* |

Virgil

| *Aen.* | *Aeneid* |

Series

ANF	Ante-Nicene Fathers
CCSL	Corpus Christianorum Series Latina
FOTC	Fathers of the Church
NPNF	Nicene and Post-Nicene Fathers
PL	Patrologia Latina
WSA	The Works of Saint Augustine: A Translation for the 21st Century

Periodicals

Ant. Chr.	*Antike und Christentum*
BJRL	*Bulletin of the John Rylands Library*
Ch. Hist.	*Church History*
JECS	*Journal of Early Christian Studies*
JEH	*Journal of Ecclesiastical History*
JTS	*Journal of Theological Studies*
Sec. Cent.	*The Second Century*
Stud. Pat.	*Studia Patristica*
Theol. Stud.	*Theological Studies*
Vig. Chr.	*Vigiliae Christianae*

The New Prophecy & "New Visions"

Introduction

IN THE LATE SECOND AND EARLY THIRD centuries, persecution against Christians erupted throughout the Roman Empire[1] as a result of either an imperial edict or localized legislation and pogroms.[2] The persecution in Carthage led to the arrest of several young catechumens and their teacher.[3] Ultimately, five of these Christians were martyred during public games held on 7 March 203.[4]

Their story was preserved in a narrative, *The Passion of Perpetua and Felicitas*, remarkable for several features. First, embedded in the account were diaries of two martyrs, who recorded their sufferings and joys amid persecution. Second, Perpetua's diary, preserved in the *Passion*, is the earliest Christian document known to be written by a woman. Third, the diaries included several visions, received by the martyrs in prison, which foreshadowed their immediate future and mirrored their eschatological expectations. Fourth, an unnamed editor assimilated the diaries with an eyewitness account of the martyrs' deaths. Finally, the editor and the martyrs exhibited possible evidence of Montanism, a movement that had gained adherents throughout the church during the previous half-century.[5]

This last feature is very intriguing to patristic historians, for, due to Catholic zeal against Montanism, few Montanist writings survived the early centuries of the church. The Montanistic character of the *Passion*, however, is not universally accepted among its commentators. Varying responses among historians include denial of any influence of Montanism in the account, acceptance of Montanism in only the editor, and affirmation of Montanism as the essential basis for the work.

The purpose of this work, therefore, is to examine the evidence that the *Passion* evinced Montanist influence throughout all its sections, which include the preface, Perpetua's diary, Saturus' vision, and the account of their martyrdom. Imbedded in the narratives, visions, and editorial framework was much of the Montanist matrix: prophecy, women's authority, eschatological expectation, rigorism, and exaltation of martyrdom. Furthermore, this thesis is supported by a detailed examination of Montanism and the *Passion* and its related issues, such as authorship, including the possibility that Tertullian was the editor; comparison among various translations and with other accounts of martyrs; and interaction with the document by the patristic church.

Brief Survey of Relevant Research

The only complete Latin manuscript of the *Passion* was discovered in 1661 in the Benedictine Monastery at Monte Cassino by Lucas Holstenius,[6] who died before it could be published. In 1663, that task was accomplished in Rome by P. Poussin, who added his notes to Holstenius'. In the next year at Paris, Henri de Valois reprinted the text with a preface in which he discussed the date and place of the martyrdom. Through the seventeenth century, other reprints followed, aided by subsequently discovered texts,[7] but the next major contribution occurred in 1889, when Rendel Harris unearthed a complete Greek text of the *Passion* in the Convent of the Holy Sepulchre in Jerusalem. When Harris, along with Seth K. Gifford, published both the Greek and Latin texts the next year, he argued for the priority of the Greek over the Latin text.[8] The next year, J. Armitage Robinson produced his work on the *Passion* complete with parallel Latin and Greek texts and a thorough introduction.[9] With painstaking attention to linguistic details, Robinson proved, even to Harris' satisfaction, that the Carthaginians' martyrdom was reported originally in Latin.[10] In 1936, C. J. M. J. van Beek provided the next edition of the *Passion*,[11] which was the definitive work[12] until 1996, when Jacqueline Amat published her critical edition.[13]

As early as 1664, de Valois recognized Montanist overtones in the editor of the *Passion*, who possibly was Tertullian, but, in 1689, Theodoric Ruinart, a Maurist monk, insisted on the editor's catholicity.[14] In 1706, Samuel Basnage, a Dutch Reformed minister, argued that not only the editor but also the martyrs were Montanist,[15] and, in response, Cardinal Giuseppe Agostino Orsi defended the orthodoxy of the martyrs.[16] Since the nineteenth century, opinions expressed in general church histories were divided predominantly along partisan lines: Catholics contended for the martyrs' orthodoxy,[17] and Protestants, for their adherence to Montanism.[18] According to James C. Robertson, an Anglican, "The Roman writers are concerned to maintain the catholicity of Perpetua and Felicitas because they are commemorated in the canon of the mass."[19] Indeed, Catholic historians who did not deny a Montanist editor were careful to claim the martyrs for orthodoxy. For example, Jean Daniélou and Henri Marrou saw a "marked Montanist outlook" in the *Passion* but attributed the taint to Tertullian's biased effort "to glorify the ideal of martyrdom."[20]

Historical surveys, of course, gave only glancing attention to the *Passion*. Monographs on subjects such as Montanism, Tertullian, martyrdom, and the *Passion* itself dealt more fully with its character. In 1878, John de Soyres contributed *Montanism and the Primitive Church*, in which he connected the martyrs with Montanism.[21]

Nathanael Bonwetsch added *Die Geschichte des Montanismus* in 1881, admitting no direct connection but seeing in their visions a relationship between the martyrs and Montanism.[22] Pierre de Labriolle, a Catholic authority on Montanism, provided a history and a source book in 1913. De Labriolle found in the visions no special Montanist phenomena but identified the editor as the Montanist Tertullian.[23] In his source book, therefore, he included the prologue but none of the visions of the *Passion.*[24]

After de Soyres, the next published English monograph on Montanism was written by Christine Trevett in 1996. Although guarded in her assertions, she maintained the probability that the martyrs were Montanists.[25] Two other recent additions to Montanist scholarship were source books compiled by Ronald Heine and by William Tabbernee. Following de Labriolle, Heine included the prologue but not the diaries of the *Passion,* implying his recognition of only the editor as a Montanist.[26] Tabbernee, noting the ambiguity of the data, acknowledged the likelihood that the editor belonged to a Montanist group but, concerning Perpetua and Saturus, conceded only the probability that they were sympathetic to the teachings of Montanism while they remained in the Catholic Church.[27]

During the last fifty years, works on other subjects related to the *Passion* contributed to the debate over its character. In *The Donatist Church,* W. H. C. Frend presented the *Passion* as representative of Montanism, a forerunner to the Donatist movement.[28] In 1971, Timothy David Barnes published his study of Tertullian, in which he stated, "The theological character of the *Passion* is Montanist through and through."[29] Some years later, however, he reversed himself, pronouncing his arguments unconvincing.[30] William C. Weinrich in *Spirit and Martyrdom* argued against Montanism in either the editor or the martyrs. He recognized in the *Passion* an emphasis upon the Spirit in revelation and empowerment but denied any relationship to similar Montanist tenets.[31] Cecil M. Robeck, Jr., gave close attention to the *Passion* as one representative of prophecy in third-century Carthage. After reviewing the debate on Montanism as a possible background to the *Passion*, he sided with Weinrich that the martyrs were orthodox Christians. Unlike Weinrich, however, Robeck took no stand on the editor's relationship to Montanism.[32]

Recently, Perpetua attracted the attention of feminist writers. In *Women and the Authority of Inspiration*, Elaine Huber examined Perpetua as an example of the prophetic Montanist movement.[33] On the other hand, Rosemary Rader, who translated and introduced the *Passion* in *A Lost Tradition: Women Writers of the Early Church*, saw no definite proof of Perpetua's affiliation with the movement.[34] Similarly, Joyce Salisbury, in a monograph on the literary character of Perpetua's diary, minimized any influence of Montanism upon the *Passion*.[35] Furthermore, Maureen Tilley, in a contribution to *A Feminist Commentary*, the second volume of *Searching the Scriptures*, contended that the "whole question of the orthodoxy of the *Passion* is nothing but a covert attack on women's wisdom."[36]

Many other recent essays and journal articles focused on women's issues raised by Perpetua.[37] Additional examinations of the *Passion* emphasized its literary importance,[38] historical context,[39] socio-political resistance,[40] early views of heaven,[41] and psychoanalysis of its dreams.[42] These writings discussed Montanism only tangentially if at all.

Only three dissertations of the past twenty years dealt substantially with the *Passion*. Zaida Maldonado-Pérez made the most recent contribution with "The Subversive Dimensions of the Visions of the Martyrs of the Roman Empire of the Second through Early Fourth Centuries." This dissertation, submitted to the Jesuit Saint Louis University, examined visions from the entire *Acts of the Mar-*

tyrs but highlighted Perpetua's and Saturus' visions. Maldonado-Pérez paid scant attention to Montanism, insisting, "Emphasis on the Montanist status of the work has served to demean Perpetua's role, and to cloud other arguments that might better elucidate our understanding of the text."[43]

The other two dissertations, which were published, have already been mentioned: Elaine Claire Huber, "Women and the Authority of Inspiration: A Reexamination of Two Prophetic Movements from a Christian Feminist Perspective";[44] and Cecil M. Robeck, Jr., "The Role and Function of Prophetic Gifts for the Church at Carthage, AD 202–258."[45] Of the two, the latter is more important for the present project. Robeck chose his topic not only as a historian but also as a Pentecostal interested in the use of spiritual gifts in the early church, specifically in the *Passion* and in the writings of Tertullian and Cyprian. He gave close attention to the influences behind the visions in the *Passion* but denied any evidence of Montanism, which he identified as heterodox.[46] Robeck's insistence on the catholicity of Perpetua's and Saturus' activities served his stated purpose to promote acceptance of his Pentecostal tradition in the current religious mainstream.[47]

Method of Study

The Latin and Greek texts of the *Passion* are available in editions by J. Armitage Robinson, C. J. M. J. van Beek, and Jacqueline Amat, and the latter two also include the shorter Latin *Acts of Perpetua and Felicitas*. Several English translations are available by R. E. Wallis,[48] E. C. E. Owen,[49] W. H. Shewring,[50] Herbert Musurillo,[51] and Rosemary Rader.[52]

Other primary sources are investigated to compare the *Passion* with Montanist teachings and with Tertullian's writings and to identify the influential resources used in the martyrs' catechism.

Montanist teachings are gleaned from the source books compiled by de Labriolle, Heine, and Tabbernee as well as from two fourth-century works: Eusebius' *Historia Ecclesiastica*[53] and Epiphanius' *Adversus Haereses* (also known as *Panarion*).[54] Tertullian's works are available in English in The Ante-Nicene Fathers[55] and in a variety of other translations[56] and in Latin in *Quinti Septimi Florentis Tertulliani Opera*, Corpus Christianorum Series Latina.[57] Catechetical resources include *The Ascension of Isaiah*,[58] *The Epistle of Barnabas*,[59] *The Ezra-Apocalypse*,[60] *The Shepherd of Hermas*,[61] and *The Revelation of Peter*.[62]

Scholars who deny that the *Passion* is a Montanist document often argue that it contains no distinctly Montanist features not found in other martyrs' accounts. To counter that argument, this project investigates such accounts as the *Martyrdom of Polycarp*, the letter of the churches of Lyons and Vienne, the *Acts of the Scillitan Martyrs*, the *Acts of Cyprian*, the *Martyrdom of Marian and James*, and the *Martyrdom of Montanus and Lucius*, which are included in the compilations by Musurillo and Owen. Augustine's references to Perpetua and Felicitas are also claimed as proof of the martyrs' orthodoxy; it was therefore necessary to research his sermons and writings.[63] The majority of these primary sources were written originally in Greek or Latin, but most are now available in English translations. Unless indicated otherwise, quotations of Latin sources cited in this book are from published translations, which will be indicated in the endnotes. The quotations from Greek sources, however, are translated by the author unless indicated otherwise.

The abundance of secondary resources attests to the importance of the *Passion* to the church. Sources from the seventeenth and eighteenth centuries are not readily available, but many nineteenth-century and early twentieth-century works were used. Many monographs, essays, journal articles, and dissertations also contributed to the research for this book.

Chapter one presents a brief history of Montanism, followed by a discussion of its message and practice. The important features of Montanism included emphasis upon the Holy Spirit and spiritual gifts, especially ecstatic prophecy; activity of women in a Spirit-based movement; eschatological expectations; rigorous discipline; and glorification of martyrdom. This chapter establishes criteria for identifying Montanism in any document, especially the *Passion*.

Chapter two addresses two issues of authorship in the *Passion*. The first is the authenticity of the diaries, and the second is the editor's identity.

The centerpiece of this project is chapter three, which analyzes the *Passion*. Each section is examined for evidence of Montanism: the preface; Perpetua's diary, including her encounters with her father and her visions; Saturus' vision; and the account of the martyrdom with its conclusion. Because the Montanists of Carthage in 203 maintained fellowship with Catholic Christians in the context of house churches, the authors of the *Passion* drew not only from Montanist sources but also from the broader Christian context. Chapter three, therefore, explores both Montanist and orthodox influences. A thematic review summarizes the findings of the chapter.

Chapter four places the *Passion* in literary and historical context and thus answers many objections to its classification as a Montanist document. First, later translations and editions that erased evidence of Montanism are discussed. Second, acceptance of Perpetua and Felicitas as orthodox saints and their subsequent praise in Augustine's sermons and other writings are investigated. Third, the *Passion* is compared to other acts of martyrs to demonstrate its uniqueness.

Finally, the conclusion summarizes the evidence that the *Passion* is a Montanist document. This chapter also evaluates the *Passion* for its significance to the church in understanding this important period of Christian history.

CHAPTER ONE

Montanism

MONTANISM received its name from its founder, Montanus, but not until the fourth century, when Cyril of Jerusalem (c. 315–86) used the term Montanists (τοὺς Μοντανοὺς) to deny their claims to be Christians.[1] At first, Montanus' detractors called his followers Cataphrygians (οἵ κατὰ Φρύγας, Latin, *cataphryges*), designating the geographical foundation of the movement.[2] The Montanists themselves, however, described their movement as the New Prophecy,[3] or simply the Prophecy,[4] and themselves as prophets or prophetesses.[5]

Other epithets assigned to the Montanists were: Priscillianists and Quintillianists, referring to other, female leaders in the movement; and Pepuzites, derived from a key city in Montanist prophecy. The various names assigned to them reveal some information about Montanists, namely a few of their early leaders and important bases for their movement. Their own name for themselves, New Prophecy, expresses the message they wanted to present about a new, fresh word to the larger movement of Christianity. Besides the leaders, location, and message, other data necessary for understanding Montanism and determining criteria for its identification are its dates of origin, character, practices, and spread from Asia to the West.

Brief History

Origin in Asia Minor

The origins of Montanism were obscured by its antiquity and its opponents. Consequently, its history must be pieced together by both research and conjecture. The elements examined in this section are the leaders of the New Prophecy, their geographical location, and the dating and purpose of their ministry.

Leaders. Very little can be ascertained about Montanus except that he lived in Phrygia during the second century, taught a new revelation, laid claim to prophetic powers, and gathered many disciples, including women.[6] The little information which the early church preserved about Montanus was generated by his opponents, so details were tainted by hostility, speculation, or late interpolation.

Jerome (c. 342–420) described Montanus as "mutilated and emasculate *(abscisum et semivirum),*" indicating Jerome's belief that Montanus formerly served as a priest of Cybele.[7] Eusebius' anonymous source alleged that, even though a recent convert, the ambitious prophet employed spiritual ecstasy, glossolalia, and prophecy to gain attention and a following. A particularly sordid rumor, comparing Montanus to Judas, claimed that he hanged himself.[8]

Montanus quickly attracted disciples, such as Maximilla and Priscilla, who provided much of the prophetic activity of the movement. The new prophets insisted that these women, following Quadratus and Ammia of Philadelphia, succeeded to the gift of Agabus, Judas, Silas, and Philip's daughters.[9] According to Jerome and Apollonius, another of Eusebius' sources, Priscilla and Maximilla were "rich and high born ladies," who left their husbands to follow Montanus and the New Prophecy.[10] As missionaries, Maximilla was active in Phrygia, including the village Koumana, and Priscilla proclaimed her message at Black Sea ports in Thrace.[11] The two women were not spiritually dependent upon Montanus but contributed equally in the prophetic activity while he not only prophesied but also organized and promoted the movement.[12]

Montanus, Priscilla, and Maximilla formed the trio most closely identified with the New Prophecy in the early decades, but other leaders were important as well. Another female prophet, Quintilla, was credited with spectacular visions. Eventually she spawned a faction within Montanism, the Quintillianists, who placed her among the founders of the New Prophecy.[13] Theodotus was identified as the financial officer ($\dot{\epsilon}\pi\dot{\iota}\tau\rho\sigma\pi\sigma\varsigma$) to whom leadership passed after Montanus. Eusebius' anonymous source repeated the gossip that Theodotus died miserably when, in a trance, he was raised up and taken into heaven, having entrusted himself to a deceitful spirit, and was hurled to the ground.[14] Themiso hindered an attempt to exorcize Maximilla and, outliving the others, assumed leadership after Theodotus' death.[15] He and Alexander gained prestige as confessors released from prison. Alexander exercised the power of the keys to bind and loose sins. With his authority, Themiso wrote a general epistle advocating the principles of the New Prophecy.[16]

Location. The geographical hub of Montanist activity was Phrygia, a region in southwestern Asia Minor. The most significant places named by the historians of the New Prophecy were Ardabau, Pepuza, and Tymion. Eusebius' anonymous source identified Ardabau, near the Phrygian border with Mysia, as the site where Montanus experienced his original ecstatic prophecies. Pepuza and

Tymion, prominent in the prophecies of Christ's return, were re-named Jerusalem by Montanus, allegedly to gather his followers into one place.[17] The exact location of these sites, indeed their actual existence, has been difficult to ascertain until recently.

Heinz Kraft connected Montanus' prophecy about Pepuza and Tymion with Revelation 21.10: "And in the spirit he carried me away to a great, high mountain and showed me the holy city Jerusalem coming down out of heaven from God" (NRSV). Therefore, according to Kraft, these towns were located on two sides of a mountain.[18]

Due to the association of that region with the seven churches of Revelation, Christine Trevett suggested that Pepuza and Tymion were located east of Philadelphia. To the Philadelphian overcomer, John the Revelator had promised to write on him "the name of the city of my God, the new Jerusalem that comes down from my God out of heaven" (Rev. 3.12 NRSV).[19] Furthermore, Philadelphia had been home to the prophetess Ammia, who figured in the line of prophetic succession to which the new prophets appealed. To escape the earthquakes of Philadelphia, the faithful had moved to the east to continue their study, to maintain their eschatological hope, and to commune with the Lord through prophecy. For Trevett, this region provided a likely locus for the Montanists' work.[20]

Recently, however, William Tabbernee published the results of his search for Pepuza (Pepouza) and Tymion, which he located more specifically about eighty-five kilometers east of Philadelphia (Philadelpheia) in West Central Phrygia.[21] He placed Pepuza in the Ulubey Canyon near Karayakuplu and Tymion due north near Susuzören. Several key proofs convinced him of his conclusion: the discovery of an inscription that contains the name Tymion; the location of the two sites in close proximity; the existence of an ancient, previously undiscovered site near Karayakuplu; and the dis-

covery of a Byzantine monastery in that region.[22] Two other significant evidences became clear as Tabbernee looked out over the sites
of Pepuza and Tymion from a nearby summit. First, he realized that
Montanus gave the name "Jerusalem" to both Pepuza and Tymion
not "because they were geographically adjacent settlements at either side of the foot of a mountain, but because they marked the
northern and southern limits of the geographic area where he expected the 'New Jerusalem' to descend out of heaven."[23] Second,
from the summit of the nearby mountain Ömerçali, he observed
that the topography and size of these sites formed "the ideal 'landing place' for the New Jerusalem. It was flat enough, level enough,
and large enough to accommodate the dimensions of the New Jerusalem as described in Revelation 21."[24]

For the identification of the other significant Montanist site,
Ardabau, Trevett looked to the Jewish apocalyptic writing 4 Ezra
(=2 Esdras). Translated into Latin and expanded by Christians, 4
Ezra offered several parallels to the New Prophecy: a vision of
Christ in female form, the descent of the promised Jerusalem, and
ascetic practices. Fourth Ezra prophesied the coming of a vast, rich
city, founded upon a verdant field, which could be reached only by
traversing a narrow, precipitous path fraught with danger.[25] The
name of the proposed site was Ardat, but variants included "Ardab"
and "Ardaf."[26] Trevett suggested that Montanus heard in the name
Ardabau an echo of the promised land. Possibly, he awarded the
name to the place where his revelations came, as they had come to
Ezra. The topography described in 4 Ezra resembled the Phrygian
terrain: difficult ascents and wide plains. Ardabau, real or symbolic,
was for Montanus an isolated, sparsely populated spot where he
first envisioned the New Prophecy.[27]

The significant sites of Montanist oracles most likely were in
Phrygia, east of Philadelphia. Historically, this region had a tradi-

tion of apocalyptic expectation derived from the Johannine tradition delivered to the seven churches. The movement engendered by these prophesies, however, was not limited to a region but spread throughout the Mediterranean basin in a very short time.

Date. Dating Montanist origins is a challenge due to the contradiction of two sources. Eusebius placed the beginning of Montanus' prophesying in the middle of Marcus Aurelius' reign (161–80), about 171, and the spread of the movement from 177.[28] Epiphanius, however, dated the origins of Montanism nineteen years after Antoninus Pius (138–61) became emperor, that is, 157.[29]

In an attempt at harmonization, R. A. Knox suggested that Epiphanius recorded the beginning of Montanus' prophetic activity in 157 and that Eusebius referred to the diffusion of the movement during the 170s.[30] Timothy David Barnes, however, shunned such a compromise. Instead, he examined the two early historians' statements, disapproved Epiphanius' dating, and supported Eusebius' assertion that Montanism originated about 170.[31] However, the presence of Montanist ideas in the West at least by 177 indicated to other scholars an earlier date.[32] For this reason, Frederick C. Klawiter, although he doubted Epiphanius, rejected Eusebius as well and opted for a date around 165.[33] The known facts about early Montanism indicate an earlier rather than a later date. Most likely, Montanus began prophesying in 157, and the movement spread to Rome by 171.

Character. The study of the character of Montanism concerns its origins and purposes. Examinations into its character can be organized under three rubrics: reclamation of primitive Christianity, heterodox sectarianism, and synthesis with the Phrygian cult of Attis-Cybele.[34]

Montanus' activity in Phrygia, as well as his alleged priesthood in the cult of Attis-Cybele, led Augustus Neander to speculate that the native Phrygian religion influenced the New Prophecy.[35] According to William Ramsay, Montanists tended to "Phrygianise their beliefs," which meant not only that Phrygia was the geographical center of their faith but also that the enthusiasm and involvement of women, typical of the Cybelene cult, shaped their religion.[36]

In an extensive comparative work, Wilhelm Schepelern uncovered four significant parallels between Montanism and the Phrygian cult.[37] First, the Phrygian ritual tattooing with red hot needles corresponded to the practice of a Montanist faction, the Tascodrougites, who reportedly pricked infants with bronze needles and used the blood in their initiation into Christ. Schepelern suggested that Montanists may have adopted Phrygian religious tattooing as part of their baptismal rite.[38] Second, Montanists known as Artotyrites celebrated the Eucharist with bread and cheese, a practice which Schepelern viewed as a possible carryover from the sacrifice to Cybele, the Magna Mater of Asia Minor, who protected agriculture and livestock.[39] Third, Schepelern compared Montanist and Cybelene virgins. Seven virgins of the Quintillian faction, dressed in white and carrying torches, inspired their congregation to penitence with weeping. For Schepelern, these virgins, grieving for Christ's suffering, recalled the Cybelene virgins who mourned the passing of Attis during their spring festival.[40] Finally, Schepelern compared women's inclusion among Montanist clergy with the high place awarded women in the Cybelene cult.[41]

Despite similarities in rituals, Schepelern decided that Montanism differed from the Phrygian cult at the significant point of penitence. Whereas the Cybelene priest had authority to forgive sin, Montanist rigorism denied forgiveness. Therefore, early Montanism did not originate from the Phrygian religion, although later

Montanist practices may have been influenced by pagan rituals.[42] Schepelern decided that, instead of a pagan origin, the New Prophecy was inspired by John's Apocalypse, which circulated first in Asia Minor. The Revelator experienced ecstatic visions while in the Spirit; he praised asceticism among the 144,000; and he exalted the martyrs in God's kingdom. Schepelern concluded, "Prophecy, asceticism, and martyrdom—that is exactly the triad that is so characteristic of Montanism in its earliest phase."[43]

Thus, Schepelern asserted that Montanism arose in an attempt to reclaim primitive Christianity at a time when, according to the new prophets' perception, the episcopal establishment was becoming secularized and was minimizing eschatological expectations. Variations upon this thesis had prevailed among nineteenth-century German scholars, particularly F. C. A. Schwegler, Albrecht Ritschl, F. C. Baur, Nathanael Bonwetsch, and Adolf Harnack.[44]

Schwegler saw Montanism as a representation of Jewish or Ebionite Christianity.[45] He compared four practices of the two faiths: ecstatic prophecy, the right of women to teach,[46] abstinence from wine and meat, and deviant Eucharistic elements.[47] Furthermore, he claimed that the Catholic Church, as it asserted its authority in opposition to Montanism, rejected ecstatic inspiration in favor of conciliar authority and subordinated ascetic demands to the goal of universality.[48]

Disputing Schwegler, Ritschl contended that Jewish Christianity had faded by the end of the second century and had been replaced by Gentile Christianity. Ritschl claimed that the original appellation, New Prophecy, derived from ecstatic prophecy, which was unknown to Hebrew prophets but familiar to New Testament writers, such as Luke, John, and Paul, and to early church fathers, such as pseudo-Ignatius, Justin Martyr, and Irenaeus.[49] Therefore, Ritschl concluded that Gentile Christianity rather than Ebionism shaped Montanism.[50]

According to Ritschl, Montanism established no new doctrines but only reacted against the moral laxity of the established church.[51] Conflict developed between Montanism and the ecclesiastical establishment over church discipline and the power of the keys *(Schlüsselgewalt)*. The bishops, on the basis of apostolic succession, claimed absolute power *(Machtvollkommenheit)* to bind and loose sins. The Montanists, although allowing bishops apostolic authority to teach *(Lehrbefugnis)*, argued that only ecstatic prophets, who succeeded to the apostolic powers of miracles *(Wunderkraft)* and prophecy, legitimately exercised absolute power of forgiveness and that forgiveness of mortal sins *(Todsünden)* was the privilege of God alone.[52] The ecclesiastical organization of the Catholic Church led to the struggle and the eventual breach with the Montanist movement.[53]

Although Baur agreed with Ritschl over the nature of the conflict between Montanists and Catholics,[54] he sided with his student, Schwegler,[55] on the influence of Judaism on Montanism. Baur recognized that Christianity and Judaism were connected most closely through the Messianic idea, though it ultimately became the sharpest antithesis between the two faiths. After Jesus' death, early Christians maintained Messianic hopes by affirming their faith in his return, but, as the delay of the *parousia* lengthened, the second- century church experienced a decline in chiliastic fervor and a growing secularization. In reaction, the emphatically millenarian Montanists arose to announce Christ's imminent return and the descent of the New Jerusalem. The Montanists' consciousness of living in the last days *(dies novissimi)* revived other tenets, such as ecstatic prophecy, rigorous discipline, and zeal for martyrdom, which they considered essential aspects of authentic Christianity but which the episcopal leadership considered impractical.[56]

Baur concluded that, having abandoned the Montanists' eschatology and rigorism, the bishops further rejected the movement's emphases on the Spirit. The Catholics denied that the Spirit moved

freely and subjectively among charismatic individuals and insisted
that the prophetic gift was now regulated by the bishops, the only
authorized representatives of the Holy Spirit.[57] Finally, the Montanist practice of ecstasy fell into disrepute. The Montanists' tran-
scendental belief in the nearness of the *parousia* placed them in between the present and the future world, thereby enabling their
minds to be transported beyond themselves. The Catholics, having
established a firm stand in the present world, determined that inspiration required self-possession, even during the operation of the
Holy Spirit.[58]

Nathanael Bonwetsch added to previous Montanist studies with
an examination of two questions. Were the rigorous moral demands
characteristic of Montanism conditioned by eschatological expectations *(Erwartung des Endes)* or by a revival of piety *(Frömmigkeit)* already present in Christianity? Was the conflict between Montanism
and the larger church due to the schismatic tendencies of the movement and, therefore, limited to ecclesiastical polity, or did the conflict extend to the entire sphere of church life?[59]

Regarding the first question, Bonwetsch asserted that Montanism was the defender of the old morals against the secularization
(Verweltlichung) of the Catholic Church, which represented progress
and freedom.[60] In Asia Minor, this otherworldly piety *(Weltflüchtig-
keit Frommer)* indeed derived from the expectation of Christ's impending return.[61] Tertullian's rejection of conformity to the world
(Weltförmigkeit) and embrace of ascetic piety *(asketischer Frömmigkeit)*, however, depended not upon his eschatological views but upon
his hope for a spiritual church *(Geisteskirche)*. Tertullian, therefore,
welcomed the advent of the New Prophecy to Carthage for its higher view of revelation, which gave authority to his rigorous demands.[62]

To the second question Bonwetsch answered that the breach between Montanism and the establishment resulted from both crises: the polity of the Catholic Church *(Krisis der Verfassung der katholischen Kirche)* and the Montanists' moral world view *(Krisis der sittlichen Weltanschauung).*[63] The schism, therefore, was not instigated by the Montanists but was the natural outcome of the basic presuppositions of the Pneumatics and Psychics, or Montanists and Catholics.[64]

Finally, Adolf Harnack summarized the conflicting viewpoints. On one side, the Catholic establishment desired a complete entrance into society, conformity to Roman customs, and, as far as possible, acknowledgment of Roman authorities, all for the sake of the worldwide mission of the church. On the other side, the Montanists demanded total separation from worldliness in imitation of Christ and in rejection of secularization.[65]

In his summary of the research conducted by these nineteenth-century German scholars, Klawiter deduced three conclusions. First, these historians explored the origin and character of Montanism in the context of the questions about the development of the Catholic Church. Second, they concluded that the Montanists' apocalyptic chiliasm demanded an otherworldly ethic in opposition to the allegedly immoral secularization of the Catholic Church. Third, in the light of these interpretations, they saw Montanism as a reformation paradigm: "prophet against bishop, holiness against catholicity, sect against universalism, the free church of the Spirit against the hierarchical, institutional church, and apocalypticism against the desire to become established." In short, Montanism was a conservation of primitive Christianity rather than a heterodox movement.[66]

In contradistinction, the third theory about the character of Montanism insisted that it was indeed a heterodox movement. The leading proponent of this explanation was Pierre de Labriolle, a

French Catholic historian, who discounted claims that Montanism was motivated by a return to primitive Christianity and doubted the alleged secularization *(mondanisation)* of the second-century church.[67] De Labriolle was scandalized, as had been the Montanists' contemporaries, by their prophetic ecstasy, which he described as convulsive agitations.[68] Furthermore, he assumed that Montanus claimed to be the incarnate Paraclete with the statement, "I am the Father, the Son, and the Paraclete."[69] Finally, he accused the Montanists of arrogantly rejecting the bishops' authority and dividing the allegiance of local congregations.[70]

Scholars in the last half of the twentieth century continued to explain Montanism according to these three categories: result of Phrygian influence,[71] conservation of primitive Christianity,[72] and heterodoxy.[73] W. H. C. Frend, however, offered a synthesis of several motifs in his description of Montanism as "a compound of provincial, in this case Phrygian, rural Christianity, protest against both compromise with the world and the continued institutionalization of the Church, and probably also, fierce reaction against a decade of sporadic repression and persecution."[74] Citing Tertullian, Frend pictured the Montanist martyr dying "under the immediate inspiration of the Holy Spirit in the assurance that he would meet his adversaries in changed roles on the Last Day."[75] Thus, he added to previous scholarship in two ways: he emphasized Montanism as a protest of martyrs against Roman persecution; and he interpreted Montanist apocalypticism as a political movement.[76]

All these characterizations are valid to an extent. The Phrygians' openness to women's religious involvement and the Cybelene custom of ecstatic enthusiasm may have played a part in the development of similar characteristics in early Montanism, as suggested by Neander and Ramsay. This explanation, however, does not account for the acceptance of Montanism in the West, which was at-

tracted to the new prophets' emphasis upon the Holy Spirit. Montanist pneumatology, not the Phrygian cult, informed their ecstatic
practices, eschatological revelations, new teachings on rigorism, and
even their acceptance of women's ministry.

As a natural outcome of their emphasis on the Spirit, Montanists did practice prophetic ecstasy, as de Labriolle complained,
but that practice did not constitute heterodoxy, as he charged. Furthermore, de Labriolle's denunciation of Montanus' identification of
himself as the Paraclete failed to consider an interpretation that he
and other Montanists merely claimed to be the Spirit's instruments.
Finally, the schism engendered by the Montanist movement cannot
be disputed, but de Labriolle's denial of secularization of the second-century church has been disputed by other historians, who
recognize the worldly tendencies of the episcopacy or, at least,
Montanists' perception of those tendencies and, therefore, the justi-
fication for the conflicts.

These two characterizations of Montanism as synthesis with
the Phrygian cult and heterodoxy, however valid in part, failed to
take into account the self-understanding of the new prophets. These
men and women viewed the increase in ecclesiastical hierarchy as
resignation to the delay of Christ's return, and they condemned the
resultant decline in eschatological vision and extraordinary manifestations of the Spirit. The new prophets attempted to establish a
prophetic movement of eschatological renewal led by the Holy Spirit. In their hostile environment, their promotion of martyrdom was
a natural consequence of their promotion of extreme rigorism.
Therefore, Montanism is most clearly characterized as a conservation of primitive Christianity in the face of ecclesiastical secularization and imperial persecution.

Spread to the West

Montanus prepared for the continuity of his movement by ap-
pointing Theodotus as trustee (ἐπίτροπος).[77] By the late fourth
century, Montanist clergy were well established and defined: first,
the patriarchs of Pepuza; second, *koinōnoi*;[78] and third, bishops.[79]

During the early decades of the movement, the persuasive power of the new prophets was demonstrated by widespread adherence
to their movement and their perseverence in Asia Minor. Two cities
in particular, Thyatira and Ancyra, were dominated by Montanism,
according to Epiphanius and Eusebius.[80] The new prophets spread
their vision also to Thrace and Syria.[81]

The larger church and its representatives harassed the Montanists wherever they thrived. Two bishops, Zoticus of Cumane and
Julian of Apamea, attempted to exorcize the lying spirit from Maximilla but were prevented by Themiso and others.[82] Serapion, bishop
of Antioch (199–211), reported similarly that "the blessed Sotas of
Anchialus wished to cast out the demon from Priscilla, but the char-
latans would not permit it."[83] Eusebius' anonymous source reported
that "those who were faithful in Asia came together many times and
in many places for this purpose: they examined the unfamiliar teachings, declared them blasphemous, and rejected the heresy. Thus, at
that point, these persons were ousted from the church and ostra-
cized from communion."[84] The actions of the bishops and their syn-
ods, however, failed to quell the movement, which spread west to
Rome and to Carthage.

Rome. The New Prophecy reached Rome by the 170s, but, as evidenced by the failure of the Novatianists in the next century, rigorist parties were never strong in the bastion of ecclesiastical
power. Even from a minority position, however, the new prophets

played key roles in three events: Irenaeus sued for peace between Rome and the new prophets; Gaius and Proclus engaged in a debate between the establishment and prophecy, respectively; and the new prophets participated in the controversy with the *Alogoi*.

In 177, the conflict between Rome and the new prophets was such that Irenaeus and the Christians of Lyons intervened. Irenaeus came to Lyons from Smyrna,[85] but, because Montanus' origins are not known for certain, and because of the lack of information about Irenaeus' early life, the latter's relationship to the New Prophecy in Asia Minor cannot be determined. Heinrich Kraft, however, surmised that Irenaeus came to Lyons as a presbyter and, therefore, as a mature Christian who was knowledgeable about Montanism and the inaccuracy of anti-Montanist accusations.[86] Many Christians of Lyons and Vienne had migrated from Asia and Phrygia,[87] and, when conflict developed between the Asian prophets and the Roman establishment, the Gallic Christians commissioned Irenaeus to take letters of rapprochement to Eleutherus, bishop of Rome (174–89).[88]

About thirty years later, Tertullian reported in *Adversus Praxean* that an unidentified "Bishop of Rome had acknowledged the prophetic gifts of Montanus, Prisca, and Maximilla, and . . . had bestowed his peace on the church of Asia and Phrygia." As a consequence of the modalist Praxeas' interference, however, this bishop recalled the "pacific letter" and denied the *charismata*.[89] Tertullian did not identify the Roman bishop, so the precise date of this episode cannot be determined, but if the occasion was the intervention of Irenaeus, then the bishop was Eleutherus, and the date, 177.[90] Regardless of the exact details, Tertullian's complaint reveals that, by the end of the second century, Montanists were known in Rome and ultimately opposed by the Roman See.

The new prophets gained prominent exposure in Rome during a

debate between the Catholic Gaius and the Montanist Proclus. During Zephyrinus' papacy, Gaius wrote a *Dialogue*, which outlined the arguments of both parties, which took in the larger clash between Roman and Asian Christians. One aspect of Gaius' polemic was his contention that the Montanists added to Scripture.[91] Much of the debate, however, centered on apostolic authority based upon possession of relics: Gaius appealed to the relics of Peter and Paul; Proclus, to those of the apostle John and Philip's daughters.[92] In the end, the Roman orthodox rejected the Prophecy.

Proclus became the leader of one camp of Montanists, who were simply called Cataproclans. Although they were reputed to promote Montanist oracles as superior to apostolic revelation,[93] they rejected the Modalistic Monarchianism of the rival Cataeschinetans, who diverged theologically from the majority of Montanists. Both Hippolytus and Pseudo-Tertullian condemned Modalistic Montanists but admitted that others were orthodox.[94] In *Adversus Praxean*, even Tertullian refuted the modalism of the wayward members of his movement.[95]

Gaius himself fell into heterodoxy when his anti-Montanist views led him to espouse the views of the *Alogoi*,[96] which assigned authorship of both the Gospel and the Apocalypse of John to the heretic Cerinthus. Gaius' hostility to Johannine literature stemmed from his attempt to rob Montanists of key Scriptures such as references to the Paraclete in John 14–16 and the apocalyptic message of Revelation. The views of the *Alogoi*, who originated in Asia Minor, were fueled by anti-Montanist extremism.[97] Their opposition to the *Alogoi*, however, did not earn acceptance for the Montanists. The orthodox, from their centrist position, rejected them both.

Carthage. Rome was an important setting for the expansion-minded new prophets, and the close relationship between the Christian communities there and in Carthage make it a likely route by which Montanism reached North Africa.[98] Tertullian's knowledge of eastern Christianity and Asian Montanism,[99] however, indicates a connection from that direction as well.

The date of Montanism's arrival in North Africa is equally uncertain. According to Trevett, although the turn of the third century is probable, a date one or two decades earlier is possible.[100] Soon after its arrival in Carthage, Montanism, with its demands for strict discipline and asceticism, attracted the attention of the rigoristic Tertullian, its most famous proponent.[101] The exact date is unknown, but, based on the dating of his Montanist writings, Barnes suggested that his adherence began before 207.[102]

Harnack insisted that western Montanism, which developed in the context of an established orthodoxy, was more acquiescent to the Catholic Church than its eastern counterpart.[103] Evidence of association between Montanists and Catholics in Carthage during the early third century confirms this appraisal.[104] In the early years, new prophets functioned within the orthodox church as an enthusiastic community, who recognized the daily work of the Holy Spirit and expected miraculous *charismata* during worship. Tertullian described a characteristic practice in his church, in which a group of Montanists remained after a regular religious service to hear a prophetess share her charismatic revelations.[105]

Tabbernee estimated that, in Tertullian's day, the Carthaginian church was organized into five or six house churches that altogether comprised three to four hundred members.[106] Because of Tertullian's literary skills and interest in prophetic activity, he recorded the content of the divine communications experienced at his church, where many, or even most, of the members adhered to the New Prophecy. This association of Montanists and Catholics could have been repeated in other house churches as well, for, although tension existed between the two factions,[107] they continued to commune together at this time.[108]

In Carthage, there is no evidence of schism between the Catholics and Montanists during the early decades of the third century. Tertullian, even as a Montanist, was not estranged totally from the Catholic community.[109] Furthermore, Cyprian, according to Jerome, considered Tertullian his master and regularly read his works,[110] proving that this decidedly Catholic bishop did not consider Tertullian a schismatic.[111]

The proselytization of the New Prophecy from the Carthaginian church has been estimated variously as minimal and as nearly overwhelming.[112] More significant than speculation about the numbers of Montanists is an evaluation of their lasting influence on Christianity in North Africa. Frend noted that Montanism, with its "hard, rigorist, martyr-inspired code," left a permanent mark on the North African church, its theology, its understanding of Christian community, and its relationship to society.[113] The rigorous nature of the North African church later gave birth to Donatism[114] and, at the same time, made it possible for a Christian to be both a Catholic and an enthusiastic ascetic,[115] as exemplified by Cyprian, Bishop of Carthage in the mid-third century.

Under Tertullian's patronage, Montanism flourished until his death, and even afterward it survived at least two more centuries in North Africa. Eventually, however, it developed into a separate movement and faced the opposition of the Catholic Church.[116] Writing in 428–29, Augustine mentioned in *De haeresibus* the Tertullianists, who were so few in number that those who remained "entered the Catholic Church and handed over their basilica" to the orthodox. Augustine, knowing that this faction was named for Tertullian, assumed that he withdrew from the Montanists and established his own group, creating yet another schism.[117] Frend inferred from this information that Tertullian became even more severe than the Montanists.[118] De Soyres, on the other hand, conjectured that Tertullian separated from the Montanists in order to reconcile with the Catholics.[119] Barnes examined the evidence, though, and determined that Tertullianists, rather than a separate faction, were simply the "Montanist party in Africa,"[120] a tenable position considering the many Montanist factions named after their leaders.[121] In many ways, however, Tertullian did extend his New Discipline beyond even the rigors of Montanism,[122] so the Tertullianists indeed may have been an extreme group of Montanists. Augustine's report indicated that the Montanist remnant in Africa was absorbed into Catholicism by the early fifth century.

Eventually, the demand for conformity initiated by the Constantinian symbiosis took its toll upon Montanism, as Constantine made the resources of the state available to the church to suppress dissension.[123] Even in its land of origin, where it persisted the longest, imperial proscriptions vanquished the remnant of new prophets in the sixth century.[124] As a result, Montanist writings and shrines were destroyed.[125]

The history of Montanism, therefore, is a history of conflict between the new prophets and the emerging Catholic Church, which ultimately proved permanent and victorious. The conflict, however, focused not only on doctrine but also, even mostly, on practice.

Message and Practice

The Montanists' call for Spirit-led revival, and their prophecies of the coming kingdom informed their doctrines, which can be arranged around these stack-poles: the Spirit, prophecy, eschatology, and rigorism. In evaluating their message, however, not only the matter but also the manner of their prophetic activity is important.

The Spirit

In his discussion of Montanist prophetic activity, Eusebius' anonymous source admitted that "the prophetic gift is necessary throughout the church until the final *parousia*,"[126] but his tone indicated embarrassment that the *charismata* were indeed becoming rare in the established church of the second century.[127] In this structured environment, Montanus and his followers claimed to have a fresh revelation from the Holy Spirit, or Paraclete, who inspired their prophecies. Before discussing the oracles, therefore, a study of their pneumatology is necessary. The basis of Montanist claims for supplementary revelation was Christ's promise to send the Paraclete (John 14.16), also called "the Spirit of truth," who "will guide you into all the truth; . . . and He will declare to you the things that are to come" (John 16.13 NRSV).[128] Montanus claimed a special relationship to the Paraclete in his oracles. Didymus the Blind (c. 313–98), an Alexandrian catechist, reported that Montanus said: "I am the Father and the Son and the Paraclete."[129] According to Epiphanius, Montanus also said, "I am the Lord God, the Almighty dwelling in a human."[130] The Catholic hierarchy misinterpreted such statements as a claim to deity. Cyril of Jerusalem, for example, complained that Montanus, "out of his mind and quite mad, . . . had the audacity to claim that he himself was the Holy Spirit."[131] Instead of divine arrogation, however, these formulas implied passive instrumentality as a mouthpiece of God, as was clear in another quotation from Montanus cited in Epiphanius: "Behold, the human being is like a lyre, and I fly over him like a pick."[132]

Basil of Caesarea (c. 330–79), assuming that Montanists identified Montanus or Priscilla with the Holy Spirit, complained facetiously that they baptized "into the Father and the Son and Montanus or Priscilla."[133] Based on such a misunderstanding of

Montanist pneumatology, the canons of several ecumenical councils required that Montanists be rebaptized for admission into the Catholic Church.[134]

Confirmation of the Montanists' error regarding the Holy Spirit and, therefore, the Trinity allegedly was provided by an undated inscription discovered in Numidia: "Flavius Avus, guardsman, has completed what he promised in the name of the Father and of the Son and of Lord Muntanus."[135] One conclusion from this statement was that later Montanists identified Montanus quite literally as the Paraclete, including him in their Trinitarian formula.[136] Tabbernee, however, examined this inscription and contended that it was not a liturgical statement referring to the founder of the New Prophecy but a pronouncement of a completed vow made to a North African martyr-saint, most likely the subject of the *Acts of Montanus and Lucius*.[137] The failure of the inscriber to include the phrase "and of the Spirit" was attributed by Tabbernee to the possibility that a layperson carved the inscription.[138] At the same time, however, the omission of the Spirit from the names of the Godhead does leave open the possibility that this inscription indeed reflected a heretical, Montanist Trinitarian formula.

Regardless of the validity of the witness of this inscription, the accusations of heresy leveled against the Montanists stemmed from critics in the fourth and fifth centuries and, if valid, demonstrated only a later shift in Montanism from orthodox doctrine to heresy.[139] The testimony regarding the early new prophets, on the other hand, showed a picture of orthodoxy completely acceptable for the late second and early third centuries.[140] Even Hippolytus ascribed to the majority of Montanists an orthodox doctrine of the Trinity.[141] Furthermore, the Montanist emphasis on the Spirit helped Tertullian develop and transmit his Trinitarian formula to the orthodox church.[142]

Women in Ministry

The New Prophecy expected the Spirit to give *charismata* not only to men but also to women,[143] so the movement granted prophetic authority to women, including such named leaders as Maximilla, Priscilla, and Quintilla, and also to others. They ordained women to the episcopate and presbyterate and supported this ordination with reference to the biblical models of Moses' sister, Miriam, and Philip's daughters. Among certain Montanists, called Quintillianists or Priscillianists by Epiphanius, seven virgins led congregations by prophesying and by encouraging them to mourn in penitence.[144]

Montanist women, finding a voice in a Spirit-based community, were not sufficiently reticent for the official church, which seized upon the women's prophetic activity as an occasion for condemnation.[145] Prominent Catholic bishops considered Maximilla and Priscilla to be victims of "counterfeit ($\nu\acute{o}\theta o\upsilon$)" spirits that were "hazardous to their mental health ($\beta\lambda\alpha\psi\acute{\iota}\phi\rho o\nu o\varsigma$)"[146] and attempted to exorcise the women.[147] Epiphanius charged Montanist prophetesses with the heresy of giving thanks to Eve "because she first ate from the tree of knowledge." Furthermore, he argued against female clergy with sacred writings that he interpreted as support for patriarchal hierarchy.[148]

Ecstatic Prophecy

Prophetic activity thrived in the Christian church through the second century. The *Didache* (c. 50–c. 150) included instructions on testing a genuine prophet.[149] In his *Dialogue with Trypho*, Justin Martyr (c. 100–c. 165) contended that prophetic gifts manifested by the church testified that Christians were the chosen people.[150] Irenaeus (c. 130–c. 200) also, in *Adversus haereses*, reported that some

Christians "have foreknowledge of future events and visions and prophetic utterances."[151] This tradition facilitated the spread of the new prophets' message and ministry.[152] At the same time, the growing influence of the clerical hierarchy marginalized and threatened Christian prophecy.[153]

Ecstasy and glossolalia, which characterized their prophecies, attracted attention and criticism for the new prophets. At the beginning of his ministry, Montanus "was swept away by spiritual enthusiasm (πνευματοφορηθῆναι) and also began suddenly to babble and to speak with strange sounds (λαλεῖν καὶ ξενοφωνεῖν), becoming possessed in some kind of trance and extreme ecstasy (κατοχῇ τινι καὶ παρεκστάσει)."[154] Furthermore, the two prophetesses, Priscilla and Maximilla, filled with a counterfeit spirit, began "to babble senselessly, inappropriately, and outlandishly" (λαλεῖν ἐκφρόνως καὶ ἀκαίρως καὶ ἀλλοτριοτρόπως), just like Montanus.[155] Maximilla was also subject to ecstatic trances, saying, "I am compelled, willing and unwilling, to attain to the knowledge of God."[156]

The ecstatic state offended many ecclesiastical authorities. When Eusebius' anonymous source first described Montanus' ecstatic behavior, he protested that it was "in a manner contrary to the tradition and the succession of the church from the beginning."[157] Miltiades, another anti-Montanist polemicist, insisted that the pseudo-prophet is carried away by his extreme ecstasy, "beginning out of voluntary stupidity but terminating in involuntary insanity."[158] Epiphanius defined Montanist ecstasy as "madness induced through standing outside of sanity (ἡ μανία διὰ τὸ ἐκστῆναι τοῦ προκειμένου)."[159]

The new prophets appealed to Scripture in defense of visionary trances and ecstatic pronouncements. From the Old Testament they drew from the examples of Adam,[160] Abraham, David,[161] Isaiah,

Ezekiel, and Daniel, and from the New Testament, Peter and John the Revelator.[162] Glossolalia also figured greatly in Montanists' prophetic ministries, and yet, they could defend themselves on the basis of Paul's statements in 1 Corinthians 12–14. As gifts of the Spirit (1 Cor. 12.8–10), prophecy and speaking in tongues continued until the end of the age (1 Cor. 13.8–10). Nevertheless, by the end of the second century, speaking in tongues was rare in the churches[163] and was practiced more often among Gnostics[164] and pagans.[165] Although Paul warned (1 Cor. 14.9–11) that speaking in tongues was strange and susceptible to various responses, it nevertheless fell within the boundaries of orthodox Christianity.[166] In its practice of prophecy through glossolalia and ecstasy, Montanism established a median position between prophetless orthodoxy and orgiastic paganism.[167]

Regarding the Montanist practice of glossolalia, Christopher Forbes argued against the majority of historians,[168] contending that "there is no unambiguous evidence whatsoever that [Montanist prophecy] took glossolalic form."[169] First, he pointed to the collections of Montanist oracles to prove that the prophecies were delivered in intelligible language. Then, he denied any evidence that these oracles had been interpreted. In a footnote, however, he admitted Maximilla's identification of herself as an "interpreter (ἑρμηνεύτην)" but then dismissed the seemingly obvious suggestion that this reference "may be taken to mean that Maximilla not only spoke her oracles, but also explained their meanings." In addition, Forbes failed to consider the probability that the new prophets utilized both intelligible and unintelligible speech in their charismatic activities.[170]

Second, Forbes focused on the language used to describe the new prophets' speech and insisted that the establishment was concerned with the content, not the form, of their message. According to Forbes, ξενοφωνεῖν, admittedly a rare word, means "to speak strange things" or "to astonish by strange words or teachings."[171] However, an etymological examination of the word, as Forbes observed, reveals that its clear meaning is "to speak as a foreigner" or "to produce a strange sound." Henry George Liddell and Robert Scott defined ξενοφωνεῖν as "to speak or sound strangely" and its nominative forms as "strange language" and "speaking or sounding strange."[172] Furthermore, ξενοφωνεῖν is coupled with λαλεῖν in the description of Montanus' activities. The latter term, while capable of being understood as "to talk or speak," is better translated as "to chatter or babble" and is often used to refer to the sounds of grasshoppers, frogs, birds, and brooks.[173] Therefore, Montanus' activity is better understood as "to babble and to speak with strange sounds." Forbes' arguments are not sufficient to overturn the historic understanding that Montanists engaged in glossolalia.[174]

Catholic critics clearly reacted against the Montanists' modes of prophecy, ecstasy and glossolalia, which they linked with irrationality and pagan and heretical behavior: "But of those who, at that time, heard those counterfeit utterances (νόθων ἐκφωνημάτων),[175] some, being offended by one who was possessed and afflicted by a demon, who was under the influence of a deceiving spirit, and who was disturbing the masses, rebuked him and hindered him from babbling, remembering the Lord's distinctiveness and also his warning to be on guard against false prophets while awaiting the *parousia*."[176] On the other hand, others were so elated and entranced by what they perceived to be the movement of the Holy Spirit and the accompanying prophetic gift that the movement could not be silenced.[177]

Although the method of prophecy caused the greatest concern among the church fathers, one aspect of the new prophets' message that was also disturbing was the claim that New Prophecy superseded the revelation given in Scripture through the apostles. According to Epiphanius' diatribe, Maximilla spoke plainly, "Do not hear me, but instead hear Christ."[178] Montanus claimed not only "I am the Lord God, the Almighty dwelling in a human" but also "Neither angel nor ambassador (οὔτε ἄγγελος οὔτε πρέσβυς), but instead I the Lord God, the Father, did come."[179] Hippolytus contended that, by such claims, Montanists deluded and captivated their followers, "asserting that they have learned more through these [Montanist books] than from the Law and the Prophets and the Gospels."[180] The ecclesiastical establishment did not consider the possibility that these statements emphasized only instrumentality in God's revelation, not superiority to it.

Tertullian, however, actually did apply prophetic revelation to contemporaneous situations in new ways. In one example, the New Prophecy prohibited a second marriage after a spouse's death, even though Paul allowed such a marriage. Tertullian defended the New Prophecy against orthodox objections: "For if Christ abrogated what Moses enjoined, . . . Christ will not therefore be reputed to have come from some other Power; why may not the Paraclete, too, have abrogated an indulgence which Paul granted . . . .?" He continued, "The New Law abrogated divorce . . . ; the New Prophecy (abrogates) second marriage."[181] Because he equated second marriage to divorce of the former marriage, Tertullian viewed this discipline not as a new revelation but as a prophetic application of a scriptural principle. Although committed to the accepted sacred writings, he considered the new revelation to be not competition but completion.

The immediacy of that revelation, though, worried the official church. Montanus insisted that God himself acted directly with neither angelic (ἄγγελος) nor human (πρέσβυς) intermediary.[182] Ignatius (30–107) said much the same thing to the Philadelphians: "For I received this word from God. . . . [T]his is not my word but God's. . . . And the Spirit proclaimed to me."[183] The difference was

that Ignatius' pronouncements affirmed the authority of the episcopacy. The new prophets rose up in the midst of such ecclesiastical
settledness to prophesy and to revive apocalyptic expectations.

Eschatological Expectation

Eschatological expectation was so integral to Montanist
thought that Bonwetsch described the movement as "an effort to
mold the whole life of the church in conformity to the expectation
of the immediate, impending return of Christ, to define the essence
of Christianity from this point of view, and to oppose everything by
which ecclesiastical conditions should acquire a more permanent
structure for the purpose of entering into a longer, historical gener-
ation."[184] As the new prophets observed the development of ecclesiastical structure, they sensed a lessening of eschatological emphasis
in the church and, therefore, a decline in prophetic *charismata*.[185]

The Christian apocryphal codicil, *The Ascension of Isaiah*, expressed similar sentiments earlier in the second century:

> And there will be many heresies at his approach, and there will be
> in those days many desiring to rule yet without wisdom. . . . And
> there will be many evil reports and much vain conceit at the advent
> of the Lord, and the Holy Spirit will withdraw from many. And
> there will not be in those days many prophets speaking strong
> messages . . . . For rivalry will be great in the final days, for each
> person will say what is pleasing in his own eyes. And they will nul-
> lify the prophecy of the prophets before me, and they will invali-
> date these visions of mine so that they will speak according to the
> impulses of their hearts.[186]

In the same way, Montanists viewed their religious context as a
Christian community replete with ecclesiastical hierarchy yet de-
void of prophecy. In response, they cast themselves in the role of
new prophets who would reinvigorate apocalyptic expectation.[187]

According to Apollonius, Montanus "named Pepuza and Tymion

'Jerusalem,' even though they were insignificant towns in Phrygia, intending to gather people from everywhere to that place."[188] G. A. Williamson, following traditional scholarship,[189] suggested that Montanus appealed to his followers to come and be among those saved at the imminent *parousia*.[190]

Douglas Powell, however, failed to see how Montanus could have expected the New Jerusalem to descend on two sites simultaneously and argued instead that Montanus' identification of Pepuza and Tymion as Jerusalem was made not in expectation of the descent of the heavenly city but in an attempt to recreate the primitive, New Testament church.[191] In contrast, the recent discovery by Tabbernee indicates that Montanus named the two towns "Jerusalem" because they were located at the northern and southern boundaries of the "ideal 'landing place' for the New Jerusalem."[192]

In conjunction with such millennialism, a prophetess delivered the following apocalypse: "Having taken the form of a woman,' she said, 'Christ came to me in a radiant garment and placed in me wisdom and revealed to me this: this place [Pepuza] is holy and in this place Jerusalem will come down from heaven."[193] The source of this oracle was uncertain to Epiphanius, who credited it to either Priscilla or Quintilla. Powell attributed the saying to Quintilla rather than to a founder of Montanism and its eschatological emphasis to a later period of the movement.[194] Neither assumption, however, is necessary. First, Anne Jensen argued for Priscilla as the source of the oracle: "The appearance explains the cultic importance of Pepuza, which from the beginning was the center of the New Prophecy: therefore, it is unlikely that the vision comes from a later phase of the movement."[195] John C. Poirier agreed and added that Priscilla's oracle preceded and inspired Montanus' words.[196] Second, as Tabbernee has shown in his discovery of Pepuza and Tymion, Montanus himself anticipated the soon return of Christ at Pepuza and infused his movement with eschatological expectations.[197]

No matter its source, this oracle drew heavily from Revelation
21 and John's vision of "new Jerusalem, coming down out of heav-
en" (Rev. 21.2 NRSV).[198] Much of Montanist dogma was inspired by
Johannine literature:[199] the promise of the Paraclete fulfilled John
14.16; the epistles confirmed to the Montanists that they lived in
the last days before the millennium;[200] their geographical context
was the region of the seven churches of Revelation 2–3, especially
Philadelphia; and the Johannine Apocalypse provided thematic content for the new prophets.[201]

Maximilla provided a veiled allusion to Revelation in her explanation of her mission: "The Lord has commissioned me as a separatist, illuminator, and interpreter of this suffering and covenant
and promise (τοῦ πόνου καὶ τῆς συνθήκης καὶ τῆς ἐπαγγελίας
αἱρεστιστὴν μηνυτὴν ἑρμηνευτην)."[202] The word πόνος, meaning "suffering" or "pain," is rare in the New Testament but appears
in Rev. 16.10–11, referring to the pain of the unrepentant, and in
Rev. 21.4, which tells of the abolition of suffering at the descent of
the New Jerusalem. Although her prediction of "wars and revolu-
tions"[203] borrowed more directly from the Lucan apocalypse (Lk.
21.9), certainly wars were a prominent motif in Revelation as
well.[204] Maximilla's role, then, was to proclaim the relationship of
the suffering of God's people and the preparation for God's redemp-
tive intervention. These two themes were common in both Jewish
and Christian literature.[205]

Furthermore, the promise (ἐπαγγελίας) of this oracle was
related to the "greatness of the promises (μεγέθους τῶν ἐπαγγελ-
μάτων)" bestowed by the Spirit at the beginning of the New Prophecy.[206] Perhaps the promised glory was the inspiration for Montanus' oracle that "the righteous ... will shine a hundred times
more than the sun, and the small ones among you who are saved
will shine a hundred times more than the moon."[207]

The prophetic message as apocalyptic expectation found a favor-

able context in Asia Minor, where chiliastic beliefs were widespread. The innovations which the New Prophecy brought centered
on immediacy and location at Pepuza. The Catholic hierarchy, however, adjusted to the delay of the *parousia* by projecting its date further into the future while relegating the prophetic era further into
the past. The orthodox position was that John the Revelator delivered the final, inspired prophecy and that later pseudo-prophets had
no right to claims of divine inspiration.[208]

This restriction of authority to biblical prophets undermined the
basis of both Montanism and the Christian movement which preceded it. Schepelern recognized that "a half-century earlier, such a
movement could reckon on ecclesiastical recognition. Between the
preaching of judgment by John and that by Montanus, there extend-
ed the decisive period of development in ecclesiastical organization
and duties, and the free expressions of the Spirit mobilized themselves against this authority in vain."[209] The ecclesiastical establishment reserved the prophetic *charismata* for themselves, making ob-
solete such reform movements as Montanism, which only served as
a paradigm by which to compare the solidification of the church's
message through fixed dogma and creed. Eventually, episcopal sta-
bility rendered prophecy superfluous to ecclesiastical ministry.[210]

Maximilla's prophecy, "After me there will be no more prophecy
but only the consummation,"[211] did not deter the faithful. The Montanist communities continued their vigil. Their apocalyptic world-
view, however, demanded a high level of discipleship in preparation
for the *parousia*.[212] This rigor was another feature of Montanist faith
and practice.

Rigorous Discipline

The Montanists' rigor focused on four areas: fasting, celibacy/
marriage, post-baptismal penitence, and martyrdom.[213] These areas

emphasized the need for holiness among the prophets. Priscilla preached that "the holy minister knows purity in order to serve, for purification is in harmony . . . and they see visions, and, further-more, turning their faces down they hear distinct voices that are as beneficial as they are also hidden."[214]

For the new prophets, the benefits of fasting consisted of prepa-ration not only for the *parousia* but also for prophetic experience. Priscilla's association of purity with visions has been noted. Mon-tanists found scriptural support in Daniel's practice: "I had eaten no rich food, no meat or wine had entered by mouth, and I had not anointed myself at all,[215] for the full three weeks . . . . I, Daniel, alone saw the vision . . . . I fell into a trance, face to the ground" (Dan. 10.2–9 NRSV). Furthermore, they drew again from 4 Ezra, which detailed Ezra's seven-day fast upon the herbs of Ardat before his vision of New Jerusalem.[216] The *Shepherd of Hermas* also linked humility, fasting, and revelation.[217] The new prophets' concern for fasting, therefore, fit the current apocalyptic pattern.

Celibacy and marriage were the next eschatological concerns, and the new prophets were aware of Paul's strictures concerning these issues now that "the appointed time has grown short" (1 Cor. 7.29 NRSV). The three founders, however, carried this ideal to an extreme. Apollonius reported that Montanus "taught the dissolu-tion of marriages," particularly in the cases of Priscilla and Max-imilla, the "foremost prophetesses," who, "once they were filled with the Spirit, abandoned their husbands." Later, Priscilla even received the title "virgin."[218]

Furthermore, remarriage after the death of a spouse was not al-lowed by the new prophets, who interpreted strictly the injunction to be "married only once" (1 Tim. 3.2 NRSV) and applied it to all Christians. Tertullian was the major opponent to digamy, but Epiphanius implied its broad prohibition among Montanists: "For they cast out everyone who has united in a second marriage (δευτέρῳ γάμῳ), and they compel everyone not to become united in a second marriage."[219] Whereas the new prophets rejected extremes of sexual asceticism and allowed marriage, they inherited from their Asian Christian context the ideal of Christian celibacy. Remarriage, therefore, was not condoned. What Paul had issued as an opinion (1 Cor. 7.40), the Paraclete codified.[220]

The third rigorous practice noted among the Montanists was the hesitation to allow post-baptismal repentance for mortal sins. Writing in the fourth century, Jerome testified to Montanists' rigidity, complaining that their attitude led them to close the church doors to errant Christians rather than to lead them back to repentance. Their strictness, according to Jerome, did not prevent sinning, only pardon.[221]

For this tenet, however, Tertullian remains the main source of information on the Montanist viewpoint, and Tertullian's own rigorous temperament and his possible modification of Montanism must be considered.[222] In *De pudicitia*, he quoted an unnamed prophet to support his position: "(I) . . . have the Paraclete Himself in the persons of the new prophets *(ipsum Paracletum in prophetis novis)*, saying, 'The Church has the power *(Potest)* to forgive sins *(donare delictum)*; but I will not do it, lest they commit others *(alia delinquant)* withal.'"[223] Tabbernee, in a study on the question, "To Pardon or Not to Pardon," determined that Tertullian utilized an oracle of a contemporary prophet or prophetess in his house church in Carthage as authority for his stand against post-baptismal repentance for such sins as murder, idolatry, fraud, apostasy, blasphemy, adultery, and fornication.[224] Tabbernee speculated further that this oracle was stimulated by Tertullian's teaching on the subject, due either to a request for special revelation or to subconscious suggestion. Either way, Tertullian's own teaching on this topic may have influenced the content of the oracle.[225]

Tertullian's rigidity may have led him to alter another Montanist teaching regarding the forgiveness of sins: the martyr's power of the keys. The testimony of Apollonius indicated that Alexander, a Montanist confessor/martyr, used his authority to pardon sin.[226] Such a prerogative, however, was not exclusively a Montanist feature. The writer of *The Letter of the Churches of Vienne and Lyons* taught that, while in prison, confessors could administer "the power of martyrdom" and grant grace to lapsed sinners.[227] At the same time, this letter implied that the writer contrasted the gracious compassion of the Gallic Christians with other, possibly Montanist, confessors, who used the power of the keys to withhold forgiveness.[228] The *Apostolic Tradition* recognized that confessors placed in chains, when released, deserved the honor of priesthood with all of the rights of that rank.[229] Tertullian, in his early treatise *Ad martyras*, acknowledged that some imprisoned confessors imparted peace to seekers who did not receive it from the church.[230]

In the later *De pudicitia*, however, Tertullian reversed himself and denied that martyrs had the power to remit others' sins. This development in his teaching about the martyrs' power of the keys was closely tied to his refusal to forgive certain post-baptismal sins and did not necessarily reflect normal Montanist practice. The overall attitude of the Montanists, therefore, was that the "spiritual" church, headed by prophets and martyrs, did possess the power of the keys but used it both to bind and to loose.[231]

The Montanists called for reform through rigorous discipline, the hallmark and goal of their Spirit-based apocalyptic preaching.[232] Their emphases on new fasts, celibacy, and post-baptismal strictures accentuated the laxity of the established church, which refused to yield to a movement demanding stricter discipline than its own.[233]

Martyrdom

Martyrdom was the fourth and highest form of asceticism in the
Montanist camp. Montanists pointed with pride to their great number of martyrs, which, for them, was a sign of the prophetic spirit in
their midst.[234]

Two Montanist oracles concerning martyrdom are extant, both
quoted by Tertullian in *De fuga in persecutione*. The first oracle com-
manded, "[S]eek not to die on bridal beds, nor in miscarriages, nor
in soft fevers, but to die the martyr's death, that He may be glorified
who has suffered for you."[235] In Tertullian's interpretation of this
oracle, this baptism of blood was sacramental in its regenerative ef-
fect: "[I]f you have to lay down your life for God, as the Comforter
(Paracletus) counsels, it is not in gentle fever and on soft beds, but in
the sharp pains of martyrdom: you must take up the cross and bear
it after your Master, as He has Himself instructed you. The sole key
to unlock Paradise is your own life's blood *(tota Paradisi clavis tuus
sanguis est)*."[236] Tertullian exalted martyrdom to the extent that only
through martyrdom did a Christian gain immediate entrance into
paradise.[237]

In the other oracle, the Spirit said, "If you are exposed to public
infamy . . . it is for your good; for he who is not exposed to dis-
honour among men is sure to be so before the Lord. Do not be
ashamed; righteousness brings you forth into the public gaze. Why
should you be ashamed of gaining glory? The opportunity is given
you when you are before the eyes of men." By submitting to persecution, the martyr was elevated to the position of judge. Tertullian
utilized this oracle to encourage voluntary martyrdom: "[I]f you
ask counsel of the Spirit, what does He approve more than that utterance of the Spirit? For, indeed, it incites all almost to go and offer
themselves in martyrdom, not to flee from it."[238]

The New Prophecy, as mediated by Tertullian, at least,[239] exhorted its followers to volunteer as martyrs and discouraged their flight, in opposition to the policy of the official church.[240] For the Montanists, martyrdom had more than just sacramental meaning. Eschatological expectation viewed persecution as a sign of the end times and martyrdom as the fulfillment of the disciplined Christian life. As Wilhelm Schepelern observed, "From the earth soaked in blood . . . of Christian martyrs, Montanism arose. And in an atmosphere saturated . . . with the apocalyptic expression of Judaism and Christianity, it thrived."[241] Thus, the Montanist theology of martyrdom was a logical derivative from Spirit-induced prophecy, apocalyptic expectation, and rigorous discipline.

In the first fifty years of the New Prophecy, opponents were forced to concede doctrinal orthodoxy among the core Montanists.[242] The official church turned its censure against paranormal activities, such as ecstatic behavior, glossolalia, apocalyptic prophecies, ethical practices, leadership by women, and a variety of rigorous disciplines, but, in every case, Montanism professed itself to be Christian.[243]

CHAPTER TWO

Authorship of the *Passion*

BEFORE EXAMINING the text of the *Passion*, it is necessary to
determine its authorship. The document consists of three separate parts, which are the two martyrs' diaries and the editorial
framework. Therefore, two problems must be investigated: the authenticity of the diaries and the identity of the unnamed editor.

Authenticity of the Diaries

The editor stated several times that the diaries were written
personally by Perpetua and Saturus.[1] After naming the catechumens
in the introduction, the editor introduced Perpetua's narrative with
a parenthetical statement: "Now from this point on the entire account of her ordeal is her own, according to her own ideas and in
the way that she herself wrote it down" (2.3). At the beginning of
Saturus' vision, the editor specified that "the blessed Saturus has
also made known his own vision and he has written it with his own
hand" (11.1). Finally, before detailing the account of their martyrdom, the editor remarked, "Such were the remarkable visions of
these martyrs, Saturus and Perpetua, written by themselves" (14.1).

Furthermore, in the opening sentences of the diaries, the editor inserted the word *inquit* ("he/she said") to reinforce the fact that the words belonged to the confessors themselves. Thus, the editor asserted the authenticity of the diaries which he or she preserved in the *Passion*.

Perpetua also testified to her authorship at the end of her diary: "So much for what I did up until the eve of the contest" (10.15). Further internal evidence for the confessors' authorship is implicit in the first person narratives.

Nonetheless, Augustine cast doubt on Perpetua's authorship of her account when he ascribed it to either the saint or "whoever wrote it."[2] Augustine, however, was the only ancient commentator to suggest that Perpetua did not write her diary.[3] Modern commentators almost universally have declared that Perpetua's and Saturus' diaries were genuine.

An important issue in this discussion of authorship is the priority of the Latin or Greek text of the *Passion*.[4] For more than two centuries after Lucas Holstenius discovered the text of the *Passion* in 1661, the Latin version was the only one known. Then in 1889, J. Rendel Harris found a Greek manuscript in Jerusalem, and, when he and Seth K. Gifford published it in 1890, they contended for its originality.[5] The next year, J. Armitage Robinson published his edition of the Latin and Greek texts with evidence that convinced even Harris of the priority of the Latin version. First, the Greek version introduced explanatory phrases that would have been extraneous to the original readers and suppressed details difficult to translate. Second, the language in the Greek version was weaker and more diffuse than that in the Latin version. Third, word play present in Latin was absent in Greek.[6]

To Robinson's linguistic evidence for the priority of the Latin version, Thomas J. Heffernan added circumstantial evidence. The

Carthaginian upper classes of this time, which included Perpetua, were overwhelmingly Roman, so, despite their ability to speak Greek, their daily language was Latin. The majority of the names listed in the *Passion*, including Perpetua's and Saturus', were Latin. Finally, the church of Carthage, founded by the Roman church and continuing under its influence, would be dominated by the Roman language.[7] Therefore, both the external and internal evidence strongly supported the priority of the Latin text.

The debate, however, did not end with Robinson.[8] Paul Monceaux contended that Saturus, because he referred to Perpetua's ability to speak Greek, must have written in Latin and that Perpetua wrote in Greek. The editor then composed the Latin *Passion*, and the Greek version was translated later.[9] Oppositely, Åke Fridh, through a metrical analysis, posited that Saturus' vision was composed in Greek, that the remainder of the *Passion* was written in Latin, and, therefore, that the original document was bilingual. In the next recension, the Greek portion was translated into Latin, and, finally, the Latin sections were translated into Greek.[10] With these conflicting hypotheses, these two scholars emphasized the linguistic variations that indicated separate authorship of the two martyrs' narratives.

In the extensive philological review found in the introduction to his 1891 edition of the *Passion*, J. Armitage Robinson examined the Latin text for differences in style and composition between the portions allegedly authored by Perpetua, by Saturus, and by the editor. As Robinson stated, "In so brief a document it would be hard to charge the redactor with falsification if no such traces were to be seen: but on the other hand their existence would confirm us in the belief that we had the actual words of the Martyrs themselves."[11]

Robinson began his analysis with the distribution of transliterated Greek words, of which most were found in the writings of Perpetua, who, according to Saturus, could speak Greek. In Saturus' and the editor's writings, the words were familiar in biblical and ecclesiastical usage, but such was not the case for Perpetua's words. Therefore, Robinson adduced individuality for Perpetua's writings.[12]

Other vocabulary further distinguished the three authors' contributions. Robinson especially noted the use of conjunctions such as *et*, *tunc*, and *ut*. These simple conjunctions differentiate the simplicity of Perpetua's and Saturus' narratives from the more rhetorical style of the editor.[13] Another difference in style is Perpetua's repetition of words and phrases where a careful writer would vary the language.

In Saturus' section, which is the shortest of the three, Robinson found much less material to compare with the rest of the *Passion*. Nonetheless, he listed the following clues: unique phrases of multiple usage, the frequent and exclusive use of *dixi* and its derivatives, and the use of *uiridarium* for garden instead of Perpetua's word *hortus*. In sum, the evidence of the authenticity of Saturus' diary, considering its brevity, is fuller than Robinson originally expected.[14]

W. H. Shewring agreed with Robinson's conclusions and added his own evidence of varying prose rhythms. He found the editor's prose followed the rhythms of a practiced writer. Perpetua's rhythms, consistently different, proved to Shewring that the editor never revised her narrative. Saturus' diary was too short to evince any regularity of rhythm but also seemed untouched by the editor.[15]

Robinson's and Shewring's works influenced scholarship so completely that the authenticity of the diaries and, hence, multiple authorship have been accepted almost universally.[16] Earlier, however, Benjamin Aubé insisted that one writer had composed the entire document. Suspicious of the editor's repeated claims of genuineness for the diaries, he also doubted that the prisoners had opportunity to write, and he contended that they delivered their narratives orally. Because he saw throughout the *Passion* not only the same hand but also evidence of Montanism, Aubé believed that the editor, undoubtedly a Montanist, fabricated the martyrs' stories in order to promote sectarian views.[17]

More recently (1995), Heffernan examined the *Passion* philologically and questioned Perpetua's authorship of her dream sequences. Like Aubé, Heffernan disputed the possibility that a prisoner was able to keep such detailed records. More important to his theory, though, were literary keys, such as the consistent use of past tense and carefully constructed phrases that indicate passage of time, both of which are not typical of diaries. Nonetheless, Heffernan did not deny the veracity of the events reported in Perpetua's narratives; instead he suggested that Perpetua orally transmitted her stories to the editor, who preserved them for the Carthaginian community in a *hypomnema*, "a vehicle that could combine some of the formal characteristics of autobiography with the jottings of diary."[18]

Heffernan's hypothesis concerning oral transmission did not diminish the authenticity of Perpetua's authorship of the diary, but it did allow for the editor's reworking.[19] Aubé's insistence on the editor's authorship of the entire document, motivated by his concern to preserve the martyrs' orthodox reputation, actually emphasized the thoroughly Montanistic flavor of the *Passion*. Neither Aubé nor Heffernan, however, took into account the philological evidence, presented by Robinson and Shewring and accepted by most scholars, that each portion of the *Passion* differed significantly from the others, nor does either scholar adequately argue against the statements of the editor that Perpetua and Saturus wrote with their own hands. Aubé's theory depended on his unproven assertion that the participants of the *Passion* were not all Montanists. Heffernan did not consider that Perpetua transmitted the account of her suffering to the editor in words that revealed her expectation that it would be preserved in writing: "About what happened at the contest itself, let him write of it who will" (10.15). The editor, then, continued the narrative, saying, "Therefore, since the Holy Spirit has permitted the story of this contest to be written down and by so permitting has willed it, we shall carry out the command or, indeed, the commission *(fideicommissum)* of the most saintly Perpetua, however unworthy I might be to add anything to this glorious story" (16.1).

In summary, the *Passion* was the composition of three authors, and the Latin text preceded the Greek. The next pressing question concerns the identity of the one who fulfilled her commission.

The Identity of the Editor

The question of the editor's identity has garnered much interest and research, most of it centered on Tertullian. Scholars' conclusions can be summarized under three headings: the editor was Tertullian;[20] the editor was not Tertullian but was another Montanist;[21] or the editor was not a Montanist.[22]

Lucas Holstenius, the first modern editor of the *Passion*, made no overt claims for Tertullian's editorship, but he did include in his edition of the *Passion* many examples of comparable vocabulary and content from Tertullian's writings.[23] Robinson, in the most complete argument for Tertullian's editorship, also compared the editor and Tertullian regarding their scriptural quotations, parallels of thought and diction, and selected similarities in vocabulary.

The first scriptural quotation examined was Acts 2.17–18 in the preface,[24] in which the sentences were disarranged compared to the Latin Vulgate.[25] In his treatise *Adversus Marcionem*, Tertullian quoted the parallel passage from Joel 2.28–29 in the same order as the editor.[26] Later in the preface, the editor conflated 1 John 1.1, 3 and used the first person plural, *contrectauimus* ("we handled"), rather than the original third person plural, *contrectauerunt* ("[our hands] handled"). Tertullian quoted 1 John 1.1 in the same way in his treatise *Against Praxeas.*[27] Robinson provided these two examples "of the way in which an individual writer may have a habit of his own in quoting a special text."[28]

Robinson discovered several parallels in words and thoughts between the writings of the editor and Tertullian. In the epilogue, the editor exclaimed: "Ah, most valiant and blessed martyrs! Truly are you called and chosen *(uocati et electi)* for the glory of Christ Jesus our Lord *(in gloriam domini nostri Iesu Christi)!*" (21.11). Thus, the editor regarded the ultimate end of martyrdom as the glory of the Lord, a theme developed by Tertullian in his treatise *De fuga in persecutione:* "The one great thing in persecution is the promotion of the glory of God."[29] In closing, Tertullian said of those who suffer, "And therefore many are called *(uocati)* but few are chosen *(electi).*"[30] Robinson saw in Tertullian's discussion similarity to the editor's statement about the martyrs, who were called and chosen to the glory of the Lord.[31]

Next, Robinson pointed out a parallel in thought rather than words. In the preface, the editor observed, "God always achieves what he promises, as a witness to the non-believer and a blessing to the faithful" (1.5).[32] In *De anima*, Tertullian stated, "God everywhere manifests signs of His own power—to His own people for their own comfort, to strangers for a testimony unto them."[33] According to Robinson, "The thought is precisely the same, and the two sentences though so differently worded are almost interchangeable."[34]

Then, Robinson presented a parallel in words rather than meaning. When reporting that Perpetua, having been tossed by the mad cow, rearranged her robe, the editor said that she was "more mindful of her modesty than of her pain" (20.4).[35] Tertullian, on the other hand, described unrepentant sinners as "more mindful of modesty than of salvation."[36]

According to Robinson, technical Montanistic language connected the *Passion* and *De anima*. The editor stated that Perpetua was unaware of the cow's attack, "so absorbed had she been in ecstasy in the Spirit *(adeo in spiritu et in extasi fuerat)*" (20.8). Similarly, Tertullian spoke of a Montanist sister and her revelations, "which she experiences through ecstacy in the Spirit *(per ecstasin in spiritu)*."[37]

The editor exhibited familiarity with Roman legal terminology, as did Tertullian. In his opening argument for the authority of the *Passion*, the editor claimed, *"uel quia proinde et haec uetera futura quandoque sunt et necessaria posteris, si in praesenti suo tempore minori deputantur auctoritati propter praesumptam uenerationem antiquitatis."*[38] The underlined, legal words were used also by Tertullian. In the *Apologeticum*, he said of the Scriptures, *"auctoritatem summa antiquitas uindicat."*[39] And, in *On the Veiling of Virgins*, he stated, *"sed nolo interim hunc morem ueritati deputare."*[40] Lastly, the editor used *instrumentum* in a way that recalled Tertullian's many uses of that term.[41]

In closing his arguments, Robinson made two statements about Tertullian and Perpetua. First, in the closing eulogy, the martyrs were described as "most valiant and blessed martyrs *(fortissimi ac beatissimi martyres)*." Tertullian described Perpetua, almost identically, as *"fortissima martyr."*[42] Second, Robinson speculated that Tertullian's portrait of Patience, who "tramples temptations under foot" was inspired by Perpetua: "Her countenance is tranquil and peaceful; . . . the motion of her head frequent against the devil, and her laugh threatening."[43]

Adhemar d'Alès delivered the next extensive argument for Tertullian's editorship of the *Passion*, utilizing circumstantial as well as philological evidence. The editor addressed the audience as "my brethren and little children" (1.6) in the paternal tone of a bishop or priest. Following Jerome, d'Alès asserted that Tertullian served as a priest in Carthage during the time of the martyrdom.[44] Tertullian's position in the church, his reputation as a writer, and his fiery nature, which resonated with the heroism of the martyrs, combined to make him the natural choice to edit their stories. Furthermore, as evidenced by his adulation of Perpetua in *De anima*, he knew her by reputation if not personally. D'Alès found it incredible that there existed, simultaneously in Carthage, two priests with the vitality, emotion, education, and linguistic ability necessary to edit the *Passion*.[45] Furthermore, the spirit and emphasis in the editor's writing paralleled Tertullian's Montanist principles and purpose.[46]

D'Alès addressed Tertullian's silence regarding his authorship of the *Passion* and its omission from his catalog of works. Tertullian's role as narrator, of necessity, kept him in the background; so also did his desire to exalt the martyrs themselves. Then, his defection to Montanism tainted the memory of the martyrs, whom the Catholics also venerated, so his involvement was repressed by the orthodox church.[47] D'Alès concluded that "all the literary, historic, and theological evidence converge toward the attribution of the *Passion* to Tertullian."[48]

In two ways, W. H. Shewring contributed to the argument that Tertullian edited the *Passion*. First, he determined the editor's prose rhythms to be not only characteristic of a practiced writer but also similar to Tertullian's style.[49] Second, he offered as an explanation for the lack of specific identification two possibilities: the extant manuscripts derived from private copies, which naturally did not include the author's name; and the liturgical purpose of the *Passion* led churches to focus on the martyrs' stories rather than the editor's framework.[50]

The arguments for Tertullian's editorship, however, did not convince all scholars, including some who recognized the editor's

Montanism. Harris and Gifford, arguing for the priority of the Greek edition, out of hand dismissed Tertullian as editor.[51] Aubé thought it likely that Tertius or Pomponius was the unknown Montanist, who recorded the confessors' oral testimonies along with an eyewitness account of their martyrdom for purposes of propaganda.[52] Following this line of thought, Julio Campos suggested that the editor was either Pomponius or another of Tertullian's disciples.[53] William Tabbernee added Pudens, the converted prison guard, to the list of possible editors.[54] René Braun presented considerable philological arguments against Tertullian as editor, but he did perceive the language of Montanism in the framework of the *Passion*.[55] Uniquely, David Scholer speculated that the editor was "very possibly a woman" contending for the Montanist cause, but he offered no evidence for his idea.[56] Christine Trevett did not suggest Tertullian as editor, but she added the interesting point of view that Tertullian, who knew and honored these Montanist martyrs, was influenced by their deaths to acknowledge openly his allegiance to their cause.[57]

Timothy David Barnes, in his important monograph on Tertullian, cautiously approached the subject of Tertullian's involvement with the *Passion*. Barnes began with the thesis that "[c]ontrary to common belief, positive arguments for attributing any literary composition to a precise author are harder to sustain than the negative ones in favour of dissociation."[58] Admitting unmistakable resemblance between the literary style and Montanist theology of the editor and Tertullian, Barnes conjectured that a contemporary, even a friend or disciple, of Tertullian imitated his rhetoric. Ultimately, Barnes concluded that Tertullian's seeming misrepresentation of the *Passion* in *De anima* decided against his editorship.[59]

In fact, the evidence offered most often against Tertullian's editorship concerned his one reference to Perpetua in *De anima:*

And how is it that, the region of Paradise, which is placed under
the altar, as revealed in John's spirit, showed no other souls in it
except those of martyrs? How is it that Perpetua, most valiant
martyr, on the day of her suffering, saw in a revelation of Paradise
only martyrs in that place, if not because the sword, the doorkeeper
of Paradise, makes way for no one except those who have died in
Christ, not in Adam?[60]

One of Tertullian's purposes in this treatise was to show that only
martyrs had immediate access to heaven, and, in this section, he
used two texts as proof: Rev. 6.9 and Perpetua's vision of Paradise.
The *Passion* recorded two visions of Paradise, one revealed to Perpetua, and the other, to Saturus. Saturus' vision included specifically
named martyrs who died "in the same persecution" (11.9).[61] Many
scholars, therefore, assumed that Tertullian's reference to "fellow-
martyrs" indicated Saturus' vision and concluded that, by his allusion to Perpetua, who saw no martyrs in her vision, he erred in such
a way that he could not have edited the *Passion*.[62]

Closer inspection, however, reveals that such conclusions are
not without flaws. First, the alleged misstatement could be a conflation[63] or a detail which Tertullian, never an exact man, easily for-
got, especially since the diaries were written by Perpetua and Saturus.[64] Or the attribution to Perpetua could have been intentional for
two reasons: she was the better known; and Montanists emphasized
that *charismata* were given to women.[65]

Second, such a conclusion is founded on the Latin *commartyres*,
"fellow-martyrs," which is visible in Peter Holmes' translation of *De
anima*.[66] This expression resembled Saturus' vision more closely
than Perpetua's but was based on a variant reading, which was less
probable than the generic *martyras*,[67] which, in turn, applied to either vision.

Next, in her first vision, Perpetua saw "many thousands of people clad in white garments *(candidati milia multa)*," who stood in Paradise and, at one point, said, "Amen."[68] This scene, obviously reminiscent of Rev. 7.9–14,[69] readily fit within the parameters of Tertullian's statement that Perpetua saw only martyrs in paradise. On the other hand, Saturus, in his vision, saw not only martyrs but also the bishop Optatus, the presbyter Aspasius, and "many of our brethren, martyrs among them *(multos fratres . . . sed et martyras)*."[70]

Finally, the passage in *De anima*, with its reference to Perpetua's vision, evinced Tertullian's view of new revelation when compared to *Scorpiace* 12.9–10:

> But the souls of the martyrs both peacefully rest in the meantime under the altar, and support their patience by the assured hope of revenge; and, clothed in their robes, wear the dazzling halo of brightness, until others also may fully share in their glory. For yet again a countless throng are revealed, clothed in white and distinguished by palms of victory, celebrating their triumph doubtless over Antichrist, since one of the elders says, 'These are they who come out of that great tribulation, and have washed their robes, and made them white *(candidauerunt)* in the blood of the Lamb.'[71]

Here, Tertullian cited two references: Rev. 6.9 and Rev. 7.9–14. In *De anima*, Tertullian supported his argument with Rev. 6.9 and Perpetua's vision, in which she saw *candidati milia multa*. Essentially, the sequence was identical in both treatises, but, in the second, Tertullian attributed the vision of the white-robed martyrs to Perpetua, not to John the Revelator. By so doing, he cited Perpetua's vision in the same way as he did John's revelation. Thus, he followed a Montanist tenet and elevated the continuing revelation of the Spirit to the level of authoritative sacred writings.[72]

In sum, Tertullian did not err when he referred to Perpetua's vision in *De anima*. However, just as the alleged mistake did not necessarily preclude his editorship of the *Passion*, so also his correct attribution did not verify his involvement. Yet, one more proof can be advanced in this regard. As Tertullian acknowledged continuing revelation, so the editor honored new prophecies and visions.[73] If not identical, the two were, at least, spiritually akin.

Despite evidence that the editor of the *Passion* was either Tertullian or another Montanist, some scholars argued otherwise. William Weinrich added a novel argument against Tertullian's editorship, contrasting Tertullian's and the editor's attitudes toward childbearing. In *Ad uxorem*, Tertullian called children a "bitter delight" and insisted that widows "will freely bear to the end whatsoever pressure and persecution, with no burdensome fruit of marriage heaving in the womb, none in the bosom."[74] This attitude, according to Weinrich, contradicted the view of the editor, who devoted an entire chapter to Felicitas' delivery in prison.[75] Weinrich found in this narrative "no hint that Felicitas' pregnancy is an encumbrance which impinges upon her preparedness for or steadfastness in persecution. Merely the timing of her pregnancy is inopportune."[76] On the contrary, Felicitas' pregnancy was such an encumbrance to her martyrdom that only the prayers of her companions alleviated the situation by precipitating her delivery. Moreover, Tertullian intended his exhortations in *Ad uxorem* to encourage men and women to abstain from second marriages, but Weinrich forced an application to Felicitas.

Not only denying that the editor was Tertullian, Weinrich also found no reason to assume that the editor was a Montanist.[77] Weinrich attributed Perpetua's ecstasy in the arena not to a Montanist ideal but to the preservation of martyrs discussed in the *Martyrdom of Polycarp* or the acts of the martyrs of Lyons.[78] In these other accounts, however, the martyrs were said to be communing with God or, at the most, not present in the flesh. The editor of the *Passion* chose a specially Montanist term, "ecstasy," to describe Perpetua's state.

Weinrich also mentioned Lyons in a comparison between the situation there and at Carthage. Just as Montanism had infected the Gallic congregation, so the movement possibly had engendered in Carthage a conflict over the Spirit, which Weinrich perceived in the preface.[79] Weinrich's argument, however, worked against himself, because the editor, who honored new prophecies, new visions, and all other gifts of the Holy Spirit, would have sided with the Montanists.

Overall, arguments for Tertullian's editorship outweigh but do not overwhelm arguments to the contrary. Nonetheless, support of the thesis that the *Passion* was a thoroughly Montanist document requires proof, not that the editor was Tertullian, but that the editor was a Montanist. The vast majority of scholars corroborate this conclusion, which is verified by examination of the editor's preface and concluding narrative.

In this regard, Perpetua, as implied by her and specified by the editor, submitted her diary to the editor and commissioned him or her to complete the story of her passion by authoring the account of her and her companions' martyrdom. Surely this trusted colleague participated in Perpetua's community of faith. Therefore, the editor's Montanism must have been shared by Perpetua, Saturus, and their companions.

CHAPTER THREE

Examination of the *Passion*

After the exploration of the authorship of the *Passion*, the next step is the examination of the document for Montanist viewpoints, which are judged by criteria established in chapter one. The *Passion* consists of four sections: a preface; Perpetua's narrative, including four visions; Saturus' vision; and the account of the martyrdom. Each section contains a variety of allusions both Montanist and Catholic. This admixture is not surprising, considering the Carthaginian Montanists' situation as members of house churches within the larger Christian community. In fact, the value of this examination of the *Passion* consists not only in the appraisal of Montanist evidence but also in the discovery of the subject matter of early catechesis. Therefore, both influences are the foci of this examination.

The Preface

In the opening lines, the editor honored contemporary acts equally with ancient deeds. In fact, he or she claimed that "the more recent events should be considered the greater *(maiora)*" against the opposition, "who would restrict the power of the one Spirit to times and seasons."[1] This assertion reflected two Montanist elements. First, Montanists were censured for introducing novelty, a charge which Tertullian disputed while arguing that the Spirit's work advanced toward "better things *(ad meliora)*" and amplified prior revelations.[2] Second, Montanists contended that the ecclesiastical hierarchy had relegated the Spirit's activity to the past.[3]

The editor considered the recent manifestation of the Spirit to be the fulfillment of the eschatological promise in Acts 2.17–18.[4] For their purposes, Montanists appropriated this passage and its Old Testament parallel in Joel 2:28–29 (3:1 in the Hebrew Scripture) with their emphases on the last days; prophecies, visions, and dreams; and the prophetic activity of women as well as men.[5] The editor extolled "new prophecies" and "new visions" *(prophetias . . . et uisiones nouas)*,[6] phrases which recalled the self-designation of New Prophecy. Furthermore, the Holy Spirit continued to administer all the *charismata*, especially the grace of martyrdom and visions.

Despite these hallmarks of the Montanist faith, William Weinrich disputed that the preface contained "Montanist argumentation."[7] He focused on the editor's statement that the current deeds "will one day become ancient and needful for the ages to come *(posteris)*" as evidence that "the redactor does not display a heightened sense of the nearness of the end-time."[8] Montanist emphasis upon Christ's return, however, never negated preparation for the future. Montanus appointed a financial officer, arranged to have offerings collected and distributed for ongoing work, and organized a Montanist hierarchy.[9] The editor, in the same way, recognized the need of posterity for a record of the *Passion*.

Weinrich concluded that "within the Church at Carthage there was a dispute concerning the continuance of certain phenomena of the Spirit within the Church. One party denied that the Spirit still

worked in the selfsame manner as in earlier periods. The other party—to which the redactor of the *Passio* would have belonged—affirmed that the Spirit continued to act in the Church as it had always acted."[10] Weinrich admitted the possibility that the conflict
derived from "the introduction of Montanism into Carthage," and
his depiction of the situation correctly mirrored the context of multiple house churches in Carthage, where one or more congregations
were dominated by new prophets.[11]

Assuming that many readers were witnesses to the events of the
Passion, the editor urged them to recall the glory of the Lord. Furthermore, the editor encouraged other readers to "have fellowship
with the holy martyrs and, through them, with the Lord Christ Jesus" (1.6). Montanist theology of martyrdom considered incarcerat-
ed confessors to be martyrs and accorded to them the power of the
keys. Apollonius, anti-Montanist polemicist writing about 200, denounced two Montanists, imprisoned and released, who claimed
prerogatives as confessor/martyrs. First, Themiso "boasting as a
martyr and imitating the apostle, presumed to compose a universal
epistle to instruct those who had been more faithful than he." Second, Alexander claimed the authority to forgive sins.[12] The confessors' authority to bind and loose sins and, therefore, to assure communion with Christ was common among Montanists.[13] The editor
attributed that authority to the martyrs of the *Passion*, and, indeed,
Perpetua and Saturus themselves claimed that authority in their
narratives.[14]

Before completing his preface, the editor introduced the arrested
catechumens: "Revocatus and Felicitas, his fellow-slave *(conserua)*,[15]
Saturninus and Secundulus; among these also was Vibia Perpetua,
nobly born, graciously raised, and honorably married" (2.1).[16] The
editor provided a detailed description of Perpetua, the main heroine
of the passion. Her noble family included her living mother and fa-

ther and two brothers, one of whom was a catechumen. Another brother, Dinocrates, had died as a boy. She was twenty-two years old and married with an infant son. Other than this reference to her marriage, however, her husband never entered this narrative. In the *Acts of Perpetua and Felicitas,* an abridged version, the husband attended the trial and urged Perpetua to choose life, not death. His absence in Perpetua's personal narrative, however, is an enigma that has elicited much speculation.[17] A possible explanation derives from the history of the early Montanists Priscilla and Maximilla, of whom Apollonius asserted: "[T]hese foremost prophetesses, once they were filled with the Spirit, abandoned their husbands."[18] This tradition could have influenced Perpetua, without officially leaving her husband, to ignore her ties to him and focus on her ties to Christ. The editor emphasized such a spiritual relationship in his later description of her "as the beloved of God, as a wife of Christ" (18.2).

Perpetua's Diary

Having introduced Perpetua and her comrades, the editor presented Perpetua's narrative, "according to her own ideas and in the way that she herself wrote it down" (2.3). Perpetua arranged her "outer" experiences around her "inner" visions: the bronze ladder, Dinocrates, and the contest with the Egyptian.[19]

The Bronze Ladder

Perpetua began her narrative with her gradual severance of familial ties, especially with her father. In the narrative portions of her diary, Perpetua revealed her father's deep affection for her. Such affection was reminiscent of another Roman father, described by Pliny the Younger, who was totally devoted to his thirteen-year-old daughter and, following her death, abandoned all restraint in his grief.[20] Likewise, throughout the narrative, Perpetua's father, in the face of her impending death, expressed the full range of grievous emotions: anger, sorrow, and intense pain.

During the first recorded confrontation, while Perpetua and her colleagues were "under legal surveillance *(prosecutoribus essemus),*"[21] her father out of affection for his daughter tried to persuade her to recant. She pointed to a vase *(uas)* and proclaimed that, just as the vase could not be called by any other name, so she could not be called anything other than "what I am, a Christian *(quod sum, Christiana)*."[22] Paul Allard suggested that this allusion was inspired by early Christian art, in which a vase carved on a tomb symbolized a Christian life.[23] This image, in turn, reflected the metaphor of 2 Cor. 4.7: "But we have this treasure in clay jars *(uasis)*." Indeed, the context of Paul's statement, which focused on persecution, could have provided the source for Perpetua's original impulse as she cast about for an illustration to give her father.[24] By identifying herself simply as a Christian, she followed the tradition of the Scillitan martyrs, who died in North Africa twenty years earlier. When urged to renounce the Christian faith, "Vestia said: 'I am a Christian *(Christiana).*' Secunda said: 'I wish to be what I am *(quod sum).*'"[25]

Perpetua reported that her father, angered by the word "Christian," threatened to "pluck my eyes out" but departed instead, "vanquished along with his diabolical arguments" (3.3). Thus, she communicated her viewpoint that Satan was behind all efforts to subvert her confession. Although the image of her threatening father reappeared in her first vision, she was, for the moment, thankful for his absence. Rigorous Montanism would have sustained her renunciation of family; such a sacrifice, however, was not unique to the new prophets but common among Christian martyrs.

During the few days between her indictment and imprisonment,

Perpetua and the other catechumens were baptized hastily because of their impending imprisonment.[26] Her first recorded experience in the Spirit occurred following baptism: "I was inspired by the Spirit not to ask for any other favour after the water but simply the perseverance of the flesh" (3.5). Her experience resembled Tertullian's exhortation to catechumens in his treatise *De baptismo:* "Therefore, . . . when you ascend from that most sacred font of your new birth, and spread your hands for the first time, . . . ask from the Father . . . that His own specialities of grace and distributions of gifts may be supplied you."[27] At baptism, then, Perpetua was inspired to ask for the *charisma* of martyrdom, the ability to confess her faith and endure persecution.[28]

Separation from her nursing baby, along with the terrors of the prison, caused her great anguish both emotionally and physically: "I had never before been in such a dark hole. What a difficult time it was! With the crowd the heat was stifling; . . . and to crown it all, I was tortured with worry for my baby there" (3.5–6). The deacons Tertius and Pomponius, however, bribed the soldiers to move the prisoners to better quarters, where Perpetua was allowed to keep her son with her. Then she wrote, "My prison *(carcer)* had suddenly become a palace, so that I wanted to be there rather than anywhere else" (3.9).

Perpetua's image of her prison as a palace is reminiscent of Tertullian's description of prison in *Ad Martyras*, written in 197 and circulated in the Christian community. Writing to imprisoned confessors,[29] Tertullian said of their prison, "It is full of darkness, but ye yourselves are light; it has bonds, but God has made you free. Unpleasant exhalations are there, but ye are an odour of sweetness. . . . The Christian outside the prison has renounced the world, but in the prison he has renounced a prison too. . . . Let us drop the name of prison *(carceris)*; let us call it a place of retirement." Tertullian pictured similarly both the suffering and the relief which Perpetua found in imprisonment. Then, he added these instructions: "Though the body is shut in, though the flesh is confined, all things are open to the spirit. In spirit, then, roam abroad; in spirit walk about, not setting before you shady paths or long colonnades, but the way which leads to God. As often as in spirit your footsteps are there, so often you will not be in bonds. The leg does not feel the chain when the mind is in the heavens."[30] Perpetua moved about often in the spirit, through her visions.

In prison, Perpetua confidently approached her visions, demonstrating experience as a prophetess. Montanism nurtured such gifted women, whom the ecclesiastical establishment limited,[31] so Perpetua's prophetic activity indicated her association with the egalitarian movement. Her brother,[32] cognizant of her reputation, occasioned a vision by requesting her to inquire about her destiny. Both Perpetua and this brother expected visions on demand, as befitted Montanists.[33] The answer came in the vision of a bronze ladder.

From her vision, Perpetua described a bronze *(aeream)* ladder, so high it reached to heaven but so narrow it must be climbed singly. Weapons of war and torture, attached to the sides of the ladder, threatened to mangle the flesh of a careless climber.[34] A possible key to interpreting this element of the vision is Jacob's ladder (Gen. 28.12), a link between earth and heaven, where a divine figure spoke to the seer.[35] Tertullian interpreted Jacob's dream of a ladder as a picture of martyrdom: some ascend and others descend in a contest, through which the martyrs conquer their persecutors and receive heavenly crowns and rewards.[36] Another biblical parallel is Jesus' statement: "For the gate is narrow and the road is hard that leads to life, and there are few who find it" (Matt. 7:14 NRSV).[37]

Some features distinctive to the bronze ladder, however, suggest another source, 4 Ezra (= 2 Esdras), a pseudepigraphic apocalypse composed in the early second century and known to Tertullian.[38] Ezra received a prophecy concerning the coming of a vast, rich city, founded upon a verdant field: "There is a city built and set on a plain, and it is full of all good things; but the entrance to it is narrow and set in a precipitous place, so that there is fire on the right hand and deep water on the left. There is only one path lying between them, that is, between the fire and the water, so that only one person can walk on the path. If now the city is given to someone as an inheritance, how will the heir receive the inheritance unless by passing through the appointed danger?" (4 Ezra = 2 Esdras 7:6–9 NRSV). In both visions, the promised refuge was attained by ascending a narrow, precipitous path fraught with danger, either Ezra's fire and water or Perpetua's metal weapons.[39]

Perpetua specified that these weapons were swords, spears, hooks, daggers, and spikes: implements of execution. Certainly she saw in these instruments the probability of capital punishment for her offense against Severus, but, in a spiritual dimension, she recognized that the Roman government, in collusion with Satan, used fear to deter Christians from the narrow way.[40]

Perpetua saw at the foot of the ladder an enormous dragon (*draco*, δράκων) who attempted to frighten aspirants from ascending. An obvious parallel was "the dragon, that ancient serpent, who is the Devil and Satan" (Rev. 20.2 NRSV), a prominent figure in the Johannine Apocalypse.[41] Thus, Perpetua pictured Satan as the one deterring her from confessing her faith through martyrdom. She previously had cast her father in the devil's role when she said that he "departed, vanquished along with his diabolical arguments."[42] Just as her father threatened and retreated, so did the dragon in her vision.

At this point, Perpetua introduced Saturus, the catechist of the young confessors.[43] He was not present when they were arrested but later surrendered himself voluntarily on their account because he had edified them.[44] Timothy David Barnes assumed that this act of voluntary martyrdom proved that Saturus was a Montanist.[45] According to William Tabbernee, however, he desired to join his catechumens in order to prevent their apostasy.[46] Weinrich further insisted that Perpetua's parenthetical statement, *quia ipse nos aedificauerat*, indicated only Saturus' concern for his pupils and that, by this phrase, she specifically intended to avoid a Montanist interpretation.[47] In actuality, the juxtaposition of his surrender *(se . . . tradiderat)* and his edification of the catechumens *(nos aedificauerat)* signified that his voluntary martyrdom modeled the Montanist training he had given his charges.

In orthodox martyrologies, voluntary martyrdom was not approved. In the mid-second century *Martyrdom of Polycarp* there is a pericope about Quintus, a Phrygian who had given himself up voluntarily and encouraged others to do likewise. Because he cowardly recanted, the writer stated, "For this reason, therefore, brothers, we do not approve those who come forward voluntarily, because the Gospel does not teach in this way."[48] A century later, Cyprian confirmed the Catholic policy: ". . . our discipline forbids anyone to surrender voluntarily."[49] Tertullian, however, balked at orthodoxy and followed instead the New Prophecy:

> Yes, and if you ask counsel of the Spirit, what does He approve more than that utterance of the Spirit? For, indeed, it incites all almost to go and offer themselves in martyrdom, not to flee from it; so that we also make mention of it. If you are exposed to public infamy, says he, it is for your good; for he who is not exposed to dishonour among men is sure to be so before the Lord. Do not be ashamed; righteousness brings you forth into the public gaze. Why should you be ashamed of gaining glory? The opportunity is given

you when you are before the eyes of men. So also elsewhere: seek
not to die on bridal beds, nor in miscarriages, nor in soft fevers, but
to die the martyr's death, that He may be glorified who has suffered
for you.[50]

Elsewhere, he said, "[I]f you have to lay down your life for God, as
the Comforter *(paracletus)* counsels, it is not in gentle fevers and on
soft beds, but in the sharp pains of martyrdom."[51] In Carthage, at
least, the attitude toward voluntary martyrdom distinguished the
Montanists from the Catholics.

When Perpetua introduced Saturus, she envisioned him ascending the ladder, which clearly symbolized martyrdom. The editor interpreted Saturus' preceding Perpetua on the ladder as a portent of
his preceding her in death: "Saturus, who being the first to climb
the stairway was the first to die" (21.8). From the top of the ladder,
he warned Perpetua about the dragon, but she answered, "He will
not harm me . . . in the name of Christ Jesus" (4.6).

This encounter recalled a vision from the *Shepherd of Hermas*, in
which Hermas was terrorized by a sea-monster, raising a cloud of
dust. After calling upon the Lord for rescue, he put on the faith of
the Lord and subdued the beast. Shortly, Hermas met a white-
haired woman in bridal clothes, symbolizing the church, who told
him that his safety resulted from "believing that you are able to be
saved by nothing except the great and glorious name."[52]

After Perpetua spoke Jesus' name, the dragon, as though afraid,
protruded his head from underneath the ladder. "Then," Perpetua
said, "using it as my first step, I trod on his head and went up" (4.7).
This symbol of Perpetua's victory over the dragon/Satan had several parallels in Scripture. First, the curse on the serpent prophesied
of the woman's seed that "he will strike your head" (Gen. 3.15
NRSV). Second, Joshua invited the men of Israel to "put your feet
on the necks of these kings," defeated in war, and then he said, "Be

strong and courageous, for thus the Lord will do to all the enemies against whom you fight" (Josh. 10.24–25 NRSV). Third, Jesus promised his disciples, "See, I have given you authority to tread on snakes and scorpions, and over all the power of the enemy" (Luke 10.19 NRSV).[53] Tertullian drew on these same writings when he wrote to the martyrs in prison, "The prison, indeed, is the devil's house as well, wherein he keeps his family. But you have come within its walls for the very purpose of trampling the wicked one under foot in his chosen abode."[54]

Once Perpetua conquered the dragon, she ascended to an immense garden, where a tall, grey-haired man in shepherd's clothing was milking sheep, surrounded by thousands of white-robed people.[55] Here biblical images abound: the garden pictures paradise;[56] the tall, grey-haired man, the Ancient of Days;[57] the shepherd, the Lord in both Old and New Testaments;[58] and the thousands of attendants, the 144,000 martyrs, who come out of the great tribulation and surround the heavenly throne.[59]

During the encounter between Perpetua and the divine shepherd,[60] he welcomed her and gave to her "a morsel of cheese" *(caseo)*[61] which she "accepted with joined hands *(iunctis manibus)* and ate *(manducaui)*"(4.9).[62] According to Herbert Musurillo's translation, the shepherd offered Perpetua a "mouthful of milk," not cheese.[63] Along this line of thought, Anne Jensen, who interpreted all of Perpetua's visions as the assimilation of her experience with the baptismal rite of initiation, saw in this scene a post-baptismal Eucharistic rite, which included drinking a mixture of milk and honey *(lactis et mellis)*.[64]

A more precise translation of *caseus*, however, recognizes that Perpetua received not milk but cheese,[65] which was significant in one Montanist tradition. In the fourth century, the use of cheese in the Eucharist was imputed to Montanists by Epiphanius, who called these sectarians, Artotyrites (Ἀρτοτυρῖται), the "bread-and-cheese people."[66] Outside of Perpetua's vision, the use of cheese in the Eucharist is not found in any extant record written before the fourth century. Nonetheless, the similarity between Perpetua's Eucharistic cheese and later practices by Montanists is suggestive. Perhaps Perpetua engaged in an act of Eucharistic piety which, indeed, was customary among Montanists by the third century,[67] or perhaps her vision influenced the later Montanist sacrament, as Douglas Powell proposed: "what is seen to have happened in heaven brought down and sacramentalised upon earth."[68] The picture of the Eucharist was completed when the white-robed attendants said, "Amen," the traditional conclusion to the rite.[69]

At the sound of this word Perpetua was aroused from her ecstatic trance, "with the taste of something sweet still in my mouth." She related the vision and her interpretation to her brother: "from now on we would no longer have any hope in this life" (4.10). Without hope in this life, Perpetua's attention continued to focus on life hereafter, the scene of her next vision.

Dinocrates

In the interim between visions, Perpetua endured another encounter with her distraught father. Upon learning that Perpetua was to be arraigned before the governor, her father hastened to the prison "from the city" (5.1).[70] As he pleaded with her to recant, he threw himself down at her feet, addressing her not as his daughter *(filiam)* but as a lady *(dominam)*. She grieved "because he alone of all my kin would be unhappy to see me suffer" (5.5–6).[71] Among her family, therefore, only her father was not a Christian, or at least a sympathizer,[72] and thus would not rejoice at her martyrdom.[73]

Next in the narrative, the prisoners were arraigned before the procurator, Hilarianus.[74] Here again, Perpetua's father arrived to dissuade her from her confession. Hilarianus joined with her father and adjured her to offer a sacrifice to the emperors. When Perpetua persisted in her identification as a Christian *(Christiana sum)*, her father continued to intercede, but this time the procurator punished him with a beating. Perpetua deplored her father's punishment, but then she rejoiced when the governor passed sentence on the confessors and condemned them to the beasts. Back in prison, she sent Pomponius to retrieve her son, but her father refused her request, separating her finally from her son. Miraculously, though, neither the baby nor Perpetua suffered from the sudden weaning.[75]

Perhaps consternation over familial separation prompted the ensuing prophetic utterance. Perpetua, during communal prayer, suddenly spoke the name of Dinocrates, her brother, who died of a facial cancer at the age of seven. Evidently he had died several years previously, for, until that moment, she had not thought of him recently. "At once I realized that I was privileged to pray for him. I began to pray *(orationem facere;* προσεύχεσθαι) for him and to sigh deeply *(ingemescere;* στεναγμῶν) for him before the Lord" (7.1–2).

In this statement, Perpetua provided two clues of Montanist faith. First, her description of prayer contained language capable of interpretation as glossolalia. The same interpretation can be made of Rom. 8.26: "for we do not know how to pray *(oremus;* προσευξώμεθα)" as we ought, but that very Spirit intercedes with sighs *(gemitibus;* στεναγμοῖς) too deep for words" (NRSV). Origen linked this verse with praying in the Spirit, private glossolalia.[76] Therefore, Perpetua's utilization in her diary of terms for praying and sighing, identical in both Greek and Latin to the Greek New Testament and Vulgate, implied that she spoke in tongues.[77] Montanus also spoke in tongues,[78] a practice which came to be identified with his followers. The second clue was her claim to be in a privileged position to intercede for Dinocrates. The belief that the con-

fessor/martyr possessed the priestly power of the keys was an expression of Montanism.[79]

Her prayers resulted in two visions of Dinocrates. In the first vision, which occurred the night after she called his name, she saw the
boy "coming out of a dark hole, where there were many others with
him, very hot and thirsty, pale and dirty. On his face was the wound
he had when he died" (7.4). A great abyss separated Perpetua from
Dinocrates, who stood next to a pool but could not drink because
the rim was too high. Perpetua awoke, "realizing that my brother
was suffering," but "confident that I could help him in his trouble"
(7.9).[80]

Perpetua continued to offer prayer (*feci . . . orationem*; προσευξ-
αμένη) for Dinocrates daily, "with tears and sighs (*gemens*; στεναγμῶν)" (7.10). During this time, the prisoners were transferred
to the military prison in preparation for their contest with the wild
beasts, which coincided with the celebration of "the emperor Geta's
birthday" (7.9).[81] When she received the next vision, Dinocrates, although in the same place, was "clean, well dressed, and refreshed
(refrigerantem)," with a scar instead of a wound (8.1). Now the rim of
the pool was within the child's reach, and a golden bowl, continual-
ly full, was available.[82] After sating his thirst, "he began to play as
children do." After rousing, Perpetua "realized that he had been
delvered from his suffering *(poena)*" (8.4).

These visions pose problems. First, the images seemingly derived from both pagan and Christian sources. Perpetua was still
susceptible to pagan conceptions of the afterlife,[83] consistently pictured in a dark, gloomy abyss.[84] Prefiguring Dinocrates' plight, the
mythological character Tantalus, who offended the gods, was placed
in a pool that receded whenever he stooped, so he remained eternal-
ly thirsty.[85] Ancient epitaphs and the writings of Homer and Virgil
reported wounded figures in Hades, such as Deiphobus, whose facial

wounds particularly resembled Dinocrates' cancer.[86] Virgil's Aeneas also discovered that premature deaths sent infant souls to Hades to suffer as they had existed on earth, that is, as children.[87] Finally, the ancients believed that the living could enable the dead to move from a state of torment to a cessation of suffering.[88]

Among Christian sources, the Old Testament also described the abode of the dead as *sheol* (LXX, ᾅδης), a shadowy pit,[89] or "dark place." Jesus added to this description in his parable about Lazarus and the rich man (Luke 16.19–31). After both died, the rich man went to Hades but could see Lazarus far away, even though the two were separated by a "great chasm." Furthermore, in Hades the rich man suffered from thirst.

From the intertestamental period came a story of prayer for the dead. Following a battle, Judas Maccabeus and his troops discovered a band of fallen Jewish soldiers, each of whom had died wearing taboo, idolatrous tokens. Judas exhorted his followers not only to collect money for a sin offering but also to pray "that the sin that had been committed might be wholly blotted out." The narrator commended Judas because to pray for the dead "was a holy and pious thought" (2 Macc. 21.39–45).

Similarly, the *Acts of Paul and Thecla*, an apocryphal work from the late second century, recorded prayer for the dead. After a pagan queen's daughter died, Christian Thecla prayed to God on behalf of the deceased for eternal salvation.[90] As a Montanist, Tertullian, who knew these *Acts*,[91] said of a widow, "Truly, she both prays on behalf of his soul and requests refreshment for him in the interim *(refrigerium interim)* and fellowship with him in the first resurrection."[92] For Tertullian, this *refrigerium interim* was a restful wait for the righteous,[93] and, significantly, as a Montanist, he urged prayer for the dead.

The second problem with Perpetua's visions of Dinocrates was her belief that, as a confessor/martyr, she possessed sufficient merit to deliver a soul from suffering to consolation. Two centuries later, Augustine asserted that, through Perpetua's intercession, her brother was transferred from punishment to respite.[94] Jacques Le Goff, in fact, presumed that the *Passion* was "the earliest document we have in which it is possible to catch a glimpse of Purgatory."[95] But was Dinocrates transferred from hell to heaven, hell to purgatory, or purgatory to heaven? Such questions are anachronistic because the doctrine of purgatory was undeveloped in the early third century.[96] Perpetua believed that Dinocrates had been delivered from *poena*, "punishment, penalty." She did not refer to *purgatio*, "purification." Most important, however, are the observations that her practice of prayer for the dead was similar to Tertullian's and that her belief in the efficacy of intercessory prayers by a confessor/martyr was shared by Montanists.

The Contest with the Egyptian

Next Perpetua introduced a prison official *(miles optio)*, Pudens, who recognized the extraordinary virtue of the confessors and, as a result, allowed them visitors for mutual comfort.[97] Among those visitors was one who did not bring comfort, Perpetua's father. When Tertullian wrote *Ad Martyras*, he warned that parents would be hindrances to the soul even at the prison,[98] and Perpetua's father certainly proved the point. He tore hairs from his beard, an ancient sign of extreme sorrow, and threw himself once more on the ground, a posture Perpetua would see recreated in her next vision.

Whereas Perpetua requested her first vision and prompted her second vison through her prayers, her final vision had no impetus other than its timing: the day before her fight with the beasts.[99] This vision consisted of three scenes, in the first of which Pomponius escorted Perpetua from her cell to the center of the arena.

Pomponius' unbelted, white tunic suggested various associations. First, the detail repeated the attire of the attendants in her first vision as well as the martyrs in Rev. 7.9–17. Second, as Hermas' white-robed lady represented the church, so Pomponius indicated the support Perpetua received from her Christian family with his words, "We are waiting for you" (10.3).[100] Third, Hermas provided another parallel to Pomponius' words in an oracle delivered by the Angel of Repentance. Pomponius said, "Perpetua, come . . . . Do not be afraid. I am here, struggling with you." The Angel of Repentance said to Hermas, "[D]o not be frightened of the devil, . . . for I will be with you." Even the context of the angel's words matched Pomponius', for the angel assured Hermas, "The devil is able to wrestle against [God's servants], but he is not able to overthrow them."[101] Just as the Angel of Repentance brought a word from the Lord, so Pomponius brought Perpetua a promise of the Lord's support in her contest.[102]

In the second scene at the arena, Perpetua was surprised to be confronted, not by wild beasts, but by an abominable *(foedus)* Egyptian.[103] She did not name him immediately, but during the course of the vision, his identity as Satan became clear. Tertullian frequently denounced Egypt, "most depraved *(foedissimam)* and superstitious," as the oppressor of God's people.[104] Furthermore, in his treatise *De baptismo*, he specifically compared the Egyptian Pharaoh, extinguished in the water of the Red Sea, with the devil, defeated through the water of baptism.[105] Perhaps Perpetua's picture of Satan as an Egyptian derived from the common conception among Roman and Carthaginian Christians of a black devil, in keeping with the way of darkness.[106] The *Epistle of Barnabas*, a pseudonymous work originating in Alexandria, referred to Satan as the "black one (ὁ μέλας)".[107] Brent Shaw asserted that this image was "a simple reflection of racism" against Egyptians, who "were the most despised, hated and reviled ethnic group in the Roman world—therefore an appropriate choice for a dark and satanic thing."[108] Later, the Egyptian added to his satanic *persona* by "rolling in the dust" (10.7), imitating God's curse on the serpent: "[U]pon your belly you shall go, and dust you shall eat all the days of your life" (Gen. 3.14 NRSV).[109]

Perpetua's preparation for the battle conjured up a striking image. Handsome young attendants[110] stripped off her clothes and rubbed her with oil, a common practice before a contest. During this process, Perpetua announced, "[A]nd suddenly I was a man *(et facta sum masculus)*" (10.7). From the writings that today constitute the Bible, no parallel was available for such a phenomenon other than Paul's egalitarian manifesto: "[T]here is no longer male and female; for all of you are one in Christ Jesus" (Gal. 3.28 NRSV).[111] The pseudepigraphic 4 Maccabees, however, provided a first-century equivalent to gender transformation in its story about a Jewish mother who watched all seven of her sons tortured and killed for their faith under the Antiochene persecution. Because "devout reason, giving her heart a man's courage in the very midst of her emotions, strengthened her to disregard, for the time her parental love," she was praised: "O more noble than males in steadfastness, and more courageous than men in endurance!" (4 Macc. 15.23, 39 NRSV).[112]

Two Gnostic writings also spoke of gender transformation. In the *Gospel of Mary*, Mary stood up before the fearful disciples and included herself as one of them, saying, "[H]e prepared us and made us into men."[113] The *Gospel of Thomas* removed gender distinctions in Jesus' eschatological declaration: "[W]hen you make the male and the female into a single one, . . . then shall you enter [the Kingdom]."[114] The conclusion of the *Gospel of Thomas*, however, resembled Perpetua's experience most closely.[115] In the disciples' conversa-

tion with Jesus, Peter said, "Let Mary go out from among us, because women are not worthy of the Life." Then Jesus answered,
"See, I shall lead her, so that I will make her male, that she too may
become a living spirit, resembling you males. For every woman who
makes herself male will enter the Kingdom of Heaven."[116] The ac-
cessibility of this document to the Carthaginian community is inde-
terminable, but the possibility exists that its androgynism could
have influenced Perpetua's vision of confessional fulfillment.[117]

Within Montanism, however, were more likely and sufficiently
egalitarian emphases to sustain Perpetua's androgynous image.
From the origins of the movement, women such as Priscilla and
Maximilla played roles equal to that of Montanus, the founder. By
the fourth century, if not earlier, Montanists ordained women as
ministers.[118] This tradition, furthermore, provided an example of
gender transformation. Epiphanius attributed to either Priscilla or
Quintilla a vision in which Christ assumed the form of a woman in a
radiant garment to bring wisdom and revelation to the prophetess.[119] Marie-Louise von Franz found another parallel to Perpetua's
transformation in Maximilla, who, inspired by the Spirit, spoke
of herself in the masculine form: "The Lord has commissioned me
as a separatist, illuminator, and interpreter (αἱρετιστὴν μηνυτὴν
ἑρμηνευτὴν) of this suffering and covenant and promise."[120] According to the Montanists' conviction, therefore, "when the prophetic spirit breathes where it will there is no sexual preference.
[Perpetua] is called bride, mother, sister, daughter, and lady; but
also leader, warrior, victor, and fighter. She is at times gentle, wom-
anly, kind, motherly, tender; at other times strong, fierce, daring,
courageous."[121] Perpetua offered, through the symbolism of gender
transformation, an example of Montanist empowerment of women
in a patriarchal society and church.

In the arena, Perpetua beheld one other image, a man who towered above the top of the arena.[122] Dressed in a purple-striped tunic, he held a staff of office as if he were the master of gladiators *(lanista)* or the superintendent of games (βραβευτὴς ἤ προστάτης μονο-μάχων).[123] Tertullian used similar terminology from athletic competitions to describe the triune God's relationship to martyrs.[124] In *Ad martyras,* he combined several elements expressed later in the *Passion:* "You are about to undergo a noble contest in which the superintendent of games *(agonothetes)* is the living God and your trainer is the Holy Spirit, . . . and, therefore, your overseer, Christ Jesus, who anoints you with the Spirit, also leads you forth into the arena."[125]

The towering figure delivered the charges to the contestants. The Egyptian, if victorious, would slay Perpetua with the sword, but Perpetua, if victorious, would receive a green branch with golden apples. Such a challenge echoed a familiar motif from the New Testament, the promise of reward to the victor, for example: "To everyone who conquers, I will give permission to eat from the tree of life that is in the paradise of God" (Rev. 2.7 NRSV); and "Blessed is anyone who endures temptation. Such a one has stood the test and will receive the crown of life" (Jam. 1.12 NRSV).[126] Once again, the *Shepherd of Hermas* provided a clue to the interpretation of Perpetua's vision. In a parable, a tall angel distributed willow branches to many people, who returned the cuttings, some withered and some green and fruit-bearing. To those whose branches bore fruit the angel presented crowns and white clothing, representing eternal life.[127] In the same way, when Perpetua received the branch after her victory, she walked triumphantly towards the Gate of Life *(portam Sanauiuariam).*[128]

Finally, in the third scene, the fight began between Perpetua and the Egyptian.[129] In the course of the battle, he attempted to grab her feet, giving her the opportunity to strike him in the face with her heels. Perpetua reported that, at one point, "I was raised up into the air and I began to pummel him without as it were touching the ground" (10.11).[130] At the conclusion, he fell on his face, and she stepped on his head.[131] The allusion to Gen. 3.15 is obvious as is the identification of the Egyptian with the dragon.[132] After waking, she postulated a two-fold interpretation of the vision. First, she would fight not wild animals but the devil, a common theme in early Christian acts of martyrdom.[133] Second, she would be victorious, following Tertullian's conception of martyrdom: "We, with the crown eternal in our eye, look upon the prison as our training-ground, that at the goal of final judgment we may be brought forth well disciplined by many a trial."[134]

After she related her fourth vision, Perpetua knew that her time was short and that someone else would finish her story as it unfolded in the arena. She concluded her diary: "So much for what I did up until the eve of the contest. About what happened at the contest itself, let him write of it who will" (10.15). Before telling that story, however, the editor inserted Saturus' vision, which Saturus also wrote in his own hand.

Saturus' Vision

In Saturus' vision, he and Perpetua had already died. Their martyrdom having been accomplished, Saturus' vision focused exclusively on the afterlife, a subject that was also present in Perpetua's visions. Similarities between their expectations resulted from Saturus' position as the confessors' catechist, whose eschatology had influenced Perpetua. On the other hand, the images communicated by Saturus revealed possible influences of ancient Christian texts which he taught to the catechumens.[135]

In the first act of this vision, Perpetua and Saturus had put off the flesh and were being carried east by four angels, who did not touch them. Their posture appeared as though they were ascending a gentle slope. Once free of the world, they saw an intense light. The experience prompted Saturus to acknowledge the fulfillment of God's promise. The angels transported them to a garden of rose bushes and tall trees, where four other angels greeted them decorously. Perpetua and Saturus met other martyrs there, but, before they were allowed to converse, the angels insisted that they first greet the Lord.[136]

In the second scene of the first act, Saturus and Perpetua come to a gated place made of light and guarded by four white-robed angels. Once inside, they heard voices endlessly chanting, "Holy, holy, holy!" (Ἅγιος, ἅγιος, ἅγιος) and saw on a throne "an aged man with white hair and a youthful face" surrounded by elders. They kissed him, and he touched their faces. Then, after exchanging the kiss of peace with the elders, they were instructed, "Go and play" (12.6).[137] Saturus said to Perpetua, "Your wish has been granted," and Perpetua responded, "Thanks be to God that I am happier here now than I was in the flesh" (12.7).

The second act took place before the gates of this place of light, where Saturus and Perpetua saw the bishop Optatus and the teaching presbyter Aspasius, each separated from the other and sad. They fell before Saturus and Perpetua and begged the martyrs to make peace between them. The martyrs, protesting their prostration, embraced them and spoke to them, Perpetua speaking in Greek. The angels, however, interrupted and scolded the ecclesiastics. The angels instructed Optatus to discipline his flock for quarreling. Next, the angels wanted to close the gates, at which time, Saturus and Perpetua recognized many martyrs there. Finally, Saturus woke up happy, sustained by a delicious, satisfying odor.[138]

About ten years after the martyrdom, Tertullian wrote in *De anima* a similar description of the post-death experience:

> Undoubtedly, when the soul . . . is released from its concretion with
> the flesh, . . . it is, moreover, certain that it escapes . . . into open
> space, to its clear, and pure, and intrinsic light; and then finds itself
> enjoying its enfranchisement from matter, and by virtue of its lib-
> erty it recovers its divinity . . . . Then it tells out what it sees; then
> it exults or it fears, . . . as soon as it sees the very angel's face, that
> arraigner of souls.[139]

Similarity of imagery and language, such as "flesh," "angel," "freedom," and "light," suggests that Tertullian either utilized Saturus'
vision in this treatise[140] or that both drew from the same source. In
either case, Saturus' description of life after death represented ideas
present in the Carthaginian congregation.[141]

Among the biblical allusions in this vision was the idea that
angels carried away the righteous dead to their reward, which
appeared also in Jesus' parable of the rich man and Lazarus.[142] Also,
the angels carried their charges to a garden "towards the east
(ἀνατολάς)," the direction of the Garden of Eden.[143] The single,
greatest biblical influence upon Saturus' vision, however, came from
Revelation.[144] Several times in the vision four angels appeared, reminiscent of the four living creatures of Revelation.[145] Another
comparison was possible between the twenty-four elders (*seniores*,
Vulgate; πρεσβυτέρους) of Revelation and the elders (*seniores*;
πρεσβύτεροι) of the vision. Although Saturus specified only four,
he did refer to others (*ceteri seniores*; πολλοὶ πρεσβύτεροι) behind
them.[146] John's beatific vision clearly was represented in Saturus' vision by the endless chanting of the Trisagion, quoted in Greek even
in the Latin version,[147] which was delivered up in praise to a towering figure, who was seated on a throne and described as "an aged
man with white hair and a youthful face" (12.3).[148] Moreover, this
divine figure "touched our faces with his hand" (12.5), a gesture
which recalled Rev. 7.17, which also concerned martyrs in heaven:
"God will wipe away every tear from their eyes" (NRSV).[149]

Two alternative readings, if accepted, provide further biblical references. In the *Passion* 12.1, four angels "put on white robes *(uestierunt stolas candidas)*." In Codex Compendiensis, however, Saturus said, "And we were dressed in white robes *(et nos uestiti stolas candidas)*." The Greek translation further amended the text, reporting that "the four angels dressed us in white robes (οἱ τέσσαρες ἄγγελοι ἐνέδυσαν ἡμᾶς λευκὰς στολάς)." Either alternative reenacted the scene in Rev. 6.11, where martyrs' souls were given white robes.

J. Armitage Robinson suggested the other emendation, which had no textual support but clarified the picture considerably.[150] According to the text of Codex Casinensis, Saturus stated, "The trees were as tall as cypresses, and their leaves were constantly falling *(quarum folia cadebant sine cessatione)*."[151] The concept of falling leaves contradicted the biblical images of heavenly trees, particularly in Ezek. 47.12: "Their leaves will not wither" (NRSV).[152] Codex Salisburgensis offered a different verb, *ardebant* ("burning"), which was no improvement. Robinson substituted a third verb, *canebant*, "singing," which had considerable biblical background, for example, 1 Chron. 16.33: "Then shall the trees of the forest sing for joy before the Lord; for he comes to judge the earth" (NRSV).[153] Robinson further supported his correction by citing the *Testament of Abraham*, where a cypress tree with a human voice cried out the Trisagion.[154] Accordingly, the leaves of Saturus' cypress-like trees were singing constantly.

As expected in a vision of the afterlife, influences from apocalyptic writings, both Jewish and Christian, abounded in Saturus' presentation. Later in the *Testament of Abraham*, a Jewish-Christian document of the second century, "Michael the archangel appeared with a multitude of angels, and they lifted up [Abraham's] precious soul in their hands in divinely woven fine linen . . . and returned to heaven singing the trisagion hymn to God, the Master of the universe."[155]

First Enoch, which originated in the intertestamental period, provided several images. Enoch, accompanied by angels, journeyed "a great distance toward the eastern region of the earth," where he "arrived at the garden of righteousness and saw . . . the tree of knowledge. . . . That same tree is tall like a pine, . . . and its fragrance traveled far from the tree."[156] Once in the new heaven, Enoch saw first "four angels of the Lord of Spirits" and then "One, who had a head of days, and His head was white like wool." There, the "resplendent" righteous dead are brought forth "in shining light."[157]

Saturus received inspiration from the *Shepherd of Hermas* as did Perpetua. The two martyrs' ascent, "carried towards the east by four angels" (11.2), echoed the close of Hermas' first vision. There the woman, who represents the church, was transported by two angels, who carried her by the arms toward the East, where earlier, four angels had transported her chair. Perhaps the method of carriage mirrored the posture of Saturus and Perpetua, who arose "as though we were climbing up a gentle hill."[158] In Hermas' third vision, this woman appeared with a beautiful, youthful face but old hair.[159]

A significant source for Saturus' vision was the *Apocalypse of Peter*, a second-century book possibly included in writings considered sacred in North Africa and very influential upon other Christian apocalypses.[160] The Petrine apocalypse described heaven as "extremely bright with light, . . . blossoming with flowers that never fade and filled with aromatic spices and garden plants, . . . and the flowery fragrance was so strong that it was carried from there all the way to us." The heavenly residents were clad in shining raiment, "and angels surrounded them in that place."[161]

Finally, similarities existed also between Saturus' and Perpetua's visions of heaven. The posture of ascent in both visions was upright, whether the flight in Saturus' vision or the ascent up the ladder in Perpetua's. Both envisioned heaven as a garden, occupied by white-robed martyrs and a divine figure with white hair. Another point of contact was provided by two towering, divine figures: one sat on the throne in Saturus' beatific vision, and the other presided over Perpetua's contest in her fourth vision.[162]

The episode with Optatus and Aspasius revealed Saturus' Montanism in two ways. First, their prostration before the confessors and their exclusion from the heavenly inner court fitted the Montanists' elevation of martyrs over clergy.[163] Second, Saturus believed, along with Montanists, that the confessor/martyr possessed the power of the keys to mediate peace between Christian factions, even when represented by ecclesiastical hierarchy.[164]

Weinrich denied any evidence of Montanism in this scene. He interpreted the confessors' attitudes to be deferential, rather than superior, because they said, "Are you not our bishop *(papa noster)*, and are you not our presbyter? How can you fall at our feet?" (13.3). For Weinrich, even the term *papa* signified respect. Furthermore, the angels' rebuked the clergy, "Allow them to rest. Settle whatever quarrels you have among yourselves" (13.6), implying to Weinrich that mediation of disputes was beyond the confessors' competence.[165] Against Weinrich's first argument, the continued relationship between the confessors and the ecclesiastics proved only that the Carthaginian Montanists had neither seceded nor been excommunicated at this time. Indeed, Perpetua respected the two clergy, but, to a Montanist, their administrative role was auxiliary to the martyrs' position, as reflected by the clerics' exclusion from Paradise.[166] Therefore, the Montanists' belief that martyrs were superior to clergy was demonstrated not by the confessors' attitude but by the clergy's position "before the gates," excluded from Paradise. Regarding the second argument, the confessors, before the angels' intervention, did not hesitate to respond to the clergy's petition. In support of this observation, Klawiter said:

Whatever the full meaning of the episode, it seems to imply at least that one destined for martyrdom has the power of the keys and can utilize it to bestow peace on other Christians. Perhaps, once the martyr enters into peace through death, he or she is no longer to be approached in prayer by Christians on earth. But that view itself rests on the assumption that while alive the destined martyr has the priestly power of the keys.[167]

The only clue to the nature of the dispute between the bishop and the teaching presbyter in Carthage was the admonition by the angels to discipline the flock, who act "as though they had come from the games *(circo)*." Lax discipline and participation in pagan amusements were targets of Montanist rigor.[168] Furthermore, the promotion of Montanist tenets may have been the cause of the tension in the Carthaginian community.[169] In any case, the object of this vision was a peaceful resolution based upon Montanist ideals.[170]

Saturus' vision ended in a manner similar to the ending of Perpetua's first vision, with an unusual sensory experience which lingered after the ecstatic trance. Just as Perpetua "came to *(experrecta sum)*, with the taste of something sweet still in my mouth" (4.10), so Saturus was "sustained by a most delicious odour that seemed to satisfy . . . and . . . woke up *(experrectus sum)* happy" (13.8).[171]

The Account of the Martyrdom

After Saturus' vision, the editor took up his role as narrator of the actual martyrdom, attributing his task to the Holy Spirit's will and Perpetua's commission.[172] The editor's narrative confirmed the validity of the visions, especially Perpetua's, as they were fulfilled in the martyrdom. Furthermore, the details of the account were consonant with Montanist beliefs.

The episode about Felicitas reveals her zeal for martyrdom and renunciation of family, both themes of Montanism. As the day of martyrdom approached, Felicitas' pregnancy had advanced only to the eighth month. Because the law prohibited the execution of pregnant women, her death would have been postponed, and her blood would have been shed alongside common criminals. Her fellow confessors, therefore, exercised their power of the keys to petition for early delivery. Their petition granted, Felicitas entered into labor. During her birth pains, she demonstrated her rigorous acceptance of martyrdom as she answered a mocking jailer: "What I am suffering now, . . . I suffer by myself. But then another will be inside me who will suffer for me, just as I shall be suffering for him" (15.6). Then she gave her daughter to a Christian sister to raise. Later, in the arena, Felicitas was "glad that she had safely given birth so that now she could fight the beasts, going from one blood bath to another, from the midwife to the gladiator, ready to wash after childbirth in a second baptism" (18.3).[173] Felicitas would have agreed with Tertullian, who, citing the Holy Spirit, said, "Seek not to die on bridal beds, nor in miscarriages . . . but to die the martyr's death, that He may be glorified who has suffered for you."[174]

The editor attributed "perseverance and nobility of soul" (16.1) to Perpetua in a story of her rebuke to the military tribune. This officer "had treated them with extraordinary severity because on the information of certain very foolish people he bacame afraid that they would be spirited out of the prison by magical spells." Exhibiting leadership characteristic of a Montanist woman, Perpetua "spoke to him directly" (16.2) and insisted on better treatment, which he ordered immediately. Not all the jailers, however, were antagonistic. Another prison official, Pudens, became a Christian, presumably from the witness of the confessors.[175]

Paul Allard read in this episode a refutation of Montanistic rigor.[176] By requesting better treatment, Perpetua neglected the discipline exalted by Tertullian in his Montanist treatise *De ieiunio ad-versus psychicos:*

> [G]o forth out of custody to (the final) conflict with all the more confidence, having nothing of sinful false care of the flesh about him, so that the tortures may not even have material to work on, since he is cuirassed in a mere dry skin, and cased in horn to meet the claws, the succulence of his blood already sent on (heavenward) before him, the baggage as it were of his soul,—the soul herself withal now hastening (after it), having already, by frequent fasting, gained a most intimate knowledge of death![177]

An analysis of the story, however, reveals that Perpetua's request resulted primarily in permission for visitation from family and Christian friends. Chronologically, the next event was the free banquet, which the prisoners celebrated as a love feast (*agapen*, ἀ-γάπην), not in avoidance of a fast. In fact, the editor, whom Allard identified as a Montanist,[178] lauded Perpetua's act as an example of steadfastness, not of lack of discipline. Perpetua's request for favor was motivated by concern for the martyrs' appearance in the arena, a concern that was repeated when she adjusted her tunic and fastened her hair after being tossed by the heifer "lest she might seem to be mourning in her hour of triumph" (20.5). Perpetua's actions, then, did not deny Montanistic rigor but, instead, prepared her and her companions for their final confession.

The martyrs converted the ritual meal before the arena, intended as a sacrifice to the pagan emperor, into a communion feast, a Christian sacrifice to the glory of God. On such an occasion, curious onlookers gathered to see the condemned prisoners. The confessors took the opportunity to warn them of God's judgment and to stress their own joy in suffering. Saturus, emphasizing the eschatological expectations common to Montanists, challenged the mob, "Yet carefully take note of our faces so that you may recognize us on that day" (17.2).[179] The three surviving men,[180] by gesticulation, repeated a similar epithet to Hilarianus from the arena: "You have condemned us, but God will condemn you" (18.8). Tertullian expressed the same sentiment in his picture of the judgment day: "I see so many . . . governors of provinces, . . . who persecuted the Christian name, in fires more fierce than those with which in the days of their pride they raged against the followers of Christ."[181]

The next day, the confessors approached death with calm and joy. Perpetua, having forsaken her husband, went "as the beloved of God, as a wife of Christ" (18.2). She was forced again to exercise her leadership in refusing to allow the group to be dressed in pagan attire. For their march into the arena, the editor appropriated Perpetua's own language to describe the scene: "Perpetua then began to sing a psalm: she was already treading on the head of the Egyptian" (18.7). And as Perpetua recognized that her fight was against not wild beasts but Satan, so the editor credited the Devil with preparing a mad heifer, chosen to match Perpetua's gender. After being tossed by the heifer, Perpetua aroused from being "in the Spirit and in ecstasy *(in spiritu et in extasi)*" (20.8), which was so deep that she was unaware of her injuries. From the arena, she exercised leadership once more by exhorting the attendant catechumens to "stand fast in the faith" (20.10).

In recognition of the confessors' self-designation as prophets, the editor deliberately detailed their prophecies concerning their death. Saturninus, eager for a contest, desired exposure to all the beasts, and he and Revocatus contended with a leopard and a bear. Saturus, on the other hand, predicted that he would die only by a leopard. As he prophesied, neither a wild boar nor a bear would attack him, but one bite from a leopard drenched him with blood so that "the mob roared in witness to his second baptism: 'Well-washed!' *(Saluum lotum)*" (21.2).[182] His last words were to Pudens, whose ring he dipped into his wound and returned as a keepsake.

The narrative concluded with descriptions of the martyrs' deaths. Bravely, the martyrs "took the sword in silence and without moving" (21.8). The editor noted that Saturus, "who being the first to climb the stairway was the first to die. For once again he was waiting for Perpetua" (21.8).[183] Perpetua's death, however, was delayed by the inexperience of the executioner, who struck a bone accidently. Ultimately, "she took the trembling hand of the young gladiator and guided it to her throat" (21.9).[184] The editor applauded Perpetua's zeal, claiming that Satan feared "so great a woman" (21.9), who could not be martyred except by her will. Implicit in this praise was the Montanist ideal of voluntary martyrdom, exhibited not only by Perpetua but also by Saturus, who earlier surrendered himself; by Felicitas, who endured an untimely parturition; and by all the "most valiant and blessed martyrs" (21.11) of the *Passion*.

In the concluding eulogy, the editor echoed his prefatory exaltation of "new prophecies" and "new visions," claiming that the church should proclaim "these new deeds of heroism which are no less significant than the tales of old." Furthermore, "these new manifestations of virtue . . . bear witness to one and the same Spirit who still operates" as well as "to the almighty Father and to the Lord Jesus Christ" (21.11).[185] This Trinitarian formula, although orthodox, reflects the Montanists' emphasis on the Holy Spirit by giving him priority in the naming of the three persons of the Godhead.

Review of Montanist Themes in the *Passion*

In summary, the *Passion* reflected all aspects of Montanism. The New Prophecy was a Spirit-based movement, featuring ecstatic prophecy, glossolalia, and new revelation and advancing women's activity. It promoted eschatological expectation, which in turn encouraged rigorous discipline and zeal for martyrdom. To confessor/martyrs the new prophets awarded the power of the keys. Historically, the movement began in the region of the seven churches of John's Apocalypse and, by the end of the second century, spread to North Africa, where Tertullian became an adherent. A thematic review of the evidence of Montanism in the *Passion* follows.

The Holy Spirit was prominent throughout the *Passion*. In the preface, the editor insisted that the power of the Spirit was not restricted to past times (1.3). On the contrary, citing Acts 2.17, the editor contended that, in the last days, God will pour out his Spirit upon men and women, resulting in new prophecies and new visions (1.4–5). This pneumatology informed the entire *Passion*, so that the Spirit's activity in each vision was understood tacitly.

The editor also acknowledged contemporary *charismata*, including the grace of martyrdom and of visions (1.5). The Holy Spirit inspired Perpetua to request the grace of martyrdom, or the perseverance of the flesh, at her baptism (3.5). Perhaps Saturus referred to this gift when, in his vision, he said to Perpetua, "Your wish is granted" (12.7).

According to the editor, the Holy Spirit willed the documentation of the *Passion* (16.1). The exhibition of virtue contained therein witnessed to the Spirit, who continues to operate in the church, along with the Father and the Son (21.11). The Trinitarian expression was orthodox but listed the Spirit first, befitting a Montanistic emphasis.

Like Montanists, the editor recognized the participation of women in Spirit-based ministries. His citation of Acts 2.17 served to emphasize the Spirit's utilization of women in prophecy and visions (1.4). Furthermore, the Holy Spirit distributed "all his gifts to all, as the Lord apportions to everyone" (1.5).

Both Perpetua and Felicitas were married, yet their husbands

were not mentioned in the longer *Passion*.[186] Although scholars
have suggested many reasons for the omission of the husbands from
the account, Montanism provides a tradition in which to understand it. As Priscilla and Maximilla renounced their marriages, so
Perpetua and Felicitas either rejected or ignored their husbands in
order that each might become "as the beloved of God, as a wife of
Christ" (18.2).

The promotion of women as prophets and leaders was evident
in the *Passion*. In prison, Perpetua's "brother" recognized that she
was "greatly privileged" and that she "might ask for a vision" (4.1).
Robeck assumed that this honor derived from Perpetua's status as a
confessor/martyr,[187] but the source could be her giftedness as a
Montanist prophetess, a more likely possibility considering Perpetua's own statement: "I knew that I could speak with the Lord,
whose blessings I had come to experience" (4.2). Evidently, she had
experienced spiritual phenomena prior to her imprisonment.

Saturus awarded Perpetua equal status with himself as he envisioned the bishop and presbyter prostrating themselves to both
confessors. This expression of gender equality was not typical of
Catholics in general.[188] In fact, after the apostolic and sub-apostolic
periods, during which Philip's four daughters and Ammia minis-
tered, prophetesses disappeared from the Catholic Church, whereas
only movements such as Gnosticism and Montanism encouraged
women's prophetic activity.[189] Apart from the link to gender transformation in the *Gospel of Thomas*, no evidence suggests that the
Passion is Gnostic, but evidence does support a Montanist connection. The editor commented further upon Perpetua's leadership in
her rebuke to the prison officials regarding severe treatment (16.2)
and pagan dress (18.5). The overall tenor of the *Passion* therefore,
reflected the respect of Montanists toward gifted and authoritative
women.

All three contributors to the *Passion*, the editor, Perpetua, and Saturus, either valued or received prophetic visions. Several acts of martyrs, of course, boast visions,[190] but *The Passion of Perpetua and Felicitas* contained the entire gamut of spiritual phenomena prized by the Montanists: ecstasy, prophecy, glossolalia, and new revelation.

The ecstatic nature of Perpetua's activity was clarified in two instances. First, immediately prior to her second vision, she stated, "Suddenly in the midst of prayer, my voice went out, and I uttered the name Dinocrates" (7.1). Not a sudden remembrance but an involuntary, ecstatic utterance prompted her to pray for her brother. Second, during her contest with the heifer, "so absorbed had she been in ecstasy *(in extasi)* in the Spirit" that she was unaware of her pain until she "awoke from a kind of sleep" (20.8). The exact nature of the visions themselves was not defined, and often scholars discuss them as dreams.[191] The Latin word for dream, *somnium*, however, was never used, and the terms for vision, *uisio* and *horoma*, were preferred (4.1; 10.1; 11.1; 14.1). Perpetua introduced her first three visions with the words: "and this was shown to me" (4.2; 7.3; 8.1). Furthermore, Perpetua stated specifically that two of her visions came during the day. Finally, both Perpetua and Saturus felt physical sensations, such as taste (4.10) and smell (13.8), during their visions. The accumulated evidence, therefore, indicates that Perpetua and Saturus experienced ecstatic trances rather than dreams.

So valuable was fulfilled prophecy to the editor that he or she took care to point out two instances during Saturus' martyrdom. First, as Perpetua saw in her vision, Saturus preceded the others in death (4.5–6; 21.8). Second, Saturus predicted that no animal other than a leopard would harm him and that only one bite would finish him (21.1–2).

The evidence for glossolalia in the *Passion* comes from the language Perpetua used to describe her prayers for Dinocrates (7.2; 7.10), which replicated the language of Rom. 8.26. Origen's interpretation that this verse discussed private glossolalia makes it possible to suggest that Perpetua, like Montanus, practiced glossolalia.

The newness of the Spirit's revelation was denoted in the very appellation, New Prophecy. Second- and third-century Catholics, however, were suspicious of novelty and claimed that prophetic activity had ceased.[192] The editor, on the other hand, sided with the new prophets in the exaltation of "new prophecies," "new visions," and "new deeds of heroism" in both the preface (1.5) and the conclusion (21.11). The stated purpose for the publication and distribution of the *Passion* was so that "no one of weak or despairing faith may think that supernatural grace was present only among men of ancient times" (1.5).

Not only did the Catholics marginalize ecstasy, prophecy, and glossolalia, and repudiate new revelation, but also they minimized eschatological expectations in favor of ecclesiastical establishment.[193] Montanism, as has been discussed, reacted against this trend and, as a significant element of their prophetic activity, emphasized the imminent *parousia*. The *Passion* expressed eschatological expectations throughout its pages, beginning with the claim that God's bestowal of *charismata* upon men and women testified to the arrival of the last days. The visionaries focused upon heaven and the afterlife, which was natural, considering their expected martyrdom. The aspect of the *Passion* which most exemplified its eschatological emphasis, however, was its utilization of apocalyptic literature.

Among the biblical allusions in the *Passion*, the majority came from Revelation, particularly the opening vision of Christ, the heavenly scene of chapters four and five, and the closing description of New Jerusalem. Even other biblical sources contained eschatological themes, such as Gen. 28.12, with its ladder to heaven, and the parable of the rich man and Lazarus. The sources later deemed non-canonical that supplied the confessors' images were almost exclusively apocalyptic literature, such as *4 Ezra, 1 Enoch*, the *Testament of Abraham*, the *Apocalypse of Peter*, and the *Shepherd of Hermas.* This evidence indicates that the catechesis which Saturus administered and Perpetua and the others received consisted largely of apocalyptic works, which Catholics diminished but which Montanists emphasized.

The obvious parallels in the *Passion* to the *Shepherd of Hermas* led Adhemar d'Alès and W. H. Shewring to deny the influence of Montanism on Perpetua and Saturus,[194] citing Tertullian's strong objection in his treatise *De pudicitia* to what he called "the 'Shepherd' of adulterers *(Pastore moechorum).*"[195] A rigorous puritan, Tertullian, after his Montanist conversion, refused the possibility of repentance from post-baptismal, mortal sin,[196] whereas the *Shepherd of Hermas* did allow one opportunity for repentance after baptism.[197]

D'Alès' and Shewring's objections are mitigated by two considerations. First, Tertullian's teaching did not represent necessarily the views of early Montanism, since he "was surely capable of using and modifying the Prophecy to his own cherished ends," and, in fact, "may be suspected of using the excuse of the Paraclete to impose a harsher discipline congenial to his own temperament."[198] Tabbernee investigated Tertullian's position on post-baptismal forgiveness and concluded that the oracle cited in the treatise *De pudicitia* was not original with the founders of the new prophets but derived from a Carthaginian prophet, who may have been influenced by Tertullian.[199] Certainly, the *De pudicitia* was among his last and most recalcitrant writings and showed a marked contrast to his treatise *De oratione*, written as a Catholic, where he cited the *Shepherd* as an authority.[200]

Second, the *Shepherd* was akin to Montanism in its severe reaction against the secularization of the church, its expectations of the end of the world, its tightening of discipline, and its ecstatic and visionary revelations.[201] Therefore, Tertullian's antagonism to the *Shepherd* does not preclude its use by Montanists.

The call to discipline, a Montanist hallmark, was evident in the *Passion* in the message of the angel to Optatus in Saturus' vision. One contention that eventually divided Montanists and the ecclesiastical hierarchy was the latter's resistance to a discipline stricter than their own.[202] In Carthage, the new prophets were still a church within a church, but the tension was present.

Important evidence of Montanism in the *Passion* derives from the new prophets' theology of martyrdom, which viewed persecution as a sign of the end times and martyrdom as the fulfillment of the disciplined Christian life.[203] All participants in the *Passion* exhibited zeal for martyrdom. Saturus, absent when his comrades were arrested, surrendered to the authorities. Felicitas, eager to die with her comrades, endured early childbirth. Perpetua guided the hand of the inexperienced executioner as he delivered the death blow, an act applauded by the editor.[204] Furthermore, the honor that Montanists gave to a confessor/martyr is expressed in Perpetua's vision of Dinocrates and Saturus' encounter with the ecclesiastics, episodes exhibiting the power of the keys.

The connection between Tertullian and the *Passion* is obvious, apart from the question of his redaction of the document itself. Allusions to his writings abounded in the preface, visions, and conclusion, and his reference to the *Passion* proved his familiarity with it. In fact, Tertullian likely sympathized with Montanists as early as 203 and possibly was inspired by the martyrdom of Perpetua and her comrades to acknowledge openly his allegiance.[205]

One final, intriguing clue that connects the *Passion* with Monta-

nism is the use of cheese in the heavenly Eucharist of Perpetua's
first vision. No other extant document linked cheese and Montanism until Ephiphanius' *Panarion* of the late fourth century. Nonetheless, two observations can be made to connect Perpetua's use of
cheese to the Montanist practice. First, Douglas Powell speculated
that the vision influenced the practice.[206] This proposal gains cre-
dence in light of the influence that other aspects of these visions had
on practice and doctrine in the early church: the visions of Dinocrates upon the doctrine of purgatory, Saturus' description of heaven
upon Tertullian's, and both Perpetua's and Saturus' depiction of
martyrs in heaven upon Tertullian's teaching that only martyrs gain
immediate access into heaven. Second, in the *Acts of Perpetua*, composed at least later than the mid-third century,[207] *caseo* ("cheese") was
changed to *fructu lactis* ("fruit of milk").[208] The redactor of the *Acts*,
which was recited on a Catholic feast day, desired to eliminate this
Montanistic reference, which may have existed as early as the third
century. These two scenarios strengthen the probability that Perpetua's reference to cheese is indeed evidence of Montanism.

This examination of the *Passion* leads to the conclusion that
every writer, every section, and every vision presents evidence of
Montanism. Maureen Tilley, however, evaluated the evidence differently. She recognized Montanist features such as ecstatic prophecy,
the authority of martyrs to forgive sins, anti-clericalism, voluntary
martyrdom, and the use of dreams and visions, but she denied that
these attributes were "*distinctively* Montanist" and contended that,
other than ecstatic prophecy, they were "characteristic of African
Christianity generally during the second through the fourth centuries."[209]

In her cursory perusal of the Montanist characteristics in the
Passion, Tilley failed to find many others discovered in research for
this chapter. Of these omissions, the most surprising is the elevation

of women in the *Passion*, a feature of Montanism that contrasted with the marginalization of women that Tilley found and decried in the church as a whole.[210] Concerning modern evaluations, she said, "When academics considered the *Passion*, many discounted the contribution of a woman as author, first, by attacking the claim of a woman's authorship, and then by minimizing the normative value of the text."[211] She recognized the dominance of males also in the early church, in the use of masculine language concerning martyrdom and in the deformation of the acts of Perpetua and Felicitas by ecclesiastical authorities such as Augustine and Quodvultdeus.[212] In contrast to such patriarchal attitudes among the early church fathers, Perpetua's prominence as a leader among her companions was a distinctively Montanist trait.

Tilley's assumption that Montanism and African Christianity shared several attributes, however, is correct and merits consideration. The reason for the similarities might be found in W. H. C. Frend's observation that Montanism found adherents among the earliest generations of Christians in North Africa and left "its mark on the North African theology of the Church, its ideas of the Christian community, and its relations to society, from the beginning to the end of its existence."[213] The next chapter shows how the affinity of North African Christianity for many of the tenets and practices of Montanism led to the acceptance of Perpetua and her companions as well as the *Passion* by the church as a whole.

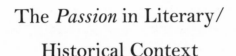

CHAPTER FOUR

The *Passion* in Literary/
Historical Context

THROUGHOUT *The Passion of Perpetua and Felicitas,* in the preface, the diaries, the visions, and the account of the martyrdom,
signs of Montanism can be observed. Yet, not all readers perceived
the Montanist beliefs of the authors, especially of Perpetua and Saturus. Despite the internal evidence, many scholars have pointed to
the response of the orthodox church to the memory of the martyrs.[1]
They were regarded as saints; the date of their martyrdom was celebrated; a basilica was erected in their honor;[2] and sermons com-
memorating them were preached by no less an authority than Augustine. These honors convinced many historians of the orthodoxy
of Perpetua and her companions. Another objection to the charge of
Montanism in the *Passion* was that the document contains no elements distinctly or overtly Montanistic but only such as were common to other acts of martyrdom in the early church.[3] This chapter,
therefore, examines the literary and historical context in which the
church read and reacted to the *Passion:* emendations in later editions;
Catholic appraisal of the *Passion* and its participants; and compar-
isons with other acts of martyrdom.

Later Editions of the *Passion*

Research into the history of transmission of the *Passion* reveals that the orthodox church emended certain elements which, in fact, it considered Montanistic. J. Armitage Robinson examined the recensions of the *Passion* in both Latin and Greek and found that certain omissions minimized its distinctly Montanistic tone. First, the Greek translation contains modified passages. Similarly, after the original Codex Casinensis, all Latin manuscripts of the *Passion* as well as the shorter Latin *Acts of Perpetua and Felicitas* lack the preface, which exalted the Holy Spirit and new prophecies and visions.[4]

Greek Translation

The Greek version, although its date is unknown, must have been translated later than the mid-third century because it ascribed the martyrdom to the period of persecution under Valerian and Gallienus from 257 to 260. According to the translator, the martyrdom occurred on February 2 (τῇ πρὸ τεσσάρων νονῶν Φευρουαρίων)[5] instead of the traditional date of March 7.[6] Another detail added in the Greek translation indicated that the martyrs were arrested in Thuburbo Minus (ἐν πόλει Θουρβιτάνων τῇ μικροτέρᾳ) before being transferred to Carthage for their trial.[7] These variations, however, have no bearing on the present thesis.

Three modifications made by the translator revealed the intent to minimize the evidence of Montanism. In the preface, the Greek translator deleted the phrase "according to the promise *(pariter repromissas)*," which tied the new prophecies and visions to Acts 2.17–18, and replaced the Latin *ceterasque uirtutes* ("and other virtues"), which included prophecies and visions among the powers of the Spirit, with the Greek πάσας τὰς δυνάμεις ("all the powers"). Thus, the translator separated the prophecies and visions not only from the promise of the Scripture but also from the Spirit's *charis-mata*. In the same context, the translator stated generically that the Holy Spirit supplies the holy church (χορηγεῖ τῇ ἁγίᾳ ἐκκλησίᾳ), whereas the Latin editor specified that the Holy Spirit's virtues, including prophecies and visions, were "intended for the instrument of the Church *(ad instrumentum Ecclesiae deputamus)*."[8] Tertullian used *instrumentum* as a term for Scripture;[9] therefore, the editor of the *Passion*, if he used the term in the same way, indicated that the visions and prophecies given by the Spirit were intended as Scripture. The translator, however, removed any reference to the possibility that new prophecies and visions constituted authoritative revelation, which was a definite Montanist tenet.

Second, in chapter sixteen, the Latin editor stated that "the Holy Spirit has permitted . . . and by so permitting has willed *(permisit et permittendo uoluit Spiritus Sanctus)*" the account of the martyrdom. The translator abbreviated the statement to say only that "the Holy Spirit permitted (ἐπέτρεψεν τὸ ἅγιον πνεῦμα)" the report.[10] The omission of the reference to the Holy Spirit's will minimized divine intervention in the communication of the martyrs' passion.

Finally, the most obvious alteration occurred in the conclusion.[11] In the Latin version, the Montanist editor gave first place to the Holy Spirit in the Trinitarian statement: "For these new manifestations of virtue will bear witness to one and the same Spirit who still operates, and to God the Father almighty, to his Son Jesus Christ our Lord" (21.11). The translator, however, removed the reference to the "new manifestations of virtue" and stated simply that "the excellent conduct of life of the blessed martyrs through whom we offer up glory to the Father of Ages, together with his only begotten Son, our Lord Jesus Christ, with the Holy Spirit." The traditional Trinitarian order betrayed the orthodox intent of the translator, who excised from the conclusion the Montanistic zeal of the Latin editor.

The Shorter Latin *Acts*

The translator made emendations to the editorial framework but not to the martyrs' diaries. The redactor of the shorter Latin *Acts*,[12] however, extensively reworked the original.[13] The two versions appeared so different to Adolf Harnack that he referred to the original as "a Montanist Latin version" and to the redaction as "a shorter Catholic Latin version."[14] Paul Monceaux, who considered the original *Passion* a Montanist polemic, regarded the *Acts* as the official Catholic edition with the traces of Montanism removed in order to make it suitable for public reading.[15]

The redactor of the *Acts* omitted first the spiritually oriented preface and began instead with a brief background, including the mistaken identification of Valerius and Gallienus as the emperors, the names of the martyrs, and their origin in Thuburbo of Africa. The redactor deleted Secundulus from the list of martyrs and added familial relationships: Saturus and Saturninus were brothers; and Felicitas was Revocatus' sister.[16]

The most significant addition to the narrative was an interrogation, led by Proconsul Minutius instead of Governor Hilarianus, which resembled the court proceedings of other acts of martyrdom, especially *The Acts of the Scillitan Martyrs*.[17] In the middle of this episode, an account of Perpetua's first vision was inserted. The redactor, however, did not mention the expectation of Perpetua and her brother that she was privileged to receive visions on demand, a characteristic of the *Passion*.

Furthermore, regarding the encounter with the dragon, the redactor of the *Acts* negated the boldness shown by Perpetua and made Saturus the dominant character: "I saw also Saturus ascending by the ladder all the way to the top. And, looking back to us, he said: 'You must not be afraid of this dragon who lies there. Be strengthened in the grace of Christ; climb and do not be afraid, so that you are able to have a portion with me'" (3.5). Perpetua's leadership, encouraged by Montanists, threatened the patriarchal presupposition of the Catholic redactor.

Another important Montanist connection in Perpetua's first vision was the use of cheese *(caseo)* in the heavenly Eucharist. In the *Acts*, however, the reference to cheese was removed and replaced with "the fruit of milk *(fructu lactis)*" (3.6).[18] Roughly a contemporary of Epiphanius,[19] the redactor knew of the Artotyrites, the "bread-and-cheese people" associated with Montanists, and amended the account of the ritual to fit orthodox parameters.

When the narrative returned to the interrogation, the redactor departed significantly from proceedings related in typical trial-transcripts of other acts. The proconsul separated the prisoners by gender, and, although he presented the males the usual demands to sacrifice, he subjected Felicitas and Perpetua to a peculiar interrogation centered around questions about their husbands and family.[20]

Furthermore, during this interchange, the redactor listed Perpetua's husband among her attendant family members.[21] One surprising feature of the *Passion* was the husband's absence despite the editor's mention of Perpetua's marriage and her own discussion of her baby. One explanation for this omission was the Montanist tradition according to which Priscilla and Maximilla abandoned their husbands, perhaps inspiring Perpetua to leave or ignore hers and focus on Christ. The redactor's inclusion of the husband restored the heroine to an orthodox family circle.

Brent Shaw observed these additions made to the account provided by the *Passion* and contended that the redactor was troubled by "the way in which these particular women feel free to move away from the normal constraints imposed by husbands, fathers, and others."[22] Shaw, however, viewing the *Passion* and the *Acts* only from a feminist perspective, attributed the redactor's emendations to male cultural expectations and ignored the possibility that the redactor acted out of Catholic concerns for the evidence of Montanism inherent in the repudiation of husbands by Perpetua and Felicitas. In fact, considering the patriarchal milieu of both Roman society[23] and the Catholic church, a Montanist context is the most likely explanation for the independence of these two women.

Disregarding Perpetua's visions of Dinocrates and, later, Saturus' vision, the redactor included only an abbreviated presentation of Perpetua's vision of the Egyptian.[24] The episode of Felicitas' premature delivery followed,[25] and next came the account of the martyrdom, which differed significantly from the report in the *Passion*. The *Acts* reported no fulfilled prophecies regarding the martyrs' manner of death and described those deaths entirely differently, saying, "Saturus and Perpetua were devoured by lions. Truly, Saturninus, wounded by a bear, was pierced by a sword. Revocatus and Felicitas completed the glorious contest by a leopard" (9.3–4). The redactor closed the *Acts* with a short epilogue, which included the date and place of the martyrdom and a doxology to God alone.[26]

The redactor made no references to the Holy Spirit in the conclusion or throughout the entire *Acts*. Visions, central to the *Passion*, were minimized. Deleting Perpetua's vision of Dinocrates and Saturus' vision of Paradise, in turn, lessened the eschatological emphasis. The *Passion* included such apocalyptic pronouncements as: "[F]rom now on we would no longer have any hope in this life" (4.10); "Thanks be to God that I am happier here now than I was in the flesh" (12.7); and "But take careful note of what we look like so that you will recognize us on the day" (17.2). In the *Acts*, the clearest statement of eschatological hope was delivered by Felicitas: "I choose to attain eternal life and everlasting splendor through temporal punishments" (Text B, 5.3). The redactor of the *Acts* stressed the martyrs' confrontation with the world and their consequent faithful suffering. The *Acts* conclude with instructions to read the martyrs' deeds in church for edification; to share faithfully in their memory; and to ask God for mercy through the prayers of the martyrs and all of the saints.[27]

In sum, the *Acts* not only was shortened but also was sterilized, prepared for liturgical purposes and orthodox consumption. The amendments and the omitted passages revealed that the redactor, like the Greek translator, assumed that the original *Passion* was a Montanist document which needed significant correction.

Catholic Appraisal of the *Passion*

The revisions to the *Passion* were made no earlier than late in the third century, but by then Perpetua and her companions had been honored as saints by the Catholic Church. To W. H. Shewring, this immediate veneration alone sufficed to vindicate the orthodoxy of the martyrs, who evidently died in communion with the Catholic Church.[28] William Weinrich added that Augustine commemorated them with sermons and referenced them in a treatise.[29] The martyrs' relationship with the church, therefore, must be explored in order to determine the reasons that the orthodox establishment accepted Montanists as saints.

Acceptance of Perpetua and Felicitas as Orthodox Saints

In Carthage at the turn of the third century, Montanists and orthodox Christians did not engage in the mutual hostility that characterized their relationship in Asia Minor. Adolf Harnack explained the comparative harmony by contrasting Asian and Carthaginian Montanism. In the middle of the second century, ecclesiastical structures were established locally but not universally, and Montanists in the East were able to oppose vigorously the secularization and moral lenience of Catholic Christianity. By the beginning of the third century, however, western Montanism emerged within a broadly established Catholic system and resisted only feebly the hierarchy of the church. As a result, Carthaginian Montanists coexisted for a time as a part, perhaps a majority, of one, or more of the house churches. Saturus' vision, in fact, reflected this very situation.[30]

Another evidence of compatibility between Montanists and Catholics in Carthage was the inherently rigorous quality of North African Christianity. The earliest, extant report of Christians in Africa was the *Acts of the Scillitan Martyrs*, which recorded their martyrdom in 180.[31] This kind of rigorous devotion, expressed twenty years before the *Passion*, appeared again a century after it in the Donatist movement.[32]

Not only a church of martyrs, the North African congregation was also a church of the Spirit.[33] Prophecy survived in Carthage well into the third century, either in spite of or because of the presence of Montanism, and the Catholics of this prophetically minded community found it possible, for a time, to co-exist with the new prophets. As evidence, the most prominent Carthaginian Christians of the third century were Tertullian, a Montanist convert, and Cyprian, a quintessential Catholic—both noted rigorists.[34]

Cyprian respected Tertullian and read his works. He agreed with much of Tertullian's thought and recognized Tertullian's authority. Cyprian, like Tertullian, gave attention to moral, practical, and disciplinary issues, so much so that he revised and reproduced many of his predecessor's works.[35] He regarded Tertullian as his "master," not a schismatic, and no churchman of the third century was more intolerant of schism than Cyprian.[36]

Just as Cyprian accepted Tertullian, despite his adherence to the

New Prophecy, so the entire Carthaginian community of the third century accepted Perpetua and her companions. Although Cyprian never referred to the *Passion*, his biographer, Pontius, testified to its significance: "Our ancestors, in their reverence for martyrdom itself, honored laymen and catechumens who had gained martyrdom so highly that they recorded many details of their sufferings."[37] Pontius likely referred to Perpetua and her companions without naming them when he specified that the martyrs whose sufferings were detailed were "honored laymen and catechumens."[38]

By the time formal schism developed between Montanists and Catholics, the *Passion* and its protagonists had become dear to the entire Christian community. The sainthood of Perpetua and her companions was assumed by the Carthaginian church immediately after their martyrdom, and the orthodox hierarchy did not revoke such honors after the schism.[39] Instead, the establishment endeavored to erase evidence of the martyrs' association with the movement.

Augustine's Use of the *Passion*

Two centuries after its composition, the *Passion* continued to affect the Christian community of North Africa. Augustine cited the document in one treatise and several sermons. Scholars have drawn different conclusions from his use of the *Passion:* either he ignored or he did not perceive its Montanist overtones,[40] or his approval testified to its orthodoxy.[41] Another possible deduction, however, is that Augustine recognized its Montanism but utilized the *Passion* to accomplish his purposes, both polemical and liturgical.[42]

In *De natura et origine animae*, Augustine repudiated Vincent Victor, a recent convert, who asserted the corporeality of the soul and the salvation of unbaptized infants.[43] This treatise is often classified as an anti-Pelagian treatise, but Kenneth B. Steinhauser argued that Victor was not a Pelagian and that Augustine never accused him of Pelagianism.[44] Instead, Steinhauser regarded Victor as a Montanist and supported this theory with three arguments. First, Victor relied exclusively on Montanist documents such as Tertullian's *De anima* and the *Passion*.[45] Second, Victor's explanation of the origin of the soul corresponded to traducianism, a doctrine associated not necessarily with Montanism but definitely with the Montanist Tertullian. Third, Augustine, in his refutation of Victor, referred explicitly and repeatedly to the Holy Spirit, attacking Victor "at the very core of his belief by denying the presence of the Holy Spirit in his teaching."[46] Specifically, Augustine satirized Victor's belief in direct inspiration by the Holy Spirit: "May the Lord be present to your mind and pour into your spirit by his spirit the readiness of humility, the light of truth, the sweetness of love, and the peace of piety so that you prefer to conquer your own mind with what is true rather than any opponent's with what is false."[47]

Victor supported both his theses with references to the *Passion*, which, for him, possessed authority equal to Scripture. To demonstrate that unbaptized people entered paradise, he cited two examples: the repentant thief and Dinocrates. He again used Dinocrates as well as Perpetua's gender transformation to prove the corporeality of the soul. In response, Augustine insisted that the *Passion* "is not part of the canonical scriptures." At the same time, he did not hesitate to utilize it himself in order to argue against Victor that no unbaptized persons are in paradise and that the soul is not corporeal.[48] When Victor cited the *Passion* as an authority, Augustine recognized both its Montanist character and its sanctity in the Christian community. Therefore, he did not dismiss it but accepted and reinterpreted it according to his purposes.[49]

The same principle governed Augustine's sermons honoring Perpetua and Felicitas. The honor accorded them immediately after martyrdom qualified them for annual commemoration. After the Constantinian symbiosis ended persecution, the memory of faithful martyrs, particularly in North Africa, became sacrosanct in Christian consciousness. Augustine could not avoid recognizing Perpetua and her companions, despite their Montanist affiliation, even if he had so desired. Therefore, he observed their feast days and preached commemorative sermons which interpreted the *Passion* according to his presuppositions.

On the anniversary of the martyrdom, or "birthday," of Perpetua and Felicitas, Augustine preached three or four sermons that are extant,[50] but his fifth-century congregation lived in a vastly different context than that of the *Passion.* "Now, however, at this time," he observed, "the descendants of those whose voices were impiously raging against the flesh of the martyrs, are raising their voices in pious praise of the martyrs' merits."[51] Augustine's church was no longer an outcast of society but its mainstay, and his responsibility was to apply the martyrs' message to the new situation.

The issue which most troubled Augustine involved the prominence of women, acceptable to Montanists but troublesome to the ecclesiastical hierarchy. He addressed the unspoken question about why the day was named for two women with a pun on their names: "Perpetua, of course, and Felicity are the names of two of them, but the reward of them all. The only reason, I mean, why all the martyrs toiled bravely for a time by suffering and confessing the faith in the struggle, was in order to enjoy perpetual felicity."[52] He stated further that the women's names were stamped on the day not because the women were ranked higher than the men but because "it was a greater miracle for women in their weakness to overcome the ancient enemy, and that the men in their strength engaged in the contest for the sake of perpetual felicity."[53]

Augustine wondered at the valor of Perpetua and Felicitas,

which he contrasted to the stereotypical estimation of feminine weakness: "What, after all, could be more glorious than these women, whom men can more easily admire than imitate?" The answer that he gave for the surprising "manliness" of these women was "But this redounds supremely to the praise of him in whom they believed, and in whose name they ran the race together with faithful zeal, so that according to the inner self they are found to be neither male nor female."[54]

Augustine also emphasized the weakness of Perpetua and Felicitas by comparing them to Eve. First, their "feminine frailty" was strengthened by Christ "with the result that women knocked out the enemy, who through woman had knocked out man."[55]

Second, Perpetua was transformed into a man for her contest with the devil, and, as a result, Satan, who "had once, of course, beguiled a man through a woman . . . , and because he sensed that this woman was reacting to him in a manly way, he very sensibly tried to overcome her through a man." This man to whom Augustine referred was Perpetua's father, not her husband, "because she was already, in her exaltation of spirit, living in heaven, and the slightest suspicion of carnal desire, would make her, for very shame, all the stronger. Instead, it was her father whom he equipped with beguiling words, hoping that a religious spirit which would not be softened by the promptings of pleasure, might be broken by the attack of family duty and feeling."[56] With these remarks, Augustine attempted to explain the absence of Perpetua's husband from her account, a circumstance which recalled the Montanist prophetesses' rejection of their husbands.

Third, when Felicitas delivered her baby, "[t]he punishment of Eve was not missing, but the grace of Mary was at hand."[57] Thus, Augustine emphasized the fall of Eve, a theme wholly absent from and, indeed, contrary to the *Passion*. The two references in the *Pas-*

sion to the pericope of Eve emphasized the victory of Eve's seed over Satan as Perpetua stepped on the heads of the dragon and the Egyptian. In his comment on Perpetua's victory over the dragon, he managed a reference to Eve's fall: "Thus the head of the ancient serpent, which had been the ruin of woman as she fell, was made into a step for a woman as she ascended."[58] In contrast to the *Passion*, therefore, Augustine sought to remind his audience that these virtuous women, who died "faithfully like men," were aberrations in a world where women normally were "the weaker sex."[59]

Augustine, troubled by the transformation of Perpetua into a man, turned this episode into a demonstration of feminine frailty, saying that, "even in them that are women in body the manliness of their soul hideth the sex of their flesh."[60] In the fourth sermon, victory over the Egyptian was not ascribed to Perpetua alone but also to her male attendant: "Perpetua being about to triumph in the Lord her Saviour, joined her hands together into a cross, having before her a young man sent by the Lord to defend her."[61] Augustine viewed Perpetua's vision as an affirmation that, in reality, women were weak and that she triumphed only by taking on manly virtues.[62] Such an inference contradicted the clear message of the *Passion*, which echoed the Montanist tradition, that the Spirit gave gifts to women as well as men.

As well as the issue of women's leadership in the *Passion*, concern over the heavenly Eucharist was implied in the fourth sermon, which substituted milk for the cheese offered by the good shepherd.[63] By Augustine's time, the association of Eucharistic cheese with Artotyrites and Montanists was recognized,[64] and so the account was changed in order to appease orthodox sensibilities.

In sum, the evidence does not support the assumption that Augustine's use of the *Passion* negates evidence of Montanism. Instead, examination of his writings reveals that he recognized the Montanist character of the *Passion* but reshaped the material to fit his Catholic milieu.

Quodvultdeus' Sermon on the *Passion*

A contemporary of Augustine and bishop of Carthage, Quodvultdeus commemorated the anniversary of the martyrdom of Perpetua and Felicitas with sermons that were probably delivered on the very site of their burial. At least one sermon has survived to reveal Quodvultdeus' attitude toward the female martyrs.[65]

Quodvultdeus' sermon used many of Augustine's themes. First, he questioned the naming of the memorial day after the women: "When there were so many men there, why were the two of them named before the others, except because the weaker sex either equaled or surpassed the fortitude of men?" He was especially surprised at the women's valor in light of the fact that Felicitas was pregnant and Perpetua was breast-feeding. He acknowledged, however, that Perpetua, in her vision, received simultaneously from the Shepherd and from the Father a mouthful of milk that imparted to her "the sweetness of perpetual felicity[66] [that] enabled her to disregard her son, to spurn her father, to give up the world, and to lose her life for Christ." Furthermore, Felicitas, "rightly named," suffered not only in child-birth but also by the attack of wild beasts and yet was joyful rather than afraid. In amazement, Quodvultdeus exclaimed, "What excellence in women! What kind of grace is it that, when it is poured out on someone, it judges no gender unworthy!"

Second, Quodvultdeus, like Augustine, contrasted Perpetua and Felicitas with Eve. Because Eve, a woman, sinned, all women had lagged behind men until grace revived the female gender through these two martyrs: "The Devil overthrew one Eve: but Christ, born of a virgin, exalted many women. Perpetua and Felicitas crushed the head of the serpent, whom Eve admitted inside to her heart."

Finally, Quodvultdeus also resorted to Gal. 3.28 to explain the women's deeds, which otherwise were beyond his understanding: "Indeed, in Christ Jesus there is neither slave nor freedman, neither is there male nor female, but all are coming together in one perfected man *(uirum)*." Notably, for Quodvultdeus, the preferred expression of consummate humanity is the gender-specific *uir* ("a man, male person") rather than the more inclusive *homo* ("a human being, man").[67]

Throughout this section of his sermon, Quodvultdeus praised Perpetua and Felicitas with amazement at their feats. He did so, however, in such a way that he minimized the female gender by his constant references to the "weaker sex" in contrast to the more typical "fortitude of men" and by his association of all women with Eve, on account of whose sin all die. Even blunter than Augustine, Quodultdeus revealed clearly the patriarchal attitudes of the Catholic Church in contrast to the inclusiveness of the Montanist congregations that encouraged the exercise of spiritual gifts by women such as Perpetua and Felicitas.

Other Accounts of Martyrs

Pierre de Labriolle investigated the *Passion* and found no specific evidence of Montanism, but he observed only that visions were familiar phenomena to the early church.[68] Not only the visionary nature of the *Passion* but also the contents of the visions and the attitudes of the martyrs displayed Montanism in the *Passion*. To support this thesis, therefore, other acts of martyrs are examined and compared to the *Passion* according to the following criteria: emphasis upon the Holy Spirit, prophetic visions, insistence on the validity of continuing revelation, involvement of women, eschatological expectations, rigorous discipline, and voluntary martyrdom.

The Martyrdom of Polycarp

In a letter to the church of Philomelium, the *Martyrdom of Polycarp* recorded an eyewitness account of martyrdoms in Smyrna during the second century. The report attested its catholicity by its address to "all the congregations of the holy, Catholic Church in every place,"[69] yet it bore similarities to the *Passion*.

First, Polycarp, "while praying, had a vision three days before he was to be arrested."[70] He saw his pillow burning and concluded that he was to be burned alive, a prophecy which the writer emphasized after the prediction came true. The editor of the *Passion* also stressed the prophecies of Saturninus and Saturus, who predicted which animals would attack them.

Second, when the governor threatened Polycarp with fire, the bishop retorted that such fire would burn only for a time and soon be extinguished, unlike the fire of everlasting punishment and judgment.[71] On the eve of martyrdom, Saturus likewise warned the mob of God's judgment. Thus, both martyrs expressed their eschatological expectations.

In the area of voluntary martyrdom, however, the *Martyrdom of Polycarp* demonstrated marked contrast to the *Passion*. Perpetua acknowledged approvingly that Saturus surrendered himself to the authorities even though he had not been arrested with the others. Such an attitude was not admired in the *Martyrdom of Polycarp*. An episode in chapter four dealt with Quintus, a Phrygian. Quintus not only volunteered for martyrdom but also encouraged others to do so. Nevertheless, when confronted with the wild animals, he turned cowardly and recanted. The writer, named Evaristus, concluded, "For this reason, therefore, brothers, we do not approve of those who come forward voluntarily."[72]

Quintus' label as a "Phrygian" as well as his willing surrender

led some scholars to identify Quintus as a Montanist.[73] This supposition, however, is complicated by questions regarding the dating of
both the *Martyrdom of Polycarp* and the origins of Montanism.[74]
Scholars inferred from internal evidence in the *Martyrdom of Polycarp* that Polycarp died about 155/56.[75] Based on Eusebius' dating
in the *Chronicon*, Hans von Campenhausen posited 167 as the date
for Polycarp's death.[76] These dates were almost contemporaneous
with the earliest possible dates for the rise of Montanism, making
Quintus' connections to the movement unlikely. Von Campenhausen, however, discovered in the *Martyrdom* three strata of redaction: the original letter; an anti-Montanistic addition; and a revision
by an *Evangelion-Redaktor*, who drew attention to parallels between
Polycarp's martyrdom and the passion of Jesus.[77] Therefore, according to von Campenhausen, the pericope of Quintus was added later
by an opponent of Montanism, who emphasized that the Gospel
does not teach voluntary martyrdom.[78]

Two other historians adjusted dates in order to fit the assertion
that chapter four alluded to Montanism. H. Grégoire and P. Orgels
placed the martyrdom late, in 177,[79] and M. Simonetti assigned the
earlier date of the 150s to the origins of Montanism.[80] Both cited
the Montanist Quintus as proof for their theories.

Not all scholars, however, were convinced that Quintus was a
Montanist.[81] First, the early date of the martyrdom relative to the
rise of Montanism led Christine Trevett tentatively to identify
Quintus as a proto-Montanist, one of the "rigorous, prophetic,
women-tolerating Christians around centres such as Hierapolis and
Philadelphia" and, perhaps, Philomelium.[82] Second, Quintus' description as a Phrygian did not identify him necessarily as a Montanist. Sources equating the two terms derived from a later date,[83] and
the further clarification that he "had only recently come from Phrygia" pointed to a geographic rather than a religious description.[84]

Whether Quintus was a Montanist, a proto-Montanist, or merely a Phrygian, his vilification sets the *Martyrdom of Polycarp* apart
from the *Passion.* The writer admired Polycarp, who avoided capture
until his vision confirmed his call to martyrdom, and praised his
testimony, which followed the Gospel of Christ.[85] However, he did
not approve of Quintus, whose surrender was against the teaching
of the Gospel. Certainly, Evaristus would have disapproved of Saturus as well.

These two acts also differed significantly in their promotion of
the Holy Spirit. The two Trinitarian formulae recorded in the *Martyrdom of Polycarp*, one in Polycarp's final prayer and the other in the
closing chapter,[86] placed the Holy Spirit in third position, as did traditional orthodoxy. The conclusion of the *Passion*, on the other
hand, elevated the Spirit to first position in the Trinity. Furthermore, although the *Martyrdom of Polycarp* referred to the Spirit a
few times,[87] it did not exalt him to the extent that the *Passion* did.
Instead, it focused on the other two members of the Trinity, "God
the almighty Father" and, especially, "our Lord Jesus Christ, the
savior of our souls, the governor of our bodies, and the shepherd of
the Catholic Church throughout the world."[88]

The Letter of the Churches of Lyons and Vienne

In the summer of 177,[89] a persecution broke out against Christians in Lyons and Vienne in Gaul. Survivors preserved the martyrs' stories in letters sent to their home churches in Asia and
Phrygia and to Eleutherus, bishop of Rome. Irenaeus, presbyter of
Lyons at the time, carried the letter to Rome, which included an appeal for help in effecting reconciliation with the Montanists. Eusebius, who is the only source for these letters, included the accounts
of martyrdom but nothing specific regarding the relationship of the
Gallic churches to Montanism. Instead, he summarized the con-

tents: "[A]s dissension began concerning [the Montanists], the Christians from Gaul, in due course, submitted their own well-considered and very orthodox judgment concerning these matters . . . in an effort to negotiate for peace among the churches."[90]

Concerning Eusebius' brevity, de Labriolle suggested that the historian simply had no more information than what he included.[91] Other scholars emphatically denied that the confessors sympathized with the Montanists and asserted that the epistle appealed to the sectarians to restore peace by ceasing their prophecies.[92] By quoting from the letter to Eleutherus, however, Eusebius indicated that he possessed a copy.[93] Furthermore, his suppression of it signified its positive nature. Had it been negative, he would have quoted from it extensively,[94] as he did with anti-Montanist sources. Such considerations led some historians to conclude that the Gallic Christians favored Montanism.[95]

Nonetheless, without the letter itself, the relationship between the Gallic Christians and the Montanists can only be inferred from the account of martyrdom and from Irenaeus' *Adversus haereses*, which alluded to Montanist issues. Irenaeus did not criticize Montanists but anti-Montanists[96] when he wrote: "To be sure, others, in order to suppress the gift of the Spirit, which, in the last days by the Father's good pleasure, has been poured out on the human race, do not allow that concept, which is favorably presented in the Gospel of John, in which the Lord promised to send the Paraclete, but, at the same time, they reject both the Gospel and the prophetic Spirit."[97] At the same time, Irenaeus, whose name means "peaceful," abhorred divisiveness and perhaps included the Montanists in his criticism of "those fools who produce schisms, lacking the love of God and thinking only of their own benefit rather than the unity of the church, and who, on account of trivial or whatever reasons, tear to pieces and divide the great and glorious body of Christ." He continued, "Indeed no reformation can be engendered by them that is as great as the damage caused by schism."[98] Thus, in the decade following the martyrdom, Irenaeus balanced a call for protection of Paraclete-inspired, prophetic activities and a warning against sectarian division.

Because of their Phrygian origins and rigorous enthusiasm, the Gallic Christians were sympathetic to Montanism. The salutation of their letter stated, "The servants of Christ in Vienne and Lyons of Gaul to our fellow Christians at Asia and Phrygia who share our faith and hope of redemption."[99] Eusebius' history and later martyrologies revealed that about half of the forty-eight martyrs had Asiatic names, and evidence indicated that the churches had been founded by recent emigrants from that region.[100] An early dating of the rise of Montanism allowed ample time for that movement to influence the evangelists who took their faith to Gaul. Indeed, the attitudes and actions reported in the letter reflected similar traits as well as contrasts.

First, the letter differed from *The Martyrdom of Polycarp* and resembled the *Passion* in its emphasis on the Spirit. The first martyr mentioned, Vettius Epagathus, was compared to Zacharias and described as "fervent in Spirit." Furthermore, although he had not been taken with the other Christians, when he observed their mistreatment, he "came forward" and "requested that he be given an audience in order to defend his fellow Christians." Because he identified himself with the Christians, he also "was transferred into the class of martyrs." In a eulogy, the writer said of Vettius: "Called the advocate (παράκλητος) of the Christians, he himself possessed the Advocate (παράκλητον), the Spirit of Zacharias, as he demonstrated through the fullness of his love when he was pleased to lay down even his own life for the defense of his fellow Christians."[101]

John de Soyres, reading that Vettius possessed the παράκλητον, considered such a description indicative of the Gauls' Montanistic leanings.[102] In opposition, de Labriolle contended that παράκλητος was a biblical term available to the entire evangelical community; and its use in reference to Vettius taught, in opposition to the Montanists, that the legitimate παράκλητος inspired, not rejection of ecclesiastical authority, but charitable fervor.[103]

Vettius' action as he "came forward" to defend his fellow Christians, which led to his martyrdom, could be compared to Saturus' surrender of himself. A similar deed, reported later in the letter, was performed by Alexander, a doctor who, at the governor's tribunal, encouraged lapsed Christians to confess Christ. The writer described Alexander as "a Phrygian by birth" and as one who was "not without a measure of the apostolic gift,"[104] suggesting ties to Montanism.[105] As with Quintus, however, Alexander's label of "Phrygian" could have been intended to be racial rather than religious.[106] Furthermore, neither action corresponded exactly to voluntary martyrdom as exemplified by Saturus. Vettius and Alexander called attention to themselves by defending or exhorting other Christians, acts which indirectly resulted in their subsequent martyrdoms. Saturus, on the other hand, surrendered himself directly to arrest and martyrdom. Nonetheless, the Gallic martyrs' zeal and the writer's Spirit-based language accentuated their similarities to Montanists in their homeland.

The next point of contact between the letter and the *Passion* was the importance of women in both narratives. Listed among the martyrs in Lyons were Biblis, one of the lapsed whose faith was revived;[107] Blandina, who, after the death of the bishop Pothinus, emerged as the inspiration for the other confessors;[108] and Blandina's mistress. Blandina, especially, became the focus of the writer because of her leadership and endurance, which was described as *imitatio Christi:* "But Blandina was hung upon a stake . . . . And, because she appeared to be hanging in the form of a cross, she, through her intense prayer, inspired great enthusiasm in those struggling in the contest, for, as they viewed her in her agony through their outward eyes, they saw in their sister the one who was crucified for them."[109] On the last day, only Blandina and a young lad named Ponticus remained, and she exhorted him until the completion of his martyrdom. Finally, "just as a noble mother, who urged her children onward and sent them ahead victorious to the king," Blandina, too, was martyred.[110]

Perpetua demonstrated similar leadership during the persecution in Carthage twenty-five years later. From the arena, "having summoned her brother and that catechumen, she addressed them, saying, 'Stand firm in the faith; and all of you love one another; and do not be scandalized by our sufferings'" (20.10). The two women differed, however, in that Blandina led as a confessor, but Perpetua, as a prophetess.

Indeed, prophetic visions received no emphasis in the letter, with a lone exception. One confessor, Alcibiades, practiced extreme asceticism, subsisting on only bread and water, even in prison. After the initial ordeal in the amphitheater, however, "it was revealed" to his comrade, Attalus, that rejecting God's provision was not a good practice or example. Alcibiades accepted the correction, and the writer concluded that "the Holy Spirit was their counselor."[111]

At first sight, this episode appears to demonstrate two Montanist practices: fasting and prophecy.[112] A closer reading, however, reveals a censure, not a promotion, of asceticism.[113] In fact, it is possible that, by including this pericope, the writer[114] and certainly Eusebius intended to criticize the Montanists, who probably influenced Alcibiades. At the same time, Attalus modeled the charismatic gift of prophetic revelation, dear to Montanists, although Eusebius took care to describe the Holy Spirit as σύμβουλον rather than παράκλητος.

Other points of comparison and contrast between the Gallic Christians and Montanists involve the martyrs' power of the keys.

Both groups affirmed the authority of martyrs, but they defined "martyrs" and applied their authority differently.

First, the survivors of the Lyonnaise persecution deflected praise by distinguishing between martyrs and confessors, saying: "They already are martyrs, whom Christ judged worthy to be taken up at their confession, putting his seal upon their testimony by their death, but we are humble and lowly confessors."[115] In contrast, two early Montanists claimed the title of martyr after their release from prison. Then, with their new authority, Themiso composed a universal letter to the church, and Alexander pardoned sins.[116]

Second, in their dealings with the lapsed, the Gallic confessors "defended all but accused none; they loosed all but bound none."[117] The new prophets, however, utilized the power of the keys to bind more than to loose, judging from Tertullian's statement in his treatise *De pudicitia:* "I have the Paraclete himself speaking in the new prophets: 'The church is able to forgive sin, but I will not do it, lest others also sin.'"[118]

In the letter from the Gallic churches, the writer revealed similarities with the Asian and Phrygian churches in the exaltation of confessors/martyrs and their authority to bind and loose. At the same time, subtle differences were delineated: confessors, whose confession was not sealed by death, reserved highest honor for the martyrs; and the power of the keys was used for forgiveness and restoration.[119] Eusebius added this editorial comment: "These matters concerning the compassion of those blessed ones for their fellow Christians who had lapsed may be presented beneficially, in view of the inhuman and uncharitable disposition of those who afterwards behaved so mercilessly towards the members of Christ's body."[120] This pointed postscript was aimed at some rigorous faction: perhaps the Novatianists or Donatists but, in this context, more likely the Montanists.[121]

In summary, these connections between the Gallic churches and

Montanism affect the interpretation of the letter. The letter included an array of Montanistic tenets: emphasis on the Spirit/Paraclete, zeal for martyrdom, women in leadership, fasting, prophetic revelation, elevation of martyrs/confessors, and the martyrs' power of the keys. At the same time, the ethical elements of Montanism, such as fasting and forgiveness, were softened. From such observations, Heinrich Kraft deduced that the Gallic Christians represented an early, proto-Montanistic *(vormontanistische)* expression of faith, which was less strict and not schismatic, due to the smaller Christian population in Gaul compared to Asia and Africa.[122]

Kraft's thesis provides an explanation for the similarities and differences between the letter and the *Passion*.[123] Both the Gallic and the Carthaginian communities were influenced by Montanism. In Lyons and Vienne, however, the influence was less direct and from an earlier, moderate source. Therefore, the *Passion*, despite its similarities to the Gallic letter, is a uniquely Montanistic document: the theology of the Spirit is more highly developed; the eschatological theme is more prominent; and, above all, the emphasis on visions and divine interventions granted to confessors is much greater.[124]

North African Acts of Martyrs

The remaining four acts to be examined transpired in North Africa. The *Acts of the Scillitan Martyrs* preceded the *Passion*, but the other three, the *Acts of Cyprian*, the *Martyrdom of Marian and James*, and the *Martyrdom of Montanus and Lucius*, occurred in the mid-third century during the persecution under Valerian.

The brief *Acts of the Scillitan Martyrs* consists entirely of court proceedings before Vigellius Saturninus,[125] proconsul of Africa, on 17 July 180.[126] Although the martyrs' homeland was mentioned only in a suspicious Greek recension, an ancient Carthaginian martyrology attested to their origin in Scillium, whose exact location is not known but is assumed to be near Carthage.[127] The earliest document of the African church, this account is noted not only for its historical value[128] but also for its literary simplicity.[129]

Its form places the *Acts of the Scillitan Martyrs* in the category of documents based on court records.[130] As such, it resembled the *Acts of Perpetua and Felicitas* rather than the *Passion*. The sparse dialogue revealed the martyrs' zeal but little of their doctrine. Speratus, the leader, made several ethical pronouncements[131] and one theological statement, which was of an eschatological nature.[132] One recension briefly concluded that the martyrs "were beheaded immediately on account of the name of Christ,"[133] but another recension closed with a traditional Trinitarian formula: "And then all were crowned with martyrdom together, and they reigned with the Father, Son, and Holy Spirit through all the ages of ages."[134] Overall, a comparison of the *Acts of the Scillitan Martyrs* with the *Passion* reveals no points of contact with Montanism. The contrast, however, is important because it accentuates the impact of the New Prophecy on the church in North Africa when the movement arrived twenty years later.

By the mid-third century, the influence of both the New Prophecy and the *Passion* could be seen in two accounts of the life and martyrdom of Cyprian. The *Life of Cyprian*, allegedly written by his deacon Pontius, often is considered the first Christian biography but more closely resembles the style of rhetorical eulogy.[135] The *Acts of Cyprian* included three separate accounts of events leading up to the bishop's martyrdom: his hearing before proconsul Paternus on 30 August 257; his return, arrest, and trial before proconsul Galerius Maximus on 14 September 258; and his execution that same day.[136]

At the time that he wrote about Cyprian, Pontius was aware of the popularity of the *Passion*, which "honored laypeople and catechumens who had gained martyrdom," and felt that "it would be unfortunate to pass over the sufferings of such a priest and martyr" as Cyprian.[137] After fifty years of contention between the new prophets and the ecclesiastical establishment of Carthage, the deacon desired to glorify his bishop by recording Cyprian's devotion, witness, and accomplishment.

The *Life* and the *Acts of Cyprian* resemble the account of the earlier bishop/martyr Polycarp. First, in the *Acts of Cyprian*, the bishop reasserted the Catholic proscription against voluntary martyrdom in his statement to the proconsul that "our discipline forbids anyone to surrender voluntarily."[138] Second, Cyprian received, as had Polycarp, a vision regarding his martyrdom.[139] In this vision, a youth "taller than a man's measure" escorted Cyprian to the tribunal of a proconsul, who, without interrogation, wrote on a tablet Cyprian's sentence. The young man, now standing behind the proconsul, gestured to Cyprian: "With his open hand as flat as a blade he imitated the stroke of the customary punishment." Cyprian responded by pleading that a delay be granted to arrange his affairs, and the youth indicated by "twisting his fingers behind each other" that the execution would be delayed one day.[140] Pontius interpreted the one day to signify one year and noted that Cyprian's martyrdom did occur exactly one year after his vision.[141]

Just as the burning pillow foreshadowed that Polycarp would be burnt alive, so the young man's gesture with his flat hand predicted that Cyprian would be beheaded. Other aspects of the vision and the *Life of Cyprian* echoed the *Passion*. The superhumanly tall youth resembled the "man of marvellous stature" who towered over the amphitheater in Perpetua's final vision.[142] More importantly, the framework of the *Life of Cyprian* was patterned after the *Passion*, with an introduction promoting the importance of the work and a conclusion extolling the glory of the martyr.[143]

This same pattern was repeated in two other North African

acts, the *Martyrdom of Marian and James* and the *Martyrdom of Montanus and Lucius.*[144] The conclusion to the *Martyrdom of Montanus* closed as the *Passion* opened, with the exaltation of recent acts alongside ancient writings.[145] Moreover, its first half consisted of a first person narrative, which was followed by an anonymous report of the martyrs' deaths. The *Martyrdom of Marian* included, as did the *Passion*, a charge from the martyrs to the writer to communicate the story of their suffering to their community of faith.[146] In other details, these two acts closely resembled each other: both involved contemporaries of Cyprian and were set during the Valerian persecution; both reflected the continuing influence of the martyred bishop Cyprian;[147] and both mentioned mothers who recalled the Maccabean heroine.[148] Such similarities evoked speculation that the same hand or, at least, the same community, strongly influenced by Cyprian, was responsible for the publication of both acts.[149]

Not only did these later acts utilize similar frameworks, but they also prominently featured visions. In one vision, Marian saw a tribunal where ranks of confessors were sentenced to die by the sword. Instead of being sentenced himself, Marian was escorted by Cyprian to the palace of the divine judge through a paradisiac country lined with cypress trees. At the conclusion of the vision, Cyprian drank from a cup filled at a crystal spring and then offered the same to Marian. After drinking gladly, Marian verbalized his gratitude to God and awoke at the sound of his voice.[150]

James had a vision in which he saw "a young man of great, incredible size," whose "feet did not touch the ground and his countenance rose above the clouds." He was dressed in a brilliant tunic, and, as he ran passed James, he tossed to him two purple belts, one each for James and Marian, and said, "Follow me quickly!"[151]

In a vision of a presbyter, Victor, the Lord appeared as a child. When Victor asked him for the location of heaven or, at least, for a sign to share with his fellow sufferers, the Lord said: "Give them the sign of Jacob," probably a reference to Jacob's ladder.[152]

An imprisoned Christian woman, Quartillosa, whose husband and son preceded her in martyrdom, saw a vision of her son and another colossal young man. This latter character carried two cups full of milk, but, although everyone drank from them, the cups were never empty. At that time, the window was opened, allowing the prisoners to see a clear picture of heaven.[153]

Three narrative elements from the *Martyrdom of Montanus* also echoed the *Passion*. First, two of the martyrs were new Christians who had only recently been baptized.[154] Second, when thrown into prison, the martyrs "were not terrified by the foul darkness of the place" but found that "the dismal prison soon began to shine with the light of the Spirit, and the ardour of our faith clothed us with the brilliance of day to protect us against the ugly shadows and the pitch-black veil of night."[155] By expressing the martyrs' inspirational response to their incarceration, perhaps the writer wished to contrast them favorably with Perpetua's slower acceptance of her experience in prison.[156] In any case, the language strongly resembled the description of the prison in the *Passion*.[157] Third, Montanus and his companions "were suddenly collected *(subito rapti sumus)* and brought to the procurator who was acting governor for the proconsul who had died."[158] Even the very words were used when Perpetua and her companions "were suddenly hurried off *(subito rapti sumus)* for a hearing" before Hilarianus, who also had replaced a recently deceased proconsul.[159] J. Rendel Harris and Seth Gifford considered unlikely the occurrence of two such similar judicial interims in North Africa within a fifty-year period.[160]

The later acts displayed striking contrasts with the *Passion*, as well as these many similarities. Instead of laypeople and catechumens, most of the protagonists of these acts were clergy.[161] The martyred Bishop Cyprian, champion of episcopal authority, was exalted in Marian's and Montanus' visions.[162] Both acts emphasized the catholicity of the church.[163] The Catholic aversion to voluntary martyrdom was implied when Marian and James "truly comprehended in their situation the long desired signs of divine esteem" and "realized that, as they were being led even now in the ripening hour into that region where the stormy tempest of persecution was raging furiously, Christ himself was guiding their footsteps directly to the place of their coronation."[164]

The authenticity of these two acts has been closely scrutinized. Harris and Gifford asserted that their similarities with the *Passion* projected the appearance of deliberate forgeries.[165] Richard Reitzenstein added that the composers borrowed and distorted elements from the *Passion* in a partisan attempt to promote the episcopacy.[166] Karl Holl described both acts as weak imitations, which tried in vain to recapture the Spirit-inspired enthusiasm of an earlier era.[167]

On the other hand, J. W. Trigg defended the authenticity of the later acts, asserting that they did not plagiarize the *Passion* but unconsciously borrowed from it due to its popularity and liturgical usage.[168] The characteristics which they shared with the *Passion* witnessed to the "fusion of 'catholic' and 'spiritual' tendencies" in the North African church of the mid-third century.[169]

Rather than a "fusion," however, these characteristics in the *Martyrdom of Marian*, the *Martyrdom of Montanus*, and even the *Life* and the *Acts of Cyprian* represented the expropriation of spiritual activities by the ecclesiastical establishment. Cyprian claimed the charismatic gifts as the prerogative of the episcopacy, utilized them for his own ends, and disallowed their use by any dissidents:[170] ". . . anyone who is not with the bishop, he is not in the Church."[171] The Montanists, therefore, "if they have torn themselves from the Church of God, can have no power or grace since all power and grace have been appointed in the Church where the elders preside. . . ."[172] From this point of view, then, the authors of the Cyprianic acts, influenced as they were by Cyprian's view of the episcopacy, were aware of the rivalry between the Catholic and the spiritual factions of the church and purposefully imitated the *Passion*,[173] its framework, narratives, visions, and language, in order to elevate the martyrs from their own community. The similarities of these acts to the *Passion*, therefore, do not minimize its uniqueness but indicate instead that evidence of its Montanism threatened the ecclesiastical establishment, which met the challenge with acts that promoted Catholic tradition and practice.

Conclusion

M ANY UNIQUE FEATURES set the *Passion* apart from other
acts of martyrdom from the patristic period. The autobio-
graphical sections written by Perpetua and Saturus and preserved
along with the eyewitness account of the editor were original with
the *Passion* and provide keen insights into the thoughts and emotions of early martyrs. Perpetua's diary is likely the earliest extant
writing by a Christian woman. In Herbert Musurillo's estimation,
the *Passion* "is also an apocalypse in its own right, reminiscent of
the book of Revelation and the *Shepherd of Hermas.*"[1] Finally, the evidence of Montanist influence in the *Passion* adds even more value
to this document for the enlightenment it provides for understanding this movement as it newly arrived in North Africa. After a summary of the evidence of Montanism uncovered in the previous chapters, an evaluation of the *Passion* in understanding Montanism in
this period of the early church follows.

Summary of the Evidence of Montanist
Influence in the *Passion*

Research into the message and practice of Montanism reveals
tenets expressed throughout the *Passion*. The exaltation of the Spirit was systemic in the *Passion;* the validity of continuing revelation
was asserted in the editorial framework; references to Revelation

and other Johannine literature were evident; visions were plentiful and available upon demand by the prophets; Perpetua's leadership was promoted unashamedly despite her gender; eschatological expectations were expressed by all the participants; disciplinary activity, although not prominent, was present in Saturus' vision; and voluntary martyrdom, specifically proscribed elsewhere, was praised in the *Passion*.

The history of the Montanist movement, particularly as it developed in Carthage, was also evident in the *Passion*. The continuing, though strained, relationship of Perpetua and Saturus with bishop Optatus and presbyter Aspasius reflected the *ecclesiola in ecclesia* formed by the Montanists before their formal schism from the Catholics. Furthermore, the *Passion* revealed mutual influence between its three authors and Tertullian, the famous Carthaginian convert to Montanism.

Indeed, the parallels between the *Passion* and Tertullian as well as his use of Perpetua's vision as new revelation indicate his possible involvement as editor. Proof of his editorship, however, is not necessary to verify the Montanist nature of the *Passion*. The significant issue related to the identity of the editor is his or her relationship to the movement, a relationship which is clear from the preface and conclusion and supported by the majority of scholars.

Not only the editor but also Perpetua and Saturus exhibited evidence of Montanism, and their diaries have been determined, through philological and internal examinations, to be independent contributions to the *Passion*. Statements by Perpetua and the editor demonstrated the kind of trusting relationship that would have been engendered in a community of faith such as a Montantist gathering.

The interaction of the Montanists with the larger church made it possible for the Catholic establishment to honor and, eventually, even to beatify the sectarian martyrs. By the time of the schism in the mid-third century, the martyrs and the *Passion* were integral parts of Christian history and liturgy. Therefore, the church modified later editions of the *Passion*, the Greek translation and the shorter *Acts*, to minimize or eliminate the Montanistic elements and make it acceptable for orthodox consumption. Furthermore, Augustine, when he cited the *Passion* in a polemical writing or in sermons, was aware not only of its Montanist origin but also of its sanctity in the Christian community, and he used it in ways that served his purposes.

Finally, although a comparison of the *Passion* with other acts of martyrdom reveals similarities as well as differences, careful investigation into the historical background of each account provides further illumination. The similarities were due, in the case of the Cyprianic acts, to deliberate copying and, in the case of the Gallic letter, to common spiritual ties to Asia and Phrygia, the homeland of Montanism. The *Passion* contrasted sharply with the *Martyrdom of Polycarp* and the *Acts of Cyprian* over the issue of voluntary martyrdom. Overall, the emphases on the Spirit, new revelation, prophetic visions, women's leadership, eschatological expectations, rigorous discipline, and voluntary martyrdom, which were displayed either to a lesser degree or not at all in other acts, clearly set apart the *Passion* as a distinctly Montanistic document.

Evaluation of the *Passion* in Understanding Montanism in the Early Church

Acceptance of the *Passion* as the product of Montanists leads to its recognition as the earliest complete work of the movement that survives. All previous Montanist writings were destroyed by zealous Catholics, and only fragments quoted by ecclesiastical opponents remain. The *Passion*, read as an expression of Montanism, adds to modern understanding of the movement and opens doors for further research into its relationship to the early church.

First, the absence of Perpetua's and Felicitas' husbands from the *Passion* suggests that Priscilla's and Maximilla's abandonment of their husbands may not have been an aberration among Montanist women. Indeed, the reappearance of both husbands in the liturgical *Acts of Perpetua* indicates Catholic concern about an ongoing Montanist practice. This interpretation is supported further by Perpetua's gender transformation, which was an image of Montanist egalitarianism.

Second, the use of cheese in the heavenly Eucharist is the earliest reference to the Montanist practice which Epiphanius associated with the Artotyrites. Three inferences, then, might be drawn from this insight. First, considering Wilhelm Schepelern's connection of the "bread-and-cheese people" to the Phrygian cult of Cybele,[2] a closer link may have existed between Carthaginian and Asian Montanism than has been assumed. Second, considering the reputation of the *Passion* among Montanists, who respected its authority, Douglas Powell may have been correct that Perpetua's vision inspired the practice.[3] Finally, Perpetua may have acted as a mediator between the early Montanists and the Artotyrites, being influenced by the Phrygian practice and perpetuating it through her vision. In any case, the overall Montanistic tenor of the *Passion* leads to the conclusion that the Eucharistic cheese was not an editorial modification but a genuine reference to a Montanist innovation.

Third, the extent of the prerogatives which Montanists awarded to confessors and martyrs is clarified in the *Passion*. Beginning with the preface, the editor called upon readers to "have fellowship with the holy martyrs and, through them, with the Lord Christ Jesus." Also, the editor credited the confessors with extraordinary powers of intercession when they prayed on Felicitas' behalf and were granted a premature delivery of her baby. Furthermore, Perpetua, confident of her privileged position as a confessor/martyr, prayed for her dead brother, Dinocrates, who, according to her vision, was released from suffering. Jacques Le Goff recognized that the *Passion* was the earliest Christian document to present an idea of purgatory and that, beginning with Augustine, scholars who developed that dogma commented upon this episode.[4] The Montanists, therefore, by their exaltation of martyrs' power of the keys, preceded and perhaps influenced the Catholic doctrines of purgatory and the treasury of merit.

Fourth, both Perpetua and Saturus saw martyrs in paradise in their visions of heaven, fulfilling the Montanists' expectation that only martyrs had immediate access to heaven. This tenet was promoted strenuously by Tertullian, who may have been inspired by the visions of the *Passion*.

Furthermore, historians long have suspected that Tertullian, with his assertive personality, recast Montanism in North Africa to fit his even more ascetic temperament. A comparison of the *Passion* with earlier Montanist oracles and logia and Tertullian's later writings could be helpful in reconstructing the possible modifications that Tertullian made, particularly in regard to post-baptismal forgiveness. Especially instructive are the contrasts between attitudes toward the *Shepherd of Hermas* and the martyrs' power of the keys. The *Shepherd* reflected many of the Montanists' concerns, and Perpetua and Saturus freely drew upon its images in their visions, but Tertullian called it "the Shepherd of adulterers" because he disagreed with its stand on the remission of sin. Asian Montanists Themiso and Alexander exercised the power of the keys, and, in the *Passion*, the confessor/martyrs were expected to wield that power, but Tertullian refused to grant such authority to confessor/martyrs because it encouraged moral laxity. Scholars who deny that the *Passion* is an inherently Montanist document often have pointed to these discrepancies as proof of their thesis. Another, equally valid viewpoint, however, is that the *Passion* is indeed a Montanist product that provides a bridge between the New Prophecy that arrived in North Africa around the turn of the third century and the Montanism presented by Tertullian in some of his later writings.

Thus, this research into the evidence of Montanism in *The Passion of Perpetua and Felicitas* adds to its value as an early Christian document, which records not only an account of martyrdom, complete with the personal memoirs of a Christian woman and her catechist, but also insights into a Spirit-based, prophetic movement, whose earlier writings were suppressed by the ecclesiastical hierarchy. Acceptance of the *Passion* as a thoroughly Montanist document makes it possible to learn more about Montanism: its beliefs; Montanist women; the movement in Africa; its relationship to the church; and its most famous convert, Tertullian.

Notes

Notes to Introduction

1. W. H. C. Frend, "Open Questions Concerning the Christians and the Roman Empire in the Age of the Severi," *JTS* 25 (1974): 336–37, listed persecutions in Carthage, Alexandria, Rome, Corinth, Cappadocia, and Antioch.

2. According to *Vita Severi*, in *The Scriptores Historiae Augustae, Severus* 17.1, trans. David Magie, Loeb Classical Library, ed. G. P. Goold (Cambridge, Mass.: Harvard University Press, 1979), 409, the Roman emperor Septimius Severus (193–211), in 202 issued an edict which "forbade conversion to Judaism under heavy penalties and enacted a similar law in regard to the Christians." See also W. H. C. Frend, *The Rise of Christianity* (Philadelphia: Fortress Press, 1984), 294. An early historian to cast doubt upon the authenticity of this edict was Hans Lietzmann, *Geschichte der alten Kirche*, vol. 2, *Ecclesia catholica* (Berlin: Verlag Walter de Gruyter & Co., 1953), 164, 158, who described the widespread persecutions of this time as "little more than phenomena of purely local significance," the result not of an imperial edict but "of local circumstances and the disposition of the governor" (my translation). K. H. Schwarte, "Das angebliche Christengesetz des Septimius Severus," *Historia* 12 (1963): 205–7, followed with evidence that the edict preserved in *Vita Severi* was a fabrication of a late fourth-century, pagan redactor. J. G. Davies, "Was the Devotion of Septimius Severus to Serapis the Cause of the Persecution of 202–3?" *JTS* 5 (1954): 73–76, added the suggestion that "the emperor's devotion to Serapis . . . induced the governors, under pressure from local devotees, to embark upon a policy of persecution in those areas where the cult was most strong." See also Timothy David Barnes, "Legislation Against the Christians," *The Journal of Roman Studies* 58 (1968): 40–41; Robert M. Grant, *Augustus to Constantine: The Emergence of Christianity in the Roman World* (San Francisco: HarperSanFrancisco, 1970; reprint, New York: Barnes and Noble Books, 1996), 100. For a discussion of the issue from an opposing view, see Frend, "Open Questions," 333–51. Frend concluded that the Severan persecution, while still an open question, was a probability.

3. The Greek text of the *Passion of Perpetua and Felicitas* and the shorter Latin *Acts of Perpetua and Felicitas* included the statement, not found in the Latin *Passion*, that the confessors were arrested in Thuburbo Minus, a city thirty-six Roman miles west of Carthage. Scholars who accepted this tradition or, at least, considered it a possibility include: Cornelius Johannes Maria Joseph van Beek, introduction to *Passio sanctarum Perpetuae et Felicitatis*, ed. Cornelius Johannes Maria Joseph van Beek (Bonn: Peter Hanstein, 1938), 3–4; Herbert Musurillo, ed., introduction to *The Acts of the Christian Martyrs* (Oxford: At the Clarendon Press, 1972), xxv–xxvi; Brent D. Shaw, "The Passion of Perpetua," *Past and Present* 139 (1993): 3 n. 3, 10–11, 25; Joyce E. Salisbury, *Perpetua's Passion: The Death and Memory of a Young Roman Woman* (New York: Routledge, 1997), 44–45; and Jacqueline Amat, introduction to *Passion*, 22–23. Amat, 23, concluded that Perpetua and her companions were arrested in Thuburbo Minus and transported to Carthage for imprisonment, trial, and execution. Scholars who rejected the authenticity of the reference to Thuburbo Minus include: J. Armitage Robinson, ed., introduction to *The Passion of S. Perpetua*, in *Texts and Studies: Contributions to Biblical and Patristic Literature*, vol. 1, part 2 (Cambridge: At the University Press, 1891; reprint, Nendeln/Liechtenstein: Kraus Reprint, 1967), 22–26; Adolf Harnack, *Die Chronologie der Altchristlichen Litteratur bis Eusebius* (Leipzig: J. C. Hinrichs'sche Buchhandlung, 1904), 2:323; Hippolyte Delehaye, *Les Passions des Martyrs et les Genres Littéraires* (Bruxelles: Société des Bollandistes, 1966), 53; and Timothy David Barnes, *Tertullian: A Historical and Literary Study* (Oxford: Clarendon Press, 1971), 72 n. 3. William Tabbernee, "Perpetua, Optatus, and Friends: Christian Ministry in Carthage c. 203 C.E.," <http://divinity.library.vanderbilt. edu/burns/chroma/clergy/Tabborders.html#N_8_> (September 2003), examined the textual history of the *Passion* and determined that the references to Thuburbo Minus, possibly resulting from the conflation of two different acts of martyrs, are quite late and untenable.

4. Timothy David Barnes, "Pre-Decian *Acta Martyrum*," *JTS* 19 (1968): 522–25, researched the dating of the *Passion* and concluded that "though the year might be doubted, the day is beyond question." Similarly, Shaw, 3 n. 2, observed, "The dates must remain conjectural. . . . [T]he day and month are probable, the year is a reasonable conjecture."

5. Philip Schaff, *History of the Christian Church*, vol. 2, *Ante-Nicene Christianity A.D. 100–325* (New York: Charles Scribner's Sons, 1910; reprint, Grand Rapids: Eerdmans, 1963), 59, suggested that Montanists' excesses motivated persecution during the reign of Septimius Severus.

6. Holstenius' manuscript, *Codex Casinensis*, is not the oldest but is the most complete. There are eight other extant manuscripts: *Codex Parisiensis*, also known as *Codex Compendiensis*; *Codex Cottonianus Nero E.I.*; *Codex Oxoniensis*, also known as *Codex Salisburgensis* or *Sarisburiensis*; *Codex Cottonianus Otho D VIII*; *Codex Cantuarius E 42*; *Codex Ambrosianus C 210 Inf.*; *Codex San-*

gallensis 577; and *Codex Einsidlensis 250.* Amat, introduction to *Passion,* 84–88. See also Robinson, 10–11.

7. These reprints included one by the Bollandists in 1668; an edition at Oxford in 1680, which followed Lactantius' *De Mortibus Persecutorum* and added some variants from another manuscript; and a recension by Theodoric Ruinart in his *Acta Sincera* with emendations from two imperfect manuscripts. Robinson, 1.

8. J. Rendel Harris and Seth K. Gifford, eds., *The Acts of the Martyrdom of Perpetua and Felicitas: The Original Greek Text* (London: C. J. Clay and Sons, 1890), 13–18.

9. *The Passion of S. Perpetua,* in *Texts and Studies: Contributions to Biblical and Patristic Literature,* vol. 1, part 2, ed. J. Armitage Robinson (Cambridge: At the University Press, 1891; reprint, Nendeln/Liechtenstein: Kraus Reprint, 1967)

10. Robinson, 3. See especially n. 1.

11. *Passio sanctarum Perpetuae et Felicitatis,* ed. Cornelius Johannes Maria Joseph van Beek (Nijmegen, Holland: Dekker & Van de Vegt, 1936).

12. Musurillo, lxv n. 20.

13. *Passion de Perpétue et de Félicité suivi de Actes,* ed. Jacqueline Amat, Sources Chrétiennes, vol. 417 (Paris: Les Éditions du Cerf, 1996).

14. Theodoric Ruinart, *Admonitio in Passionem SS. Perpetuae, Felicitatis, etc.,* in *Acta Martyrum* (Regensburg: G. Josephi Manz, 1859), 135–36. See also Nathaniel Lardner, *The Credibility of the Gospel History,* in *The Works of Nathaniel Lardner,* vol. 2 (London: William Ball, 1838), 585–86.

15. Samuel Basnage, *Annales politico-ecclesiastici* (1706), 203, cited in Lardner, 585.

16. Giuseppe Agostino Orsi, *Dissertatio Apologetica pro Sanctarum Perpetuae, Felicitatis et sociorum martyrum Orthodoxia adversus Samuelem Basnagium* (Florentiae: Typis Bernardi Paperini, 1728), cited in John de Soyres, *Montanism and the Primitive Church: A Study in the Ecclesiastical History of the Second Century* (Cambridge: Deighton, Bell, and Co., 1878; reprint, Lexington, Ky.: The American Theological Library Association, 1965), 44. See also Benjamin Aubé, *Les chrétiens dans l'Empire romain,* Studia Historica, vol. 103 (Paris: Ristampa Anastatica Invariata dell'Edizione, 1881; reprint, Roma: "L'Erma" di Bretschneider, 1972), 513; and Adhemar d'Alès, "L'Auteur de la *Passio Perpetuae,*" *Revue d'histoire ecclesiastique* 8 (1907): 15.

17. The Catholic surveys researched include: John Alzog, *History of the Church,* trans. F. J. Pabisch and Thomas S. Byrne, vol. 1 (New York: Benziger Brothers, 1874), 269 n. 2; Fernand Mourret, *A History of the Catholic Church,* vol. 1, *Period of Early Expansion,* trans. Newton Thompson (St. Louis, Mo.: B. Herder Book Co., 1931), 325 n. 37; Philip Carrington, *The Early Christian Church,* vol. 2, *The Second Christian Century* (Cambridge: At the University Press, 1957), 427–28; Louis J. Rogier, ed. *The Christian Centuries,* vol. 1, *The*

First Six Hundred Years, by Jean Daniélou and Henri Marrou, trans. Vincent Cronin (New York: McGraw-Hill Book Company, 1964), 144, 154; Jean Daniélou, *A History of Early Christian Doctrine Before the Council of Nicæa*, vol. 3, *The Origins of Latin Christianity*, trans. David Smith and John Austin Baker, ed. with a Postscript by John Austin Baker (Philadelphia: The Westminster Press, 1977), 59; and Hubert Jedin and John Dolan, eds., *History of the Church*, vol. 1, *From the Apostolic Community to Constantine*, by Karl Baus, with an Introduction by Hubert Jedin (New York: The Seabury Press, 1980), 218–19.

18. Protestant surveys researched include: John C. L. Gieseler, *A Compendium of Ecclesiastical History*, vol. 1, rev. from 4th ed., trans. Samuel Davidson (New York: Harper and Brothers, 1849), 195 n. 9; Henry Hart Milman, *The History of Christianity*, vol. 2, new and rev. ed. (New York: W. J. Widdleton, Publisher, 1866), 170; Philip Schaff, *History of the Christian Church*, vol. 2, *Ante-Nicene Christianity A.D. 100–325* (New York: Charles Scribner's Sons, 1910; reprint, Grand Rapids: Eerdmans, 1963), 58; Johann Heinrich Kurtz, *Church History*, trans. John MacPherson, in *The Foreign Biblical Library*, vol. 1, ed. W. Robertson Nicoll (New York: Funk and Wagnalls Company, 1888), 228; Albert Henry Newman, *A Manual of Church History*, vol. 1, *Ancient and Mediæval Church History (To A.D. 1517)* (Philadelphia; American Baptist Publication Society, 1899), 161; Charles Bigg, *The Origins of Christianity*, ed. T. B. Strong (Oxford: At the Clarendon Press, 1909), 299; Henry Melvill Gwatkin, *Early Church History to 313* (London: MacMillan and Co., 1909), 1:124; Joseph Cullen Ayer, Jr., *A Source Book for Ancient Church History from the Apostolic Age to the Close of the Conciliar Period* (New York: Charles Scribner's Sons, 1913), 145; B. J. Kidd, *A History of the Church to A.D. 461*, vol. 1, *To A.D. 313* (Oxford: At the Clarendon Press, 1922), 286–87; and Lietzmann, 2:161–62. While Lietzmann does not specifically identify the martyrs as Montanists, his description of their activities corresponds exactly to his description of Montanism, 196–205.

19. James C. Robertson, *History of the Christian Church from the Apostolic Age to the Reformation: A. D. 64–1517*, new and rev. ed., vol. 1 (London: John Murray, 1876), 98 n. f.

20. Daniélou and Marrou, 144, 154.

21. De Soyres, 44.

22. G. Nathanael Bonwetsch, *Die Geschichte des Montanismus* (Erlangen: Verlag von Andreas Deichert, 1881; reprint, Hildesheim: Verlag Dr. H. A. Gerstenbert, 1972), 185.

23. Pierre de Labriolle, *La Crise Montaniste* (Paris: Ernest Leroux, 1913), 345–52.

24. Pierre de Labriolle, *Les Sources de L'histoire du Montanisme: textes grecs, latins, syriaques*, Collecteanea Friburgensia 24 (Paris: Ernest Leroux, 1913), 9–11.

25. Christine Trevett, *Montanism: Gender, Authority, and the New Prophecy* (Cambridge: Cambridge University Press, 1996), 177–78.

26. Ronald E. Heine, ed., *The Montanist Oracles and Testimonia*, Patristic Monograph Series, no. 14, North American Patristic Society (Macon, Ga.: Mercer University Press, 1989), 60–63.

27. William Tabbernee, ed., *Montanist Inscriptions and Testimonia: Epigraphic Sources Illustrating the History of Montanism*, Patristic Monograph Series, no. 16, North American Patristic Society (Macon, Ga.: Mercer University Press, 1997), 57–59.

28. W. H. C. Frend, *The Donatist Church* (Oxford: At the Clarendon Press, 1952), 116–17.

29. Barnes, *Tertullian*, 77.

30. Timothy David Barnes, *Tertullian: A Historical and Literary Study*, rev. ed. (Oxford: Clarendon Press, 1985), 329. See also J. F. Matthews, review of *Tertullian: A Historical and Literary Study*, by Timothy David Barnes, *JTS* 24 (1973): 245–49.

31. William C. Weinrich, *Spirit and Martyrdom* (Washington, D. C.: University Press of America, 1981), 241–42.

32. Cecil M. Robeck, Jr., *Prophecy in Carthage: Perpetua, Tertullian, and Cyprian* (Cleveland: The Pilgrim Press, 1992), 13–18. Robeck doubted that Tertullian edited the *Passion*.

33. Elaine C. Huber, *Women and the Authority of Inspiration: A Reexamination of Two Prophetic Movements from Contemporary Feminist Perspective* (Lanham, Md.: University Press of America, 1985), 21.

34. Rosemary Rader, "The *Martyrdom of Perpetua*: A Protest Account of Third-Century Christianity," in *A Lost Tradition: Women Writers of the Early Church*, ed. Patricia Wilson-Kastner and others (Lanham, Md.: University Press of America, 1981), 17 n. 45.

35. Joyce E. Salisbury, *Perpetua's Passion: The Death and Memory of a Young Roman Woman* (New York: Routledge, 1997), 158.

36. Maureen A. Tilley, "The Passion of Perpetua and Felicity," in *Searching the Scriptures*, vol. 2, *A Feminist Commentary*, ed. Elisabeth Schüssler Fiorenza (New York: Crossroad Publishing Company, 1994), 835. Tilley, 836, tempered her statement with a correct observation: "Even if one were to decide that not only the editor's program but that of Perpetua herself was Montanist, this ought not to handicap the investigation of the *Passion*, nor can it invalidate Perpetua's own experience."

37. Francine Cardman, "Acts of the Women Martyrs," *Anglican Theological Review* 70 (April 1988): 144–50; Gillian Cloke, "*Mater* or Martyr: Christianity and the Alienation of Women within the Family in the Later Roman Empire," *Theology and Sexuality* 5 (1996): 37–57; Kate Cooper, "The Voice of the Victim: Gender, Representation and Early Christian Martyrdom," *BJRL* 80 (1998): 147–57; Giselle de Nie, "'Consciousness Fecund through God': From Male Fighter to Spiritual Bride-Mother in Late Antique Female Sanctity," in *Sanctity and Motherhood: Essays on Holy Mothers in the Middle Ages*, ed. Anneke B. Mulder-Bakker, Garland Medieval Casebooks, ed. Joyce E. Salisbury and

Christopher Kleinhenz, 101–61 (New York: Garland Publishing, 1995); Anne Jensen, *God's Self-Confident Daughters: Early Christianity and the Liberation of Women*, trans. O. C. Dean, Jr. (Louisville, Ky.: Westminster John Knox Press, 1996), 93–111; Scholer, 10–15; and Brent D. Shaw, "The Passion of Perpetua," *Past and Present* 139 (1993): 3–45.

38. Peter Dronke, *Women Writers of the Middle Ages: A Critical Study of Texts from Perpetua (203) to Marguerite Porete (1310)* (Cambridge: Cambridge University Press, 1984); J. W. Halporn, "Literary History and Generic Expectations in the *Passio* and *Acta Perpetuae*," *Vig. Chr* 45 (1991): 223–41; and Thomas J. Heffernan, "The Passion of Saints Perpetua and Felicitas and the *Imitatio Christi*," in *Sacred Biography: Saints and Their Biographers in the Middle Ages* (New York: Oxford University Press, 1988), 185–230.

39. James Rives, "The Piety of a Persecutor," *JECS* 4:1 (1996): 1–25; and Andrzej Wypustek, "Magic, Montanism, Perpetua, and the Severan Persecution," *Vig. Chr.* 51 (1997):276–97.

40. Alvyn Pettersen, "Perpetua—Prisoner of Conscience," *Vig. Chr.* 41 (1987): 139–53; and Lisa M. Sullivan, "'I Responded, "I Will Not . . .'": Christianity as Catalyst for Resistance in the *Passio Perpetuae et Felicitatis*," *Semeia* 79 (1997): 63–74.

41. A. P. Orbán, "The Afterlife in the Visions of the *Passio SS. Perpetuae et Felicitatis*," in *Fructus centesimus: mélanges offerts à Gerard J. M. Bartelink à l'occasion de son soixante-cinquième anniversaire*, ed. A. A. R. Bastiaensen, A. Hilhorst, and C. H. Kneepkens, 269–77, Instrumenta patristica 19 (Dordrecht: Kluwer, 1989).

42. Marie-Louise von Franz, *The Passion of Perpetua*, trans. Elizabeth Welsh, Jungian Classics Series, vol. 3 (Irving, Tex.: Spring Publications, 1980); E. R. Dodds, *Pagan and Christian in an Age of Anxiety: Some Aspects of Religious Experience from Marcus Aurelius to Constantine* (Cambridge: At the University Press, 1965); Mary Ann Rossi, "The Passion of Perpetua, Everywoman of Late Antiquity," in *Pagan And Christian Anxiety: A Response to E. R. Dodds*, ed. Robert C. Smith and John Lounibos (Lanham, Md.: University Press of America, 1984); Mary R. Lefkowitz, "Motivations for St. Perpetua's Martyrdom," *Journal of the American Academy of Religion* 44 (1976): 417–21.

43. Zaida Maldonado-Pérez, "The Subversive Dimensions of the Visions of the Martyrs of the Roman Empire of the Second through Early Fourth Centuries" (Ph.D. Diss., Saint Louis University, 1999), 242.

44. Elaine Claire Huber, "Women and the Authority of Inspiration: A Reexamination of Two Prophetic Movements from a Christian Feminist Perspective," (Ph.D. Diss., Graduate Theological Union, 1984).

45. Cecil Melvin Robeck, Jr., "The Role and Function of Prophetic Gifts for the Church at Carthage, AD 202–258," (Ph.D. Diss., Fuller Theological Seminary, 1985).

46. Robeck, *Prophecy in Carthage*, 15–16.

47. Ibid., xi.

48. *The Martyrdom of Perpetua and Felicitas*, trans. R. E. Wallis, in ANF, vol. 3, ed. Alexander Roberts and James Donaldson (Edinburgh: T. and T. Clark, 1873; reprint, Grand Rapids: Eerdmans, 1978), 697–706.

49. *Passion of SS. Perpetua and Felicitas*, in *Some Authentic Acts of the Early Martyrs*, trans. E. C. E. Owen (London: Society for Promoting Christian Knowledge, 1927), 74–92.

50. *The Passion of Perpetua and Felicity: A New Edition and Translation of the Latin Text together with the Sermons of S. Augustine upon These Saints*, trans. W. H. Shewring (London: Sheed and Ward, 1931).

51. *The Martyrdom of Perpetua and Felicitas*, in *The Acts of the Christian Martyrs*, trans. with Introduction by Herbert Musurillo (Oxford: At the Clarendon Press, 1972), 106–31.

52. *The Martyrdom of Perpetua*, trans. Rosemary Rader, *A Lost Tradition: Women Writers of the Early Church*, ed. Patricia Wilson-Kastner and others (Lanham, Md.: University Press of America, 1981), 19–32.

53. Eusebius, *The History of the Church from Christ to Constantine*, ed. and trans. with an introduction by G. A. Williamson (New York: Dorset Press, 1965); *Eusebius Werke*, vol. 2, part 1, *Ecclesiasticae Historiae*, books 1–5, ed. Eduard Schwartz, Die Griechischen Christlichen Schriftsteller der Ersten Drei Jahrhunderte (Leipzig: J. C. Hinrichs'sche Buchhandlung, 1903).

54. Epiphanius, *The Panarion of Epiphanius of Salamis: Books II and III*, trans. Frank Williams (New York: E. J. Brill, 1994); *Panarion haer. 34–64*, ed. Karl Holl, Die Griechischen Christlichen Schriftsteller der Ersten Jahrhunderte (Berlin: Akademie-Verlag, 1980).

55. ANF, vols. 3 and 4, ed. Alexander Roberts and James Donaldson (Edinburgh: T. and T. Clark, 1873; reprint, Grand Rapids: Eerdmans, 1978 and 1982).

56. See bibliography for a list of selected English translations.

57. *Quinti Septimi Florentis Tertulliani Opera*, 2 vols, CCSL (Turnhout: Brepols, 1954).

58. *The Ascension of Isaiah*, ed. R. H. Charles (London: Adam and Charles Black, 1900); *Ascensio Isaiae: Textus*, vol. 7, Corpus Christianorum Series Apocryphorum (Turnhout: Brepols, 1995).

59. *Epistle of Barnabas*, in *The Apostolic Fathers*, trans. J. B. Lightfoot, ed. and rev. Michael W. Holmes (Grand Rapids: Baker, 1999), 270–321.

60. *The Ezra-Apocalypse*, trans. G. H. Box. London: Sir Isaac Pitman and Sons, Ltd., 1912.

61. *Shepherd of Hermas*, in *The Apostolic Fathers*, trans. J. B. Lightfoot, ed. and rev. Michael W. Holmes (Grand Rapids: Baker, 1999), 368–73; *Hermae Pastor Graece: Addita Versione Latina Recentiore e Codice Palatineo*, ed. Oscar de Gabhardt and Adolfus Harnack (Lipsiae: J. C. Hinrichs, 1877).

62. J. Armitage Robinson and Montague Rhodes James, eds., *The Gospel*

According to Peter, and The Revelation of Peter: Two Lectures on the Newly Recovered Fragments Together with the Greek Texts, 2d ed. (London: C. J. Clay and Sons, 1892).

63. Augustine, *Sermons*, trans. Edmund Hill, in WSA, part 3, vol. 8, ed. John E. Rotelle (Hyde Park, N.Y.: New City Press, 1994); idem., *The Nature and Origin of the Soul*, trans. Roland J. Teske, in *The Works of Saint Augustine: A Translation for the 21st Century*, part 1, vol. 23, *Answer to the Pelagians*, ed. John E. Rotelle (Hyde Park, N.Y.: New City Press, 1995).

Notes to Chapter 1

1. "And these Montanists are called, although falsely, by our same name, 'Christian.'" Cyril of Jerusalem, *Cat.* 16.8. Unless otherwise indicated, all translations of Greek sources are mine. Translations of Latin texts will be indicated in the references.

2. See, for example, Epiphanius, *Haer.* 48.12.4; 51.33.3; and Augustine, *Haer.* 26–27.

3. See Serapion's description: "this false order nicknamed the New Prophecy (νέας προφετείας)." Serapion, cited in Eusebius, *Hist. Eccl.* 19.2. Tertullian also used the term New Prophecy *(nova prophetia)* repeatedly, for examples, *Marc.*, 3.24.4, 4.22.4; *Resur.*, 63.9; and *Jejun.* 1.3. Latin texts for Tertullian's writings are from *Tertulliani Opera*, 2 vols., CCSL (Turnhout: Prepols, 1954).

4. See the reference by Eusebius' anonymous source, cited hereafter as Anonymous: "the Prophecy, so-called by them (τῆς κατ' αὐτοὺς λεγομένης προφητείας)." Anonymous, cited in Eusebius, *Hist. Eccl.* 5.16.14.

5. Trevett, *Montanism*, 2.

6. De Soyres, 31. De Soyres posited as the beginning date of Montanus' ministry A.D. 130, which is earlier than most estimates. See below for a fuller discussion.

7. Jerome, *Ep.* 41.4, trans. W. H. Fremantle, in NPNF, 2d series, vol. 6, ed. Philip Schaff and Henry Wace (Grand Rapids: Eerdmans, 1954), 56; PL (Paris: J. P. Migne, 1879), 22:476. See also William Tabbernee, ed., *Montanist Inscriptions and Testimonia*, 18–19; and W. H. C. Frend, "Montanism: A Movement of Prophecy and Regional Identity in the Early Church," *BJRL* 70 (Autumn 1988): 27.

8. Even the anonymous source doubted this gossip. Anonymous, cited in Eusebius, *Hist. Eccl.* 5.16.13.

9. Anonymous, cited in Eusebius, *Hist. Eccl.* 5.17.3. See also Acts 11.28; 15.32; 21.8–10. Nothing is known of Ammia other than that she was recognized as a prophet by both Catholics and Montanists. Quadratus, perhaps, was the second-century apologist, whom Eusebius described as a prophet. Eusebius, *Hist. Eccl.* 3.37.1. See also Trevett, *Montanism*, 34.

10. Jerome, *Ep.* 133.4, NPNF 2:6:275; Apollonius, cited in Eusebius, *Hist. Eccl.* 5.18.3.

11. Anonymous, cited in Eusebius, *Hist. Eccl.* 5.16.17; Serapion, cited in Eusebius, *Hist. Eccl.* 5.19.3. Frend, "Montanism," 27, located Koumana in Pamphylia of Southern Asia Minor; Tabbernee, *Montanist Inscriptions and Testimonia*, 21 n. 20, however, identified this village as Konana, or modern Gönen, in Phrygia.

12. Jensen, 135–36, 173, suggested that the titles of "founder and head" of the New Prophecy were more appropriate for Priscilla than for Montanus. Trevett, *Montanism*, 158–62, however, argued correctly that "Montanus was the first to manifest the Prophecy" and, at the same time, that the prophetesses were as significant as Montanus in the establishment and spread of the movement.

13. Epiphanius, *Haer.* 49.1.1–3; 49.2.1.

14. Anonymous, cited in Eusebius, *Hist. Eccl.* 5.16.14-5. See also Tabbernee, *Montanist Inscriptions and Testimonia*, 52–53.

15. Anonymous, cited in Eusebius, *Hist. Eccl.* 5.16.17; Apollonius, cited in Eusebius, *Hist. Eccl.* 5.18.5. See also de Soyres, 35.

16. Apollonius, cited in Eusebius, *Hist. Eccl.* 5.18.5-7. See also Frederick C. Klawiter, "The Role of Martyrdom and Persecution in Developing the Priestly Authority of Women in Early Christianity: A Case Study of Montanism," *Ch. Hist.* 49 (September 1980): 255.

17. Anonymous, cited in Eusebius, *Hist. Eccl.* 5.16.7; Apollonius, cited in Eusebius, *Hist. Eccl.* 5.18.2.

18. Heinz Kraft, "Die altkirchliche Prophetie und die Enstehung des Montanismus," *Theologische Zeitschrift* 11 (1955): 260–61.

19. Unless otherwise indicated, the Scripture quotations contained herein are from the New Revised Standard Version Bible, copyright (c) 1989 by the Division of Christian Education of the National Council of the Church of Christ in the U.S.A., and are used by permission. All rights reserved. The text used is *The New Oxford Annotated Bible with the Apocryphal/Deuterocanonical Books*, ed. Bruce M. Metzger and Roland E. Murphy (New York: Oxford University Press, 1994).

20. Trevett, *Montanism*, 23–24. See also Rev. 3.11–12: "I am coming quickly" (NRSV).

21. William Tabbernee, "Portals of the Montanist New Jerusalem: The Discovery of Pepouza and Tymion," *JECS* 11 (2003): 87–93.

22. Ibid., 93.

23. Ibid., 92.

24. Ibid., 93.

25. "There is a city built and set on a plain, and it is full of all good things; but the entrance to it is narrow and set in a precipitous place, so that there is fire on the right hand and deep water on the left. There is only one path lying

between them, that is, between the fire and the water, so that only one person can walk on the path. If now the city is given to someone as an inheritance, how will the heir receive the inheritance unless by passing through the appointed danger?" (4 Ezra = 2 Esdras 7:6–9 NRSV)." See also *The Ezra-Apocalypse*, trans. G. H. Box (London: Sir Isaac Pitman and Sons, 1912), 100–101, 3.

26. "[P]robably, . . . the name has a mystic or eschatological significance; it represents a mysterious place entirely removed from contact with ordinary human life. . . . Cf. Hermas, *Simil.* ix. 1, 4." Box, 213 n. *p.*

27. Trevett, *Montanism*, 25–26.

28. Eusebius, *Hist. Eccl.* 4.27.1; 5.3.4; 5 *preface*; 1.4. See also Timothy David Barnes, "The Chronology of Montanism," *JTS* 21 (1970): 403–4.

29. Epiphanius, *Haer.* 48.1.2. See also Barnes, "The Chronology of Montanism," 404.

30. R. A. Knox, *Enthusiasm: A Chapter in the History of Religion* (Oxford: At the Clarendon Press, 1950), 29. Grant, *Augustus to Constantine*, 133, had a similar proposal: the later date marks the condemnation of Montanism in Asia Minor. See also Bonwetsch, 142–48; and Adolf Harnack, *Die Chronologie der Altchristlichen Litteratur bis Eusebius* (Leipzig: J. C. Hinrichs'sche Buchhandlung, 1897), 1:380–81.

31. For a full discussion of the issues and possible resolutions, see Barnes, "The Chronology of Montanism," 403–8, especially 404 nn. 6–10.

32. G. S. P. Freeman-Grenville, "The Date of the Outbreak of Montanism," *JEH* 5 (1954): 14–15.

33. Frederick C. Klawiter, "The New Prophecy in Early Christianity: The Origin, Nature and Development of Montanism AD 165–220" (Ph.D. Diss., University of Chicago, 1975), 63.

34. Ibid., 1.

35. Augustus Neander, *General History of the Christian Religion and Church*, vol. 1, 11th American ed. (New York: Hurd and Houghton, 1871), 513.

36. W. M. Ramsay, *The Church in the Roman Empire before A.D. 170* (New York: G. P. Putnam's Sons, 1893), 438.

37. Wilhelm Schepelern, *Der Montanismus und die phrygischen Kulte: Eine religionsgeschichtlich Untersuchung*, trans. W. Baur (Tubingen: Verlag von J. C. B. Mohr. 1929), 122–30.

38. Schepelern, 125. See also Prudentius, *Discourse of the Martyr St. Romanus against the Pagans*, trans. M. Clement Eagan, in FOTC, vol. 43, *The Poems of Prudentius*, ed. Roy Joseph Deferrari (Washington, D.C.: The Catholic University of America Press, 1962), 237; Jerome, *Ep.* 41.4; Augustine, *Haer.* 26; Epiphanius, *Haer.* 48.14.5; 48.15.7.

39. Schepelern, 126. See also Epiphanius, *Haer.* 49.2.6. Augustine cited as reasoning for this aberration "that the first humans made offerings from the products of earth and of sheep." Augustine, *Haer.* 28, trans. Roland J. Teske, in WSA, part 1, vol. 18, *Arianism and Other Heresies*, ed. John E. Rotelle (Hyde Park, N.Y.: New City Press, 1995), 38.

40. Schepelern, 127. Epiphanius, *Haer.* 49.2.3–4.

41. Schepelern, 128. See also Epiphanius, *Haer.* 49.2.5.

42. Schepelern, 129–30.

43. Ibid., 161 (my translation).

44. For an excellent survey of these historians' views of Montanism, see Klawiter, "The New Prophecy in Early Christianity," 2–21.

45. F. C. A. Schwegler, *Der Montanismus und die Christliche Kirche des Zweiten Jahrhunderts* (Tübingen: Ludwig Friedrich Fues, 1841), 93–94.

46. Ibid., 83–84, 88. Schwegler contended that Paul's opposition in Corinth were Ebionites, who emphasized ecstatic prophecy and women's right to teach.

47. Ibid., 117–19, 121. From the pseudo-Clementine homilies, which Schwegler identified with Jewish Christianity, he compared the Ebionite use of bread and salt in the Eucharist with the Montanist/Artotyrite use of bread and cheese, which he cited from *The Passion of Perpetua and Felicitas* 4.9.

48. Ibid., 234, 236–37.

49. Albrecht Ritschl, *Die Entstehung der altkatholischen Kirche: Eine kirchen- und dogmengeschichtliche Monographie* (Bonn: Adolph Marcus, 1857), 468–70. Ritschl accepted William Cureton's thesis that only Ignatius' letters to Polycarp, to the Ephesians, and to the Romans were genuine. According to Cureton, the rest were from the late second century. Ibid., 403 n. 1. This thesis was refuted by J. B. Lightfoot, ed., *The Apostolic Fathers*, part 2, vol. 1., *Ignatius and Polycarp*, 2d ed. (n.p.: Macmillan, 1889; reprint, Peabody, Mass.: Hendrickson Publishers, 1989), 284–327.

50. Ibid., 477.

51. Ibid., 492.

52. Ibid., 515–18. Ritschl based his assertions on Tertullian, *Pud.* 21.

53. Ritschl, 518. See also Klawiter, "The New Prophecy in Early Christianity," 9.

54. Ferdinand Christian Baur, *The Church History of the First Three Centuries*, 2 vols., trans. Allan Menzies, 3d ed. (London: Williams and Norgate, 1878–9), 1:251.

55. Another point of agreement between these two scholars was the minimization of Montanus in the origins of Montanism. Schwegler, 241–43, denies outright the historicity of Montanus. Taking a more moderate stance, Baur merely questions Montanus' significance in the development of the movement, whose followers first were not called Montanists but Cataphrygians for the place where they lived and awaited the *parousia*. Baur, 1:255. For a view opposed to Schwegler and Baur, see Neander, 509–10.

56. Baur, 1:246–54.

57. Ibid., 2:53. The same point was made by James L. Ash, Jr. in "The Decline of Ecstatic Prophecy in the Early Church," *Theol. Stud.* 37 (1976): 251–52.

58. Baur, 2:55.

59. Bonwetsch, 15.

60. Ibid., 105.

61. Ibid., 126, 139.

62. Ibid., 126–27.

63. Ibid., 137. See also Ritschl, 520.

64. Bonwetsch, 138. Tertullian derived the term "Psychics" from 1 Cor. 2.14: "Those who are unspiritual (ψυχικὸς, "natural") do not receive the gifts of God's Spirit, for they are foolishness to them, and they are unable to understand them because they are spiritually (πνευματικῶς) discerned" (NRSV).

65. Adolf Harnack, "Montanism," *Encyclopaedia Britannica*, 11th ed.

66. Klawiter, "The New Prophecy in Early Christianity," 20. Mention should be made of the nineteenth-century work by de Soyres, the only monograph in the English language until Klawiter's dissertation (1975) and Trevett's published work (1996). De Soyres, 107–9, also concluded that Montanism revealed nothing contrary to the Catholic faith but insisted upon a return to primitive Christianity.

67. De Labriolle, *La Crise Montaniste*, 129–30, 137. De Labriolle's denunciation of Montanism as a heresy and his devotion to Catholicism were not coincidental. The same denominational loyalties led Catholic historians consistently to deny Montanism in the *Passion of Perpetua*. See the Introduction above. One exception to this rule is the Catholic Ernest Renan, who calls the *Acts* of St. Perpetua Montanist. Ernest Renan, *The History of the Origins of Christianity*, Book 7, *Marcus-Aurelius* (London: Mathieson and Company, n.d.), 137.

68. Ibid., 130.

69. Ibid., 131, 135. Other oracles cited in de Labriolle included "I am the Lord God the Father who came;" "I am the Lord, the all-powerful one who resides in man;" "I am Word, Spirit, Power;" and "Do not hear me, but hear Christ."

70. Ibid., 136.

71. For more recent discussions of possible Phrygian influences upon Montanism, see Greville Freeman, "Montanism and the Pagan Cults," *Dominican Studies* 3 (1950): 297–316; Balfour William Goree, Jr., "The Cultural Bases of Montanism" (Ph.D. Diss., Baylor University, 1980); Melanie Starks Kierstead, "The Socio-Historical Development of the New Prophecy: An Historical Inquiry to the Foundations of Montanism" (Ph.D. Diss., Drew University, 1996); and Susanna Elm, "Montanist Oracles," in *Searching the Scriptures*, vol. 2, *A Feminist Commentary*, ed. Elisabeth Schüssler Fiorenza, 131–38 (New York: Crossroad Publishing Company, 1994).

72. J. Massingberd Ford, based on criteria used by Schwegler, has argued for a Jewish-Christian background to Montanism in an article, "Was Montanism a Jewish-Christian Heresy?" *JEH* 17 (1966): 145–58. Carrying on the tradition of German scholarship are Kurt Aland, "Bermerkungen zum Mon-

tanismus und zur frühchristlichen Eschatologie," in *Kirchengeschichtliche Entwürfe* (Gütersloh, 1960), 105–43, cited in Klawiter, "The New Prophecy in Early Christianity," 31; and Hans von Campenhausen, *Ecclesiastical Authority and Spiritual Power in the Church of the First Three Centuries*, trans. J. A. Baker (London: A. and C. Black, 1969; reprint, Peabody, Mass.: Hendrickson Publishers, 1997), 181–92. A feminist perspective views the New Prophecy as a trajectory of Pauline egalitarianism and apocalypticism and its opposition as another Pauline trajectory of patriarchal assimilationism. See Sheila Elizabeth McGinn-Moorer, "The New Prophecy of Asia Minor and the Rise of Ecclesiastical Patriarchy in Second Century Pauline Traditions" (Ph.D. Diss., Northwestern University, 1989).

73. R. A. Knox, the Catholic apologist, disputed the arguments of Ritschl, Harnack, and de Soyres and insisted that Montanism was an innovative fanaticism, which foreshadowed the enthusiasm of such as Joachim of Fiore, the Fraticelli, John of Leyden, Jansenists, Quakers, Shakers, and the Salvation Army, all of whom he disdained. Knox, 25–49.

74. W. H. C. Frend, *Martyrdom and Persecution in the Early Church: A Study of a Conflict from the Maccabees to Donatus* (Garden City, N.Y.: Doubleday and Company, 1967), 217–19. Frend, holding to a date of 172 for the appearance of Montanus, referred to the decade of persecution which began under Marcus Aurelius.

75. Ibid., 264. See Tertullian, *Scorp.* 6; and *An.* 55.

76. Klawiter, "The New Prophecy in Early Christianity," 35.

77. Anonymous, cited in Eusebius, *Hist. Eccl.* 5.16.14. William Tabbernee, "Montanist Regional Bishops: New Evidence from Ancient Inscriptions," *JECS* 1 (1993): 258–59, suggested that ἐπίτροπος could refer to a "guardian" of the new prophetic movement.

78. Jerome, *Ep.* 41.3. Tabbernee, "Montanist Regional Bishops," 257–68, acknowledged that the second rank of Montanist clergy is difficult to define. Jerome used the Latinized word *cenonas* in place of the original Greek word, which was thought at one time to be derived from οἰκονόμους but is now understood to be from κοινωνούς. Interpretations of this term have varied among scholars to include: financial officers; associates of the original founders; exclusively female clergy; social leaders similar to those in a Jewish community; companions of Christ, in the sense of sharing in Christ's sufferings; and companions of the Spirit, in the sense of guardians of the Montanist prophetic message. Tabbernee argued from epigraphic evidence that these *koinōnoi* were regional bishops.

79. Jerome, *Ep.* 41.3, disdained the Montanists' relegation of bishops to third place, which ignored apostolic succession. Trevett, *Montanism*, 210.

80. "[T]hese Cataphrygians settled there [in Thyatira] and, like wolves, stole away the affections of unsuspecting believers and converted the entire city to their heresy." Epiphanius, *Haer.* 51.33.3. "Recently, being in Ancyra of

Galatia, I discovered the church in that place deafened by this new thing: not prophecy, as they say, but, very much more likely, false prophecy, as will be proven." Anonymous, cited in Eusebius, *Hist. Eccl.* 5.16.4.

81. Trevett, *Montanism*, 51–54.

82. Anonymous, cited in Eusebius, *Hist. Eccl.* 5.16.17.

83. Serapion, cited in Eusebius, *Hist. Eccl.* 5.19.3.

84. Anonymous, cited in Eusebius, *Hist. Eccl.* 5.16.10.

85. Evidence of possible Montanist activity in Smyrna appears in the episode involving the Phrygian Quintus in *The Martyrdom of Polycarp* 4, in *The Acts of the Christian Martyrs*, trans. with an introduction by Herbert Musurillo (Oxford: At the Clarendon Press, 1972), 4–5. See chapter four below.

86. Heinrich Kraft, "Die Lyoner Märtyrer und der Montanismus," in *Pietas: Festschrift für Bernhard Kötting*, ed. Ernst Dassmann and K. Suso Frank, *Jahrbuch für Antike und Christentum*, vol. 8, ed. Franz Joseph Dölger (Münster Westfalen: Aschendorffsche Verlagsbuchhandlung, 1980), 256–57.

87. Frend, *Martyrdom and Persecution*, 2–3.

88. Eusebius, *Hist. Eccl.* 5.3.4.

89. Tertullian, *Prax.* 1.5, trans. Peter Holmes, in ANF, vol. 3, ed. Alexander Roberts and James Donaldson (Edinburgh: T. and T. Clark, 1873; reprint, Grand Rapids: Eerdmans, 1978), 597, continued, "By this Praxeas did a twofold service for the devil at Rome: he drove away prophecy, and he brought in heresy; he put to flight the Paraclete, and he crucified the Father." All quotations from Tertullian's writings are from ANF.

90. Trevett, *Montanism*, 58–60. Eleutherus' successors, Victor (189–99) and Zephyrinus (199–217) have also been suggested as this bishop.

91. Eusebius, *Hist. Eccl.* 6.20.3.

92. Eusebius, *Hist. Eccl.* 2.25.6–7, 3.31.4, 5.24.2–3. William Tabbernee summarized the tension between West and East with the title of his article, "'Our Trophies are Better than your Trophies': The Appeal to Tombs and Reliquaries in Montanist-Orthodox Relations," in *Stud. Pat.*, vol. 31, ed. Elizabeth A. Livingstone (Leuven: Peeters Press, 1997), 206–17.

93. Pseudo-Tertullian, *Haer.* 7.2.

94. Hippolytus, *Haer.* 8.19.2; Pseudo-Tertullian, *Haer.* 7.2.

95. Jaroslav Pelikan, "Montanism and Its Trinitarian Significance," *Ch. Hist.* 25 (1956): 102.

96. Epiphanius coined the term *Alogoi*, which not only indicated their rejection of John who utilized *logos* in his writings but also carried the derogation, "without reason." Epiphanius, *Haer.* 51.3.1–3.

97. Trevett, *Montanism*, 138–41. See also F. F. Bruce, *The Spreading Flame*, vol. 1 of The Advance of Christianity Through the Centuries, ed. F. F. Bruce (Grand Rapids: Eerdmans, 1958), 220.

98. Trevett, *Montanism*, 71. See also Robeck, *Prophecy in Carthage*, 14.

99. Tertullian, *Bapt.* 17.5, knew of the Asian *Acts of Paul and Thecla*. Ac-

cording to Jerome, *Vir. ill.* 53, Tertullian wrote the last book of *De ecstasi* against the Asian anti-Montanist Apollonius. See also Trevett, *Montanism,* 71–72.

100. Assuming Montanist association with *The Passion of Perpetua and Felicitas,* the Prophecy must have arrived by 203. Assuming also that Tertullian converted to Christianity in the mid-190s and then allied himself to Montanism at a later date, then the influence of the movement must not have been felt in Carthage until the turn of the century, else the rigorous Tertullian would have been attracted to it immediately. Trevett, *Montanism,* 70–71.

101. Morton S. Enslin, "Puritan of Carthage," *The Journal of Religion* 27 (1947): 206; Eric Osborn, *Tertullian, First Theologian of the West* (Cambridge: Cambridge University Press, 1997), 210. See also Stuart A. Donaldson, *Church Life and Thought in North Africa A.D. 200* (Cambridge: University Press, 1909), 168–69, who thought it possible that Tertullian came in contact with Montanism in Rome.

102. Barnes, *Tertullian,* 47.

103. Harnack, "Montanism."

104. Douglas Powell, "Tertullianists and Cataphrygians," *Vig. Chr.* 29 (1975): 33–38, argued against a Montanist schism in North Africa and deftly interpreted Tertullian's pronouncements concerning the Prophets and the psychics to conclude that the Carthaginian Montanists "[o]riginally . . . formed, not a schismatic body, but an *ecclesiola in ecclesia* - not, indeed, content to be such, but prepared to be such while they strove still to secure the official recognition of that New Prophecy which they themselves obeyed." See also William Tabbernee, "Remnants of the New Prophecy: Literary and Epigraphical Sources of the Montanist Movement," in *Stud. Pat.,* vol. 21, ed. Elizabeth A. Livingstone (Leuven: Peeters Press, 1989), 195–97.

105. Tertullian, *An.* 9.4. On another occasion, a woman described as "a certain sister of ours" received a revelation from an angel. Tertullian, *Virg.* 17.3. See also Powell, 37. De Labriolle, however, assumed that such ceremonies proved a Montanist schism. Pierre de Labriolle, *History and Literature of Christianity from Tertullian to Boethius,* trans. Herbert Wilson with an introduction by Aidan Gasquet (New York: Alfred A. Knopf, 1925), 64.

106. William Tabbernee, "To Pardon or not to Pardon?: North African Montanism and the Forgiveness of Sins," in *Stud. Pat.,* vol. 36, ed. M. F. Wiles and E. J. Yarnold (Leuven: Peeters Press, 2001), 381.

107. Tertullian, *Jejun.* 1.

108. Tabbernee, "To Pardon or not to Pardon," 385–86.

109. Tertullian addressed *De fuga in persecutione* to "My brother Fabius,"who had opposed Tertullian regarding other questions and had not accepted the Paraclete. *Fug.* 1.1. He also referred to a certain man who took a second wife as "among our brethren." *Exh. cast.* 12.6. See also Powell, 33–35; and Trevett, *Montanism,* 73–74. Osborn, *Tertullian,* 176, suggested that Ter-

tullian remained in the Catholic Church, "despite (or because of) his allegiance to the New Prophecy." For an opposing view, see Paul McKechnie, *The First Christian Centuries: Perspectives on the Early Church* (Downers Grove, Ill.: Inter-Varsity Press, 2001), 175; and idem., "'Women's Religion' and Second-Century Christianity," *JEH* 47 (1996): 427. McKechnie, in opposition to Powell, insisted that Tertullian and his own faction, the "Tertullianists," split from the Carthaginian church in 206. McKechnie assumed that Tertullian's adherence to Montanism constituted a split from Catholicism.

110. Jerome, *Vir. ill.* 53. See also Powell, 38.

111. Osborn, *Tertullian*, 177.

112. De Labriolle, *History and Literature of Christianity*, 64, declared, "However, the Montanist group at Carthage could never have been very numerous," while Barnes, *Tertullian*, 131, claimed, "The evidence . . . indicates that the church of Carthage nearly succumbed." Neither provided convincing proof for his assertion.

113. Frend, *Martyrdom and Persecution*, 267–68; and idem., *Saints and Sinners in the Early Church: Differing and Conflicting Traditions in the First Six Centuries*, Theology and Life Series, vol. 11 (Wilmington, Del.: Michael Glazier, 1985), 72.

114. For a comparison of Montanism and Donatism see W. H. C. Frend, *The Donatist Church: A Movement of Protest in Roman North Africa* (Oxford: At the Clarendon Press, 1952), 116–24.

115. Trevett, *Montanism*, 74; Osborn, *Tertullian*, 177.

116. Robeck, *Prophecy in Carthage*, 14.

117. Augustine, *Haer.* 86, WSA 1:18:54–55.

118. Frend, *Martyrdom and Persecution*, 271.

119. De Soyres, 53. De Soyres based his suggestion on Praedestinatus: *[Tertullianus] fundit a se omnem Phrygiae vanitatem et Tertullianistarum conventicula propagavit.* "Tertullian poured out of himself every untruth of the Phrygians and propagated assemblies of Tertullianists" (my translation). Praedestinatus, *Haer.* 1:86; PL 53:616–17.

120. Barnes, *Tertullian*, 258. See also J. M. Fuller, "Tertullian," *Dictionary of Christian Biography*, vol. 4, ed. William Smith and Henry Wace (London: John Murray, 1887).

121. For example, the Priscillianists and Quintillianists.

122. Trevett, *Montanism*, 114–18.

123. Ibid., 223.

124. Ibid., 227–29.

125. For example, in the sixth century, John, bishop of Ephesus, discovered a shrine inscribed "Of Montanus and the women." Inside were the skeletons of Montanus, Maximilla, and Priscilla with golden plates fastened across their mouths. Included in the reliquary were Montanist books, but they were destroyed along with the founders' bones. Tabbernee, *Montanist Inscriptions and Testimonia*, 1.

126. Anonymous, cited in Eusebius, *Hist. Eccl.* 5.17.4.

127. Jaroslav Pelikan, *The Christian Tradition: A History of the Development of Doctrine*, vol. 1, *The Emergence of the Catholic Tradition (100–600)* (Chicago: The University of Chicago Press, 1971), 99–100.

128. De Soyres, 58.

129. Didymus, *Trin.* 3.41, in *The Montanist Oracles and Testimonia*, ed. Ronald E. Heine, 8–9.

130. Epiphanius, *Haer.* 48.11.1.

131. Cyril of Jerusalem, *Cat.* 16.8.

132. Epiphanius, *Haer.* 48.4. See also William Tabbernee, "'Will the Real Paraclete Please Speak Forth!': The Catholic-Montanist Conflict over Pneumatology," in *Advents of the Spirit: An Introduction to the Current Study of Pneumatology*, ed. Bradford E. Hinze and D. Lyle Dabney, Marquette Studies in Theology, vol. 30, ed. Andrew Tallon (Milwaukee, Wis.: Marquette University Press, 2001), 105.

133. Basil, *Ep.* 188.1. See also Tabbernee, "The Catholic-Montanist Conflict," 113–14.

134. Synod of Laodicea, Canon 8, in NPNF, 2d series, vol. 14, ed. Philip Schaff and Henry Wace (Edinburgh: T. and T. Clark, 1892; reprint, Grand Rapids: Eerdmans, 1979), 128.

135. *Flabius Abus dome-sticus i<n> nomine Patris et Filii do<mi>ni Muntani quod promi-sit complevit.* Tabbernee, *Montanist Inscriptions and Testimonia*, 445–47 (my translation).

136. Trevett, *Montanism*, 219.

137. Tabbernee, *Montanist Inscriptions and Testimonia*, 448–52; idem., "The Catholic-Montanist Conflict," 113–14.

138. Tabbernee, *Montanist Inscriptions and Testimonia*, 449.

139. Pelikan, *The Emergence of the Catholic Tradition*, 103–4.

140. For a thorough discussion and defense of the Montanist pneumatology, see Tabbernee, "The Catholic-Montanist Conflict," 97–115.

141. "These [Phrygians], in a similar manner to the church, confess God to be the father of the universe and creator of everything and also as many things concerning Christ as the Gospel testifies." Hippolytus, *Haer.* 8.19.2.

142. Tertullian, *Prax.* 3. See also Pelikan, *The Emergence of the Catholic Tradition*, 105: "The early writings of Tertullian tended to stress the Father and the Son at the expense of the Holy Spirit; those which definitely dated from the Montanist period, on the other hand, did contain a more metaphysical doctrine of the 'Trinity.' . . . The emphasis in Montanism on the Spirit is the explanation of this shift that suggests itself most insistently."

143. Spirit-based movements throughout the history of the church have been more open to the Spirit's utilization of women in ministry, including Quakers, Shakers, Quietists, and Pentecostals.

144. Epiphanius, *Haer.* 49.2.2–3.

145. Trevett, *Montanism*, 175. See also Elaine C. Huber, *Women and the Authority of Inspiration*, 62; and Jensen, 169–73.

146. Eusebius, *Hist. Eccl.* 5.16.9, 13.

147. Anonymous, cited in Eusebius, *Hist. Eccl.* 5.16.17; Serapion, cited in Eusebius, *Hist. Eccl.* 5.19.3.

148. Gen. 3.16, 1 Cor. 11.8, and 1 Tim. 2.12, 14. Epiphanius, *Haer.* 49.2.1–3.3.

149. *Did.* 11–13, trans. J. B. Lightfoot, in *The Apostolic Fathers: Greek Texts and English Translations*, ed. and rev. Michael W. Holmes (Grand Rapids: Baker, 1999), 263–67.

150. Justin Martyr, *Dial.* 82.

151. Irenaeus, *Haer.* 2.32.4.

152. The new prophets' practice of ecstatic prophecy and glossolalia did not prevent their oracles from being interpreted, recorded, and collected and their books, circulated. Hippolytus, *Haer.* 8.19.1. These documents, unfortunately, were destroyed by ecclesiastical authorities during anti-Montanist campaigns. For an example, see Tabbernee, *Montanist Inscriptions and Testimonia*, 1.

153. Trevett, *Montanism*, 86.

154. Anonymous, cited in Eusebius, *Hist. Eccl.* 5.16.7.

155. Anonymous, cited in Eusebius, *Hist. Eccl.* 5.16.9.

156. Epiphanius, *Haer.* 48.13.1.

157. Anonymous, cited in Eusebius, *Hist. Eccl.* 5.16.7.

158. ἀρχομένου μὲν ἐξ ἑκουσίου ἀμαθίας, καταστρέφοντος δὲ εἰς ἀκούσιν μανίαν ψυχῆς. Miltiades, cited in Eusebius, *Hist. Eccl.* 5.17.2.

159. Epiphanius, *Haer.* 48.4.6. In fact, however, other terms such as μανία and κατοχή did not describe explicitly abnormal behaviors associated with trance, such as collapse, frenzy, and delirium. David E. Aune, *Prophecy in Early Christianity and the Ancient Mediterranean World* (Grand Rapids: Eerdmans, 1983), 21.

160. "And God brought a trance (ἔκστασιν) upon Adam, and he slept." Gen. 2.21 (LXX). See also Dennis E. Groh, "Utterance and Exegesis: Biblical Interpretation in the Montanist Crisis," in *The Living Text: Essays in Honor of Ernest W. Saunders*, ed. Dennis E. Groh and Robert Jewett (Lanham, Md.: University Press of America, 1985), 85.

161. "And I said in my amazement (ἐκστάσει), Every man is a liar." Ps. 116.11 (LXX, 115.2).

162. Epiphanius, *Haer.* 48.3.5, 7, 9; 4.4; 7.3, 8; 10.1. See also Trevett, *Montanism*, 88.

163. William Tabbernee, "The Opposition to Montanism from Church and State" (Ph.D. Diss., University of Melbourne, 1978), 98.

164. For a reference to the practice of glossolalia by Gnostics, see Irenaeus, *Haer.* 1.13.3.

165. An example of pagan glossolalia is the practice of the Pythia at Delphi. After researching oracles at Delphi, Tabbernee, "The Opposition to Montanism from Church and State," 99, observed, "Ancient references to the Pythia's speech imply that her replies were confused and incoherent, suggesting a form of glossolalia. See also H. W. Parke, *Greek Oracles* (London: Hutchinson University Library, 1967), 84.

166. Irenaeus, *Haer.* 5.6.1, wrote that "we also hear about brothers in the church who have prophetic gifts and who speak in all kinds of languages through the Spirit and . . . who clarify the mysteries of God." See also Trevett, *Montanism*, 89–91.

167. Trevett, *Montanism*, 252 n. 42.

168. See, for example, Schwegler, 86; and de Labriolle, *La Crise Montaniste*, 170–72.

169. Christopher Forbes, *Prophecy and Inspired Speech in Early Christianity and its Hellenistic Environment* (Peabody, Mass.: Hendrickson, 1997), 160–62.

170. William Tabbernee, "The Opposition to Montanism from Church and State," 97, observed, "In Montanus' case, his intelligible statements were accompanied by other phenomenon [*sic*] which could only be described as babble or strange talk which made no sense. The same was true of Maximilla and Priscilla for they too 'chattered crazily . . . like Montanus himself." Later, Tabbernee posited that "the New Prophets declared their utterances . . . through a mixture of intelligible statements and a form of glossolalia." Ibid., 548.

171. Forbes, 161, cited G. W. H. Lampe, ed., *A Patristic Greek Lexicon* (Oxford: At the Clarendon Press, 1961).

172. Henry George Liddell and Robert Scott, ed., *A Greek-English Lexicon*, rev. Henry Stuart Jones (Oxford: At the Clarendon Press, 1968).

173. Ibid.

174. For views opposed by Forbes, see Nils Ivar Johan Engelsen, "Glossolalia and Other Forms of Inspired Speech According to 1 Corinthians 12–14" (Ph.D. Diss., Yale University, 1970), 43–45; and Mattie Elizabeth Hart, "Speaking in Tongues and Prophecy as Understood by Paul and at Corinth, with Reference to Early Christian Usage" (Ph.D. Diss., University of Durham, 1975), 106.

175. Trevett, *Montanism*, 87, translated this phrase "bastard utterances."

176. Anonymous, cited in Eusebius, *Hist. Eccl.* 5.16.8.

177. Ibid.

178. Epiphanius, *Haer.* 48.12.4.

179. Epiphanius, *Haer.* 48.11.1, 9. Note similarity to Is. 63.9 LXX: "Not an ambassador (πρέσβυς), nor a messenger (ἄγγελος), but he himself saved them." Tertullian, *Marc.* 4.22.11, cited this verse also.

180. Hippolytus, *Haer.* 8.19.1.

181. *Nova lex abstulit repudium . . . . Nova prophetia, secundum matrimonium.*

Tertullian, *Mon.* 14.3–4. Two other examples were fasting innovations, such as prolonged fasts, xerophagies, or dry fasts, and abstinence from bathing; and prohibition to serve in the army. Tertullian, *Jejun.* 11; and *De Corona* 1–15.

182. Groh, 90.

183. Ignatius, *Phld.* 7 (longer recension).

184. Bonwetsch, 139 (my translation). Other scholars who recognized the millennialism and eschatological emphases of Montanism were Baur, 1:245–48; de Soyres, 77–78; de Labriolle, *La Crise Montaniste*, 107–8; Schepelern, 28–33; Klawiter, "The Role of Martyrdom and Persecution," 253; and Frend, "Montanism," 26–27.

185. Pelikan, *The Emergence of the Catholic Tradition*, 98–99.

186. *Asc. Isa.* 3.22–31.

187. Pelikan, *The Emergence of the Catholic Tradition*, 99.

188. Apollonius, cited in Eusebius, *Hist. Eccl.* 5.18.2.

189. See, for example, de Labriolle, *La Crise Montaniste*, 16–17, 487; de Soyres, 77; Schepelern, 29–30; and Knox, 38.

190. G. A. Williamson, ed., *The History of the Church from Christ to Constantine*, trans. with an introduction by G. A. Williamson (New York: Dorset Press, 1965) 223 n. 2.

191. Powell, 44. Ultimately, Powell, 46, disputed the "apocalyptic futurism usually ascribed to the Montanists" and advocated instead "an eschatology largely realised in a present spiritual experience for the more visionary Elect." Other scholars who doubted any extraordinary millennialism in Montanism include William Tabbernee, "Revelation 21 and the Montanist 'New Jerusalem,'" *Australian Biblical Review* 37 (1989): 52–60 (but see the next note below); Trevett, *Montanism*, 103–5; Jensen, 151–58; and John C. Poirier, "Montanist Pepuza-Jerusalem and the Dwelling Place of Wisdom," *JECS* 7 (1999): 505–7.

192. Tabbernee, "Portals of the Montanist New Jerusalem," 92. Following his discovery, Tabbernee decided that Montanus indeed did expect the descent of New Jerusalem onto Pepuza and Tymion. Earlier, in "Revelation 21 and the Montanist 'New Jerusalem,'" 53–57, he questioned the assumption that eschatological innovation was the purpose behind Montanus' identification of these two towns as Jerusalem and preferred the suggestion that Montanus' intention was the organization of his movement. In this earlier article, Tabbernee found the inspiration for the name "Jerusalem" not in Revelation but in Acts. Once he discovered the ancient sites of Pepuza and Tymion, however, he reported that he stood on a nearby mountain and envisioned Montanus looking out over the plain where the New Jerusalem would descend out of heaven, "as described in Revelation 21." Tabbernee, "Portals of the Montanist New Jerusalem," 93.

193. Epiphanius, *Haer.* 49.1.3.

194. Powell, 44.

195. Jensen, 166.

196. Poirier, 495–96 n. 13.

197. The expectation of the descent of Jerusalem was featured in Montanism for a long time. See Frend, "Montanism," 32. Furthermore, Tertullian, *Marc.* 3.24.3–4, discussed "the divinely-built city of Jerusalem, 'let down from heaven' *(in civitate divini operis Jerusalem coelo delata)*."

198. *Contra* Poirier, 491–507, who contended that Sirach 24 was a possible source for this oracle.

199. Ronald E. Heine, "The Role of the Gospel of John in the Montanist Controversy," *Sec. Cent.* 6 (1987): 1–19, contended that the inspiration from Johannine writings came to the Montanists not during the early years in Phrygia but later in Rome and Carthage.

200. Frend, "Montanism," 32.

201. Ford, 147.

202. Epiphanius, *Haer.* 48.13.1.

203. Anonymous, cited by Eusebius, *Hist. Eccl.* 5.16.18.

204. See Rev. 11.7; 12.7, 17; 13.4, 7; 17.14.

205. Trevett, *Montanism*, 102–3.

206. Anonymous, cited in Eusebius, *Hist. Eccl.* 5.16.9.

207. Epiphanius, *Haer.* 48.10.3.

208. Pelikan, *The Emergence of the Catholic Tradition*, 106. See also Heine, "The Role of the Gospel of John in the Montanist Controversy," 15.

209. Schepelern, 162 (my translation). See also Pelikan, *The Emergence of the Catholic Tradition*, 107.

210. Pelikan, *The Emergence of the Catholic Tradition*, 107. See also Ash, 251–52.

211. Epiphanius, *Haer.* 48.2.4.

212. Trevett, *Montanism*, 104–5. Osborn, *Tertullian*, 177, observed that Tertullian's allegiance to Montanism may have intensified his eschatological expectation, which in turn emphasized the need for the church to purify itself for Christ's return.

213. Osborn, *Tertullian*, 210–13.

214. Tertullian, *Exh. cast.* 10.5.

215. As Daniel had done before them, Montanists, too, abstained from bathing during the xerophagy. Tertullian, *Exh. cast.* 1.5.

216. *The Ezra-Apocalypse*, Box, 213–14.

217. *Herm. Vis.* 2.2, 3.1. See also Trevett, *Montanism*, 107–8.

218. Apollonius, cited in Eusebius, *Hist. Eccl.* 5.18.2–3.

219. Epiphanius, *Haer.* 48.9.7. See also Jerome, *Ep.* 41.3.

220. Trevett, *Montanism*, 114.

221. Jerome, *Ep.* 41.3.

222. H. J. Lawlor, "The Heresy of the Phrygians," *JTS* 9 (1908): 490; Cahal B. Daly, *Tertullian the Puritan and His Influence: An Essay in Historical Theol-*

ogy (Dublin, Ire.: Four Courts Press, 1993), 15; and Trevett, *Montanism*, 117.

223. Tertullian, *Pud.* 21.7.

224. Tertullian, *Pud.* 19.25.

225. Tabbernee, "To Pardon or Not to Pardon," 385–86. See also Jensen, 130.

226. Apollonius, cited in Eusebius, *Hist. Eccl.* 5.18.7. See also Klawiter, "The Role of Martyrdom and Persecution," 255.

227. *The Letter of the Churches of Lyons and Vienne,* cited in Eusebius, *Hist. Eccl.* 5.2.4–6. See also Klawiter, "The Role of Martyrdom and Persecution," 255.

228. Klawiter, "The Role of Martyrdom and Persecution," 256.

229. Hippolytus, *Trad. ap.* 9.1 (10.1).

230. Tertullian, *Mart.* 1.6.

231. Trevett, *Montanism*, 117–18.

232. Robin Lane Fox, *Pagans and Christians* (New York: Alfred A. Knopf, 1989), 408–9.

233. Trevett, *Montanism*, 108, 120.

234. Anonymous, cited in Eusebius, *Hist. Eccl.* 5.16.20. Eusebius' anonymous source was skeptical of the Montanists' claims, but his report confirmed their high evaluation of martyrdom.

235. Tertullian, *Fug.* 9.4.

236. Tertullian, *An.* 55.5.

237. William Tabbernee, "Early Montanism and Voluntary Martyrdom," *Colloquium: The Australian and New Zealand Theological Review* 17 (1985): 36.

238. Tertullian, *Fug.* 9.4.

239. Tabbernee, "Early Montanism and Voluntary Martyrdom," 43, denied that Asian Montanism differed from orthodoxy regarding voluntary martyrdom *contra* Schwegler, 65–67; Knox, 49; Klawiter, "The Role of Martyrdom and Persecution," 251–61; and W. H. C. Frend, *Martyrdom and Persecution in the Early Church*, 293. He acknowledged, however, that Tertullian did exalt voluntary martyrdom.

240. *Mart. Pol.* 4; *Acts Cyp.* 1.5.

241. Schepelern, 162 (my translation). See also Pelikan, *The Emergence of the Catholic Tradition*, 98.

242. Frend, "Montanism," 32.

243. Trevett, *Montanism*, 91.

Notes to Chapter 2

1. *Passion* 2.3, 3.1, 11.1, 11.2, 14.1. Unless indicated otherwise, all quotations from the *Passion* are from Musurillo's translation, and all translations from Greek texts are mine.

2. Augustine, *Nat. orig.* 1.10.12, trans. Roland J. Teske, in WSA, part 1,

vol. 23, *Answer to the Pelagians*, ed. John Rotelle (Hyde Park, N.Y.: New City Press, 1995), 479.

3. Thomas J. Heffernan, "Philology and Authorship in the *Passio Sanctarum Perpetuae et Felicitatis*," *Traditio* 50 (1995): 316.

4. For a history of research, see Julio Campos, "El autor de la *Passio SS Perpetuae et Felicitatis*," *Helmantica* 10 (1959): 358–61.

5. Harris and Gifford, 13–18. Benjamin Aubé, *Les chrétiens dans l'Empire romain*, Studia Historica, vol. 103 (Paris: Ristampa Anastatica Invariata dell'Edizione, 1881; reprint, Roma: "L'Erma" di Bretschneider, 1972), 515, suggested the possibility of a Greek original before the discovery of the Greek text. See also A. H. Salonius, *Passio S. Perpetuae: Kritische Bemerkungen mit besonderer Berücksichtigung der griechisch-lateinischen Überlieferung des Textes* (Helsingfors: Helsingfors Centraltryckeri Och Bokbinderi Aktiebolag, 1921), 63.

6. Robinson, 2–9, especially 3 n. 1.

7. Thomas J. Heffernan, "The Passion of Saints Perpetua and Felicitas and the *Imitatio Christi*," in *Sacred Biography: Saints and Their Biographers in the Middle Ages* (New York: Oxford University Press, 1988), 199.

8. Van Beek (1936), 90*, for example, suggested that the editor composed the *Passion* first in Latin and then in Greek, an idea which René Braun, "Séance du 26 Mars 1955," *Revue des études latines* 33 (1955): 81, refuted. Ernst Rupprecht, "Bemerkungen zur *Passion SS. Perpetuae et Felicitatis*," *Rheinisches Museum für Philologie* 90 (1941): 179–80; and Campos, 362–67; argued that the Greek text was a translation but of a different Latin text which is not preserved. Many scholars agreed with Robinson, including de Labriolle, *La Crise Montaniste* (Paris: Ernest Leroux, 1913), 339; W. H. Shewring, introduction to *The Passion of Perpetua and Felicity: A New Edition and Translation of the Latin Text together with the Sermons of S. Augustine upon These Saints*, trans. W. H. Shewring (London: Sheed and Ward, 1931), xix; Barnes, "Pre-Decian *Acta Martyrum*," 521; Musurillo, xxvii; Johannes Quasten, *Patrology*, vol. 1, *The Beginnings of Patristic Literature* (Westminster, Md.: Christian Classics, 1986), 181–82; Peter Habermehl, *Perpetua und der Ägypter oder Bilder des Bösen im Frühen Afrikanischen Christentum* (Berlin: Akademie Verlag, 1992), 3; and Robeck, *Prophecy in Carthage*, 12.

9. Paul Monceaux, *Histoire Littéraire de l'Afrique Chrétienne depuis les Origines jusqu'a l'Invasion Arabe*, vol. 1, *Tertullien et les Origines* (Paris: n.p., 1901; reprint, Brussels: Culture et Civilisation, 1963, 83. See also Adolf Harnack, *Die Chronologie der Altchristlichen Litteratur bis Eusebius*, 2:322; Adhemar d'Alès, "L'Auteur de la *Passio Perpetuae*," *Revue d'histoire ecclesiastique* 8 (1907): 10; E. R. Dodds, *Pagan and Christian in an Age of Anxiety: Some Aspects of Religious Experience from Marcus Aurelius to Constantine* (Cambridge: At the University Press, 1965), 50; and Louis Robert, "Une vision de Perpétue, martyre à Carthage en 203," *Comptes rendus de l'Academie des Inscriptions et Belles-Lettres* (1982), 253–56.

10. Åke Fridh, *Le problème de la Passion des Saintes Perpétue et Félicité.* Studia Graeca et Latina Gothoburgensia, 26 (Göteborg: Acta Universitatis Gothoburgensis, 1968), 82–83. See also Barnes, *Tertullian*, 265–66.

11. Robinson, 43.

12. Ibid., 43–44.

13. "These may seem trifling points; but we must remember that it is in the use of particles that we find the surest evidence of the sameness or differences of styles, where there is any room for the suspicion that a forger has been at work." Ibid., 44–45.

14. Ibid., 46–47.

15. W. H. Shewring, "Prose Rhythm in the *Passio S. Perpetuae*," *JTS* 30 (1928): 56–57.

16. Paul Allard, *Histoire des persécutions*, vol. 2 (Paris: Librairie Victor Lecoffre, 1919), 102–3; Jacqueline Amat, introduction to *Passion*, 67; Barnes, "Pre-Decian *Acta Martyrum*," 521; de Labriolle, *History and Literature of Christianity*, 103–4; Hippolyte Delehaye, *Les Passions des Martyrs et les Genres Littéraires* (Bruxelles: Société des Bollandistes, 1966), 49–50; de Soyres, 139; Habermehl, 241–43; Klawiter, "The Role of Martyrdom and Persecution," 257; Dronke, 1; Fridh, 83; Harnack, *Die Chronologie der Altchristlichen Litteratur bis Eusebius*, 2:321; Musurillo, xxv; E. C. E. Owen, introduction to *The Passion of SS. Perpetua and Felicitas*, in *Some Authentic Acts of the Early Martyrs*, trans. E. C. E. Owen (London: Society for Promoting Christian Knowledge, 1927), 74–75; Quasten, 181; Rader, "A Protest Account of Third-Century Christianity," 1; Robeck, *Prophecy in Carthage*, 12; Trevett, *Montanism*, 176.

17. Aubé, 510–15. Harris and Gifford, 7, suggested that Aubé saw uniformity throughout the *Passion* because he knew only the Latin text, which they believed to be a translation of the Greek. They continued, "Our own impression is that the differences of style are quite sufficient to discriminate the various hands in the book."

18. Heffernan, "Philology and Authorship," 320–23.

19. Ibid., 323. Heffernan also reminded the reader that oral testimony carried significant authority in this period.

20. A. Cleveland Coxe, introduction to *The Martyrdom of Perpetua and Felicitas*, trans. R. E. Wallis, in ANF, vol. 3, ed. Alexander Roberts and James Donaldson (Edinburgh: T. and T. Clark, 1873; reprint, Grand Rapids: Eerdmans, 1978), 697; Bonwetsch, 185; Robinson, 47–58; Harnack, *Die Chronologie der Altchristlichen Litteratur bis Eusebius*, 2:321; Adhemar d'Alès, "L'Auteur de la *Passio Perpetuae*," 5–18; de Labriolle, *La Crise Montaniste*, 353; idem, *History and Literature of Christianity*, 104; Owen, 77; W. H. Shewring, *The Passion of Perpetua and Felicity*, xx; idem, "Prose Rhythms," 57; van Beek, 95*; idem, introduction to *Passio sanctarum Perpetuae et Felicitatis*, ed. Cornelius Johannes Maria Joseph van Beek (Bonn: Peter Hanstein, 1938), 2; Delehaye, *Les Passions des Martyrs*, 50–52; Quasten, 181; Hans von Campenhausen, *The Fathers of the*

Latin Church, trans. Mandred Hoffman (London: Adam and Charles Black, 1964), 32; and Robert, 235 n. 35.

21. C. E. Freppel, *Tertullien*, vol. 1 (Paris: Ambroise Bray, 1864), 347–49; Aubé, 515; Harris and Gifford, 28, cf. 2–3; Monceaux, 83; Henri Le Clercq, *Les Martyrs*, vol. 1, *Les Temps Neroniens et le Deuxième Siècle* (Paris: H. Oudin, 1902), 121; Allard, 105–6; F. J. Dölger, "Antike Parallelen zum leidenden Dinocrates in der Passio Perpetuae," *Ant. Chr.* 2 (1930): 40 n. 108; idem, "Der Kampf mit dem Ägypter in der Perpetua-Vision: Das Martyrium als Kampf mit dem Teufel," *Ant. Chr.* 3 (1932): 188; René Braun, 80–81; idem, "Nouvelles Observations Linguistiques sur le Rédacteur de la *'Passio Perpetuae,'" Vig. Chr.* 33 (June 1979): 105–17; Campos, 381; Jacques Fontaine, *Aspects et problémes de la prose d'art Latine au IIIe siècle: La genèse des styles Latins chrétiens* (Torino: Bottega d'Erasmo, 1968), 73–75; Amat, introduction to *Passion*, 68; Barnes, "Pre-Decian *Acta Martyrum*," 522; idem, *Tertullian*, 79–80; Musurillo, xxvi; David Scholer, "'And I Was a Man': The Power and Problem of Perpetua." *Daughters of Sarah* 15 (September 1989): 11; Habermehl, 3; Tabbernee, ed., *Montanist Inscriptions and Testimonia*, 55–57; Trevett, *Montanism*, 177–78; and Rachel Moriarty, "The Claims of the Past: Attitudes to Antiquity in the Introduction to *Passio Perpetuae*," in *Stud. Pat.*, vol. 31, ed. Elizabeth A. Livingstone (Leuven, Belgium: Peeters, 1997), 309. At least three scholars considered that the editor was not Tertullian, but they made no comment about Montanism, because their concern was with the priority of the Latin and Greek texts: Salonius, iv; Rupprecht, 177–92; Fridh, 11.

22. Ruinart, 135–36; Weinrich, 223–24, 228–36; Robeck, *Prophecy in Carthage*, 16–18.

23. Robinson, 47.

24. *In nouissimis enim diebus, dicit dominus, effundam de Spiritu meo super omnem carnem, et prophetabunt filii filiaeque eorum; et super seruos et ancillas meas de meo Spiritu effundam; et iuuenes uisiones uidebunt, et senes somnia somniabunt. Passion* 1.4.

25. *Et erit in nouissimis diebus, dicit Dominus, effundam de Spiritu meo super omnem carnem, et prophetabunt filii uestri et filiae uestrae; et iuuenes uestri ruisiones uidebunt et seniores uestri somnia somniabunt; et quidem super seruos meos et super ancillas meas in diebus illis effundam de Spiritu meo, et prophetabunt.* All references to Latin Scriptures are taken from *Nouum Testamentum Latine*, trans. Jerome, ed. Johannes Wordsworth and Henricus Iulianus White (Oxford: Oxford University Press, 1911). The Vulgate postdated the *Passion* by more than 160 years, but the Old Latin text, which Jerome consulted in his translation, was begun in Africa in the second century. Because only fragments of the Old Latin text were preserved as quotations in patristic writings, the Vulgate provides the only insight into the Latin text of third-century North Africa. See J. N. D. Kelly, *Jerome: His Life, Writings and Controversies* (Gerald Duckworth and Co., 1975; reprint, Peabody, Mass.: Hendrickson, 1998), 86–87. *Nouum Testamentum Latine* hereafter cited as Vulgate.

26. *In nouissimis diebus effundam de meo Spiritu in omnem carnem, et prophetabunt filii filiaeque eorum; et super seruos et ancillas meas de meo Spiritu effundam.* Tertullian, *Marc.* 5.8.6. Latin texts for Tertullian's writings are from *Tertulliani Opera*, 2 vols., CCSL (Turnhout: Prepols, 1954). See also Robinson, 47–48.

27. Compare *Passion* 1.6 with 1 John 1.1, 3 Vulgate, and Tertullian, *Prax.* 15.2. See also Robinson, 48–49.

28. Robinson, 49.

29. Tertullian, *Fug.* 1.6. All translations of Tertullian's writings are from ANF, vols. 3 and 4, ed. Alexander Roberts and James Donaldson (Edinburgh: T. and T. Clark, 1873; reprint, Grand Rapids: Eerdmans, 1978).

30. Ibid., 14.3.

31. Robinson, 50.

32. "... *semper Deus operetur quae repromisit, non credentibus in testimonium, credentibus in beneficium.*"

33. "... *ubique Deus potestatis suae signa proponit, suis in solatium, extraneis in testimonium.*" Tertullian, *An.* 51.7.

34. Robinson, 51.

35. "... *pudoris potius memor quam doloris*" (my translation).

36. "... *pudoris magis memores quam salutis.*" Tertullian, *Paen.* 10.1.

37. Tertullian, *An.* 9.4 (my translation). See also Robinson, 52.

38. "For indeed these too will one day become ancient and needful for the ages to come, even though in our own day they may enjoy less prestige because of the prior claim of antiquity." *Passion* 1.2.

39. "Their high antiquity, first of all, claims authority for these writings." Tertullian, *Apol.* 19.1.

40. "But I will not, meantime, attribute this usage to Truth." Tertullian, *Virg.* 2. See also Robinson, 52–53.

41. Robinson, 53. See also *Passion* 1.5 and Tertullian, *Cor.* 8.1. De Labriolle, *La Crise Montaniste*, 348, called *instrumentum* "Tertullian's favorite word to designate the Scripture," citing Tertullian, *Prax.* 20.2; *Mon.* 4.1, 7.1; *Marc.* 4.2.1; and *Pud.* 10.12. In the prologue, the editor stated his intent to enter new visions and prophecies into the *instrumentum Ecclesiae*, a legal term for a document dealing with faith or a written testimony. De Labriolle, *La Crise Montaniste*, 353.

42. Tertullian, *An.* 55.4. See also Robinson, 54–55.

43. Tertullian, *Pat.* 15.2, 4–5. See also *Passion* 4.7 and 10.11 where Perpetua trampled on the heads of the dragon and the Egyptian, symbols of Satan. Robinson's identification of Perpetua with Tertullian's Patience was fanciful, but Barnes, *Tertullian*, 55, did date *Pat.* about 203. Quasten, 181, evidently agreed with Robinson.

44. D'Alès, "L'Auteur de la *Passio Perpetuae*," 8. See also Jerome, *Vir. ill.* 53. *Contra* Jerome, see Barnes, *Tertullian*, 11, citing Tertullian, *Exh. cast.* 7.3; and *Mon.* 12.2.

45. D'Alès, "L'Auteur de la *Passio Perpetuae*," 9–10, believed that Perpetua wrote her diary in Greek; therefore, for d'Alès, Tertullian's ability to work with both Latin and Greek added to the evidence of his editorship.

46. "These parallels in the texts appear decisive; one recognizes there the same spirit and accent. . . . [The *Passion*] appeals to the principles of Montanism against the abuses that it wants to eradicate from the church; it exploits to the profit of Montanism the glory of the Carthaginian martyrs." Ibid., 12 (my translation). See also de Labriolle, *La Crise Montaniste*, 353.

47. D'Alès, "L'Auteur de la *Passio Perpetuae*," 12–13. See Owen, 77, for the same suggestion.

48. D'Alès, "L'Auteur de la *Passio Perpetuae*," 13 (my translation).

49. Shewring, "Prose Rhythms," 57.

50. Shewring, ed., introduction to *The Passion of Perpetua and Felicity*, xxi.

51. They did speculate, however, that Tertullian addressed *Ad Martyras* to Perpetua and her companions. In doing so, they admitted that he knew the martyrs and, at least, had sympathy for their Montanist cause. Harris and Gifford, 28.

52. Aubé, 515.

53. Campos, 381.

54. Tabbernee, *Montanist Inscriptions and Testimonia*, 56.

55. Braun, "Séance du 26 Mars 1955," 80, claimed that previous philological support for Tertullian's editorship by Robinson, d'Alès, and de Labriolle had been "pressed and even peremptory" (my translation) and that Shewring's study of prose rhythms offered no sure indication. See also idem, "Nouvelles Observations Linguistiques sur le Rédacteur de la '*Passio Perpetuae*,'" 105. Like Aubé and Campos, Braun opted for Pomponius as editor.

56. Scholer, 11. Robeck, *Prophecy in Carthage*, 16, although he denied the editor's Montanism, wrote, "This suggestion merits further consideration in light of the feminist concerns of Perpetua, the obvious leadership role she is granted in the vision of Saturus, and the redactor's own personal interest to convey the story of this young woman so vividly."

57. Trevett, *Montanism*, 71.

58. Barnes, *Tertullian*, 80.

59. Ibid. See also idem, "Pre-Decian *Acta Martyrum*," 522.

60. Tertullian, *An.* 55.4.

61. See also *Passion* 13.8.

62. Dölger, "Antike Parallelen zum leidenden Dinocrates," 40 n. 108; Rupprecht, 181–82; Braun, "Séance du 26 Mars 1955," 80; idem, "Nouvelles Observations Linguistiques sur le Rédacteur de la '*Passio Perpetuae*,'" 105 n. 1; Fridh, 9–10; Amat, introduction to *Passion*, 68; Barnes, *Tertullian*, 80; Weinrich, 224; Robeck, *Prophecy in Carthage*, 17.

63. W. H. C. Frend, "Blandina and Perpetua: Two Early Christian Heroines," in *Women in Early Christianity*, ed. David M. Scholer, Studies in Early

Christianity: A Collection of Scholarly Essays, vol. 14, ed. Everett Ferguson (New York: Garland Publishing, 1993), 172–73, committed the same conflation in his discussion of the *Passion:* elements of Saturus' vision are presented as if they were seen by Perpetua.

64. D'Alès, "L'Auteur de la *Passio Perpetuae*," 13. Amat, introduction to *Passion*, 68, declared Tertullian's editorship of the *Passion* an impossibility due to his inexact citation in *De anima* and yet admitted in the same paragraph that Tertullian rarely was concerned about exact quotations.

65. D'Alès, "L'Auteur de la *Passio Perpetuae*," 13.

66. Tertullian, *A Treatise on the Soul* 55.5, trans. Peter Holmes, in ANF, vol. 3, ed. Alexander Roberts and James Donaldson (Edinburgh: T. and T. Clark, 1873; reprint, Grand Rapids: Eerdmans, 1978), 321.

67. J. H. Waszink, ed., *Quinti Septimi Florentis Tertulliani De Anima* (Amsterdam: J. M. Meulenhoff, 1947), 561–62.

68. *Passion* 4.8.

69. "After this I looked, and there was a great multitude that no one could count, . . . standing . . . , robed in white, . . . , singing, 'Amen!' . . . Then one of the elders addressed me, saying, 'Who are these, robed in white, and where have they come from?' I said to him, 'Sir, you are the one that knows.' Then he said to me, 'These are they who have come out of the great ordeal; they have washed their robes and made them white in the blood of the Lamb'" (NRSV).

70. *Passion* 13.1, 8. The translation of the last phrase indicates that the group included not only martyrs. See also Robinson, 55 n. 1.

71. Tertullian, *Scorp.* 12.9–10.

72. A. A. R. Bastiaensen, "Tertullian's Reference to the *Passio Perpetuae* in *De Anima* 55, 4," in *Stud. Pat.*, vol. 17:2, ed. by Elizabeth A. Livingstone (Oxford: Pergamon Press, 1982), 791–93.

73. *Passion* 1.5.

74. Tertullian, *Ux.* 1.5.1, 3. Weinrich also cited, less appropriately, *Exh. cast.* 12.5; and *Mon.* 16.8.

75. *Passion* 15.

76. Weinrich, 224–25.

77. Ibid., 228–29.

78. *Passion* 20.8. See also the *Mart. Pol.* 2; and Eusebius, *Hist. Eccl.* 5.1.26.

79. Weinrich, 235–36.

Notes to Chapter 3

1. Unless indicated otherwise, all translations of *The Passion of Perpetua and Felicitas* are from *The Martyrdom of Saints Perpetua and Felicitas*, in *The Acts of the Christian Martyrs*, trans. with an introduction by Herbert Musurillo (Oxford: At the Clarendon Press, 1972). Latin and Greek texts are from *Passio sanctarum Perpetuae et Felicitatis* 1.3, in *Passion de Perpétue et de Félicité suivi de*

Actes, ed. Jacqueline Amat, Sources Chrétiennes, vol. 417 (Paris: Les Éditions du Cerf, 1996). *Passion of Perpetua and Felicitas* hereafter cited as *Passion*, and quotations will be cited parenthetically.

2. Tertullian, *Virg.* 1.8. See also idem, *Mon.* 14.7. All translations of Tertullian's writings, unless indicated otherwise, are from ANF, vols. 3–4, ed. Alexander Roberts and James Donaldson (Edinburgh: T. and T. Clark, 1873; reprint, Grand Rapids: Eerdmans, 1978). Latin texts for Tertullian's writings are from *Tertulliani Opera*, 2 vols., CCSL (Turnhout: Brepols, 1954). William Weinrich, *Spirit and Martyrdom: A Study of the Works of the Holy Spirit in Contexts of Persecution and Martyrdoms in the New Testament and Early Christian Literature* (Washington, D.C.: University Press of America, 1981), 233–35, argued that *maiora* was not an absolute comparative adjective and that the editor intended to emphasize the equality of recent and ancient events.

3. Trevett, *Montanism*, 134.

4. "For in the last days, God declares, I will pour out my Spirit upon all flesh and their sons and daughters shall prophesy and on my manservants and my maidservants I will pour my Spirit, and the young men shall see visions and the old men shall dream dreams." *Passion* 1.4.

5. Trevett, *Montanism*, 177. Tertullian frequently quoted Joel: *Marc.* 5.4.2; 5.8.6; 5.11.4; 5.17.4; *An.* 47.2; *Fug.* 6.6; *Res.* 10.2; 63.7. In the last passage, he specifically stated that the New Prophecy descended from the Spirit. Robinson, 47–48, compared the quotation in the *Passion* and Tertullian's quotation in *Marc.* 5.8.6 in his defense of Tertullian's authorship of the *Passion*.

6. *Passion* 1.5.

7. Weinrich, 234.

8. Ibid. See also *Passion* 1.2.

9. Anonymous, cited in Eusebius, *Hist. Eccl.* 5.16.14; Apollonius, cited in Eusebius, *Hist. Eccl.* 5.18.2; Jerome, *Ep.* 41. See also Tabbernee, "Montanist Regional Bishops," 250.

10. Weinrich, 235–36, compared this situation to that of Irenaeus' church, where some, in over-reaction to Montanism, rejected the Gospel of John and continued prophetic activity. See Irenaeus, *Haer.* 3.11.9.

11. This situation was reflected in Saturus' vision, *Passion* 13, and in Tertullian, *An.* 9.4.

12. Apollonius, cited in Eusebius, *Hist. Eccl.* 5.18.5. Unless indicated otherwise, all translations of Greek texts are mine. See also Frederick C. Klawiter, "The Role of Martyrdom and Persecution," 255.

13. Klawiter, "The Role of Martyrdom and Persecution," 256–57. See also Trevett, *Montanism*, 116–19.

14. *Passion* 7 and 13.

15. Jensen, 95, raised the question that Felicitas was Revocatus' wife, since, in Christian circles, *conserua* had taken on the connotation of a wife as "fellow Christian." The redactor of the shorter Latin *Acts* certainly did not un-

derstand the relationship of Felicitas and Revocatus in this way. See the *Acta sanctarum Perpetuae et Felicitatis*, 5.3–6, in *Passion de Perpétue et de Félicité suivi de Actes*, ed. Jacqueline Amat, Sources Chrétiennes, vol. 417 (Paris: Les Éditions du Cerf, 1996), 284. *Acta sanctarum Perpetuae et Felicitatis* hereafter cited as *Acts*.

16. My translation. Musurillo translated the description of Perpetua as "newly married *(matronaliter nupta)*," but the fact that she had an infant indicated otherwise.

17. First, an early reviser suppressed Perpetua's statements about her husband for unknown motives, which might include his apostasy. Second, a later redactor, with an idealized view of ascetic women, might have excised Perpetua's marital relationship to emphasize the ideal of a virgin martyr. In this case, Perpetua's encounters with her father may have been substituted for scenes with her husband. Third, her husband was either dead or absent from Carthage. Fourth, Perpetua excluded her husband, even though he was alive and in Carthage, for unknown reasons, possibly a "father-fixation" or her husband's estrangement following her conversion. Dronke, 282 n. 3. Shaw, 25, contended that the husband, hostile to Christianity, agreed with the punishment meted out and that Perpetua omitted him from her narrative because she had rejected him and his views. Carolyn Osiek, "Perpetua's Husband," *JECS* 10 (2002): 287–90, suggested that Saturus was Perpetua's husband and her child's father. Ross Shepard Kraemer, *Her Share of the Blessings: Women's Religions among Pagans, Jews, and Christians in the Greco-Roman World* (New York: Oxford University Press, 1992), 161, includes as one of several suggestions what she admitted was an "extreme reading": "we may even wonder whether there ever was a husband and whether the true father of the baby was Perpetua's own father."

18. Apollonius, cited in Eusebius, *Hist. Eccl.* 5.18.3. See also Harris and Gifford, 5–6; Kraemer, 161, 171.

19. Dronke, 1.

20. Pliny the Younger, *Ep.* 5.16.

21. Dronke, 2. Musurillo, 109, described the catechumens as "under arrest," but Amat, *Passion de Perpétue et Félicité*, 194, indicated that *prosecutoribus* was a late Latin term and translated it "in the company of our guards *(en compagnie de nos gardes)*.

22. *Passion* 3.1–2.

23. Allard, 110. See also Mourret, 317 n. 22.

24. "[W]e are afflicted in every way, but not crushed; perplexed, but not despairing; persecuted, but not forsaken; struck down, but not destroyed" (2 Cor. 4.8–9 NRSV).

25. *Mart. Scill.* 9, in *The Acts of the Christian Martyrs*, trans. with an introduction by Herbert Musurillo (Oxford: At the Clarendon Press, 1972).

26. Anne Jensen, 100–111, found in Perpetua's visions repeated images

and symbols not only from baptismal liturgy but also from the entirety of Christian initiation including baptism, confirmation, and Eucharist.

27. Tertullian, *Bapt.* 20.5. See also Kilian McDonnell, "Communion Ecclesiology and Baptism in the Spirit: Tertullian and the Early Church," *Theol. Stud.* 49 (1988): 679–84.

28. Cecil M. Robeck, Jr., *Prophecy in Carthage: Perpetua, Tertullian, and Cyprian* (Cleveland: The Pilgrim Press, 1992), 19.

29. For speculation that Tertullian wrote *Ad Martyras* to Perpetua and her companions, see Theofried Baumeister, "Martyrium als Thema Fruhchristlicher Apologetischer Literatur," in *Martyrium in Multidisciplinary Perspective,* ed. M. Lamberigts and P. Van Deun (Leuven, Belgium: Leuven University Press, 1995), 325–26.

30. Tertullian, *Mart.* 2.4–10.

31. To see the impact Montanism made on Tertullian's view of women, compare his misogynist statement in *Cult. fem.* 1.1 with his expressions of appreciation for Montanist women in *Marc.* 5.8.12; *An.* 9.4; *Virg.* 17.6; and *Res.* 11.2.

32. Either her brother who was a catechumen (2.2), as suggested by Robeck, *Prophecy in Carthage,* 20; or a fellow prisoner, whom she addressed as "brother," as suggested by Salisbury, *Perpetua's Passion,* 98.

33. Tertullian, *Exh. cast.* 10.5. See also Tabbernee, ed., *Montanist Inscriptions and Testimonia,* 58.

34. *Passion* 4.3.

35. Pettersen, 147. See also Frend, "Blandina and Perpetua," 172; Robeck, *Prophecy in Carthage,* 27.

36. Tertullian, *Fug.* 1.3.

37. See Tertullian's citation of this passage: "It is not asked who is ready to follow the broad way, but who the narrow *(angustam).* And therefore the Comforter *(Paracletus)* is requisite, who guides into all truth, and animates to all endurance." Tertullian, *Fug.* 14.2–3.

38. Montague Rhodes James, introduction to *The Fourth Book of Ezra,* ed. Robert L. Bensly (Cambridge: 1895), xxx, xlii.

39. Robeck, *Prophecy in Carthage,* 28. Fourth Ezra offered several parallels to the New Prophecy: a vision of Christ in female form, the descent of the promised Jerusalem, ascetic practices, and a possible link to Montanus' home town, Ardabau. Trevett, *Montanism,* 23–24.

40. Robeck, *Prophecy in Carthage,* 29. See also Christopher Rowland, *The Open Heaven: A Study of Apocalyptic in Judaism and Early Christianity* (New York: Crossroad, 1982), 399.

41. The entire Christian church, of course, utilized Revelation, but Johannine literature, with its references to the Paraclete and emphasis upon eschatology, was favored by Montanists. Frend, "Montanism," 32. Ronald E. Heine, "John and the Montanist Debate in Rome," in *Stud. Pat.,* vol. 21, ed. Elizabeth A. Livingstone (Leuven: Peeters Press, 1989), 95–100, contended that Johan-

nine literature did not motivate the early Montanists in Phrygia but that it did
have a significant impact on Montanism in Rome and North Africa.

42. *Passion* 3.3.

43. A feature of the Severan persecution was its proscription against conversion to Judaism and Christianity, which led to widespread arrests of catechumens and catechists. Frend, *The Rise of Christianity*, 293–94. For the identification of Saturus as catechist, see Rader, "A Protest Account of
Third-Century Christianity," 1.

44. . . . *postea se propter nos ultro tradiderat, quia ipse nos aedificauerat* . . . .
Passion 4.5.

45. Barnes, *Tertullian: A Historical and Literary Study* (Oxford: Clarendon
Press, 1971), 78.

46. Tabbernee, "Early Montanism and Voluntary Martyrdom," 42. At the
same time, Tabbernee said of Saturus, "He appears to have belonged to a
Montanist circle within the Carthaginian catholic church."

47. Weinrich, 228, 247 n. 19.

48. *Mart. Pol.* 4. The writer referred to the Gospel teaching in Matt.
10.23: "When they persecute you in one town, flee to the next" (NRSV). The
possibility that this pericope was inserted by a later anti-Montanist is discussed in chapter four.

49. *Acts Cyp.* 1, in *The Acts of the Christian Martyrs*, trans. with an introduction by Herbert Musurillo (Oxford: At the Clarendon Press, 1972).

50. Tertullian, *Fug.* 9.4.

51. Tertullian, *An.* 55.5.

52. *Herm. Vis.* 4.1.1–2.4.

53. Robeck, *Prophecy in Carthage*, 26.

54. Tertullian, *Mart.* 1.4.

55. *Passion* 4.8.

56. The terms "garden" and "paradise" are identical in the Septuagint,
which referred to the garden of Eden as παράδεισος. Gen. 2.8 (LXX).

57. ". . . an Ancient One took his throne, his clothing was white as snow,
and the hair of his head like pure wool" (Dan. 7.9 NRSV). See also Robeck,
Prophecy in Carthage, 30–31.

58. Ps. 23.1; Isa.40.11; Jer. 31.10; Ezek. 34.12–16; Matt. 25.32–33; Jn.
10.11, 14. For a non-canonical parallel, see *Herm. Rev.* 5.1.1.

59. Rev. 7.9–14.

60. *Passion* 5.2. Because Perpetua's description of the grey-haired *(canum)*
shepherd resembled her father with his grey hairs *(canis)*, she seemed to con-
jure in her vision a new father figure, who accepted rather than rejected her.
Petterson, 144.

61. Dodds, 51 n. 2, supposed that "the 'curds' *(caseo)* offered by a male per-
sonage at the top of a 'ladder' could well have a latent sexual meaning."

62. My translation.

63. Musurillo, 113.

64. Jensen, 103–4, cited Hippolytus, *Trad. ap.* 21.28, and Tertullian, *Cor.* 3.3, as examples of this common practice in the early church.

65. *The Martyrdom of Perpetua*, trans. Rosemary Rader, 21. See also Robeck, *Prophecy in Carthage*, 36.

66. Epiphanius, *Haer.* 49.1.1.

67. Schwegler, 121–22; de Soyres, 140; and Kenneth B. Steinhauser, "Augustine's Reading of the *Passio sanctarum Perpetuae et Felicitatis*," in *Stud. Pat.*, vol. 33, ed. Elizabeth A. Livingstone (Leuven, Belgium: Peeters, 1997), 244. For an opposing view, see Andrew McGowan, *Ascetic Eucharists: Food and Drink in Early Christian Ritual Meals*, Oxford Early Christian Studies, ed. Gillian Clark and Andrew Louth (Oxford: Clarendon Press, 1999), 100–103. McGowan thought a connection between Perpetua and Artotyrites unlikely, but, in doing so, he ignored the use of cheese in the vision and focused instead on the significance of milk, which, for him, formed a "powerful opposition with the bloodshed of the arena." Ultimately, he conjectured that, instead of a witness to the use of milk or cheese in the Eucharist, the *Passion* perhaps intended to present oppositions between "bloodshed, meat-eating, and sacrifice on the one hand, and idyllic peace and avoidance of meat on the other."

68. Powell, 47.

69. Tertullian, *Spect.* 25.5.

70. The Greek text included the statement that the confessors were arrested in Thuburbo Minus (Θουρβιτάνων τῇ μικροτέρᾳ), a city thirty-six Roman miles west of Carthage. *Passion* 2.1. Barnes, *Tertullian*, 72 n. 3, doubted the Greek text at this point, but Shaw, 10, inferred from this information that Perpetua's noble family prospered in this rich, agricultural region. See the introduction above for a more complete discussion of this question.

71. Contemporaneous with Perpetua's martyrdom, Tertullian wrote: "Since, then, there is certainty as to the resurrection of the dead, grief for death is needless, and impatience of grief is needless. For why should you grieve, if you believe that (your loved one) is not perished? Why should you bear impatiently the temporary withdrawal of him who you believe will return? That which you think to be death is departure. He who goes before us is not to be lamented, though by all means to be longed for." Tertullian, *Pat.* 9.2–3.

72. In the Roman Empire, the *pater familias* presided over the religious faith of his family, but Perpetua's family exemplified a new paradigm, in which Christianity divided familial loyalties. Only Perpetua and one brother were described as catechumens, but her mother and other brother were either sympathetic or baptized since Perpetua assumed that they would rejoice at her suffering. Salisbury, 6, 62, 89–90.

73. Shaw, 24–25, inferred that Perpetua referred not to her natal family but to her husband's family, to which her father was related. "In that case, only

her father out of all of the relatives on his side of the family sympathized with her plight." Shaw missed the point entirely. Because he rejected a theological interpretation of the *Passion* (Shaw, 16 n. 41), he failed to apprehend the Christian understanding of martyrdom as honor and assumed that members of Perpetua's family, hostile to the "newfangled cult of Christianity," would rejoice merely at her death.

74. For an extensive discussion of Hilarianus' historical background as well as his involvement in the persecution of the Carthaginian Christians, see James Rives, "The Piety of a Persecutor," *JECS* 4:1 (1996): 1–25.

75. *Passion* 6.

76. Origen, *Or.* 2.4. See also Gordon D. Fee, *God's Empowering Presence: The Holy Spirit in the Letters of Paul* (Peabody, Mass.: Hendrickson Publishers, 1994), 580.

77. Robeck, 247 n. 6.

78. Anonymous, cited in Eusebius, *Hist. Eccl.* 5.16.7. See also Schwegler, 86; Pierre de Labriolle, *La Crise Montaniste*, 170–72; and Tabbernee, "The Opposition to Montanism from Church and State," 97, 548.

79. Klawiter, "The Role of Martyrdom and Persecution," 256–57, showed that "in the New Prophecy, one road to the power of the keys was by way of confession and imprisonment" and that "[t]he visions of both Perpetua and Saturus reveal that the imprisoned confessor possessed the priestly power of the keys." See also Barnes, *Tertullian*, 77–78.

80. Salisbury, 105, suggested that Perpetua, having renounced her maternal role nursing her infant son, took up responsibility for her thirsty, dead brother.

81. Barnes, "Pre-Decian *Acta Martyrium*," 522–25, established this date as the Nones, or seventh, of March.

82. Golden bowls were mentioned twice in Revelation (5.7; 15.7), but the nearer parallel was Rev. 22.17: "And let everyone who is thirsty come. Let anyone who wishes take the water of life as a gift" (NRSV).

83. Dölger, "Antike Parallelen zum leidenden Dinocrates in der Passio Perpetuae," 37–38. See also Robeck, *Prophecy in Carthage*, 49–51.

84. For example, see Virgil, *Aen.* 6:576–81. The reference to Virgil is especially apt, considering Aeneas' legendary connections to Rome and, through his love affair with Dido, to Carthage.

85. Homer, *Od.* 11:582–92. See also Edith Hamilton, *Mythology* (New York: New American Library, 1942), 237.

86. Dölger, "Antike Parallelen zum leidenden Dinocrates in der Passio Perpetuae," 28–31. See also Homer, *Od.* 11:23–50; Virgil, *Aen.* 6:444–46, 449–50, 494–98.

87. Virgil, *Aen.* 6:425–29.

88. Virgil, *Aen.* 6:119–23, 156–235.

89. *The Westminster Dictionary of the Bible*, ed. John D. Davis, rev. Henry Snyder Gehman (Philadelphia: The Westminster Press, 1944), s.v. "Hell."

90. *The Acts of Paul and Thecla* 28–29, trans. R. McL. Wilson, in *New Testament Apocrypha*, vol. 2, ed. Edgar Hennecke and Wilhelm Schneelmelcher (Philadelphia: The Westminster Press, 1964), 361. Immediately prior to Thecla's prayer, the queen saw in a dream her daughter, who said, "Mother, thou shalt have in my place the stranger, the desolate Thecla, that she may pray for me and I be translated to the place of the just."

91. Tertullian, *Bapt.* 17.5.

92. Tertullian, *Mon.* 10.5.

93. Tertullian, *Marc.* 4.34.13. See also Jacques Le Goff, *The Birth of Purgatory*, trans. Arthur Goldhammer (Chicago: The University of Chicago Press, 1984), 46–48.

94. Augustine, *Nat. orig.* 1.10.12.

95. Le Goff, 48. He added, however, that the "importance of the *Passion of Perpetua and Felicitas* in the prehistory of Purgatory should neither be exaggerated nor minimized. It is not Purgatory as such that is being discussed here, and none of the images contained in Perpetua's two visions recur in medieval imagery associated with Purgatory." Ibid., 50.

96. Barnes, *Tertullian*, 78. See also Dölger, "Antike Parallelen zum leidenden Dinocrates in der Passio Perpetuae," 38.

97. *Passion 9.*

98. *Cetera aeque animi impedimenta usque ad limen carceris deduxerint uos, quousque et parentes uestri.* Tertullian, Mart. 2.1.

99. Robeck, *Prophecy in Carthage*, 57.

100. Compare with *Herm. Vis.* 4.2.1–2. See also Robeck, *Prophecy in Carthage*, 60. Jacqueline Amat, *Songes et Visions: L'au-delà dans la littérature latine tardive* (Paris: Ètudes Augustiniennes, 1985), 77, perceived a double entendre in Pomponius words' to Perpetua: the deacon represented not only the Christian community but also "the celestial assembly of the saints and angels who were ready to welcome Perpetua." For Amat, this second interpretation is made clearer with Pomponius' next words that allude to "Christ's real presence at the martyrs' sides" (my translation).

101. *Passion* 10.3–4; *Herm. Mand.* 12.4.6–7, 5.2.

102. Robeck, *Prophecy in Carthage*, 62. See also Weinrich, 239.

103. *Passion* 10.6.

104. Tertullian, *Marc.* 2.14.4. See also ibid., 3.13.10; *Spect.* 3.8; and *Scorp.* 2.2. Furthermore, see Habermehl, 131–33.

105. Tertullian, *Bapt.* 9.1.

106. Van Beek (1938), 34 n. 9. See also Robeck, *Prophecy in Carthage*, 62–63.

107. *Barn.* 4.9. See also *Barn.* 20.1: "But the way of the black one is crooked and thoroughly cursed."

108. Shaw, 28 n. 62.

109. Robeck, *Prophecy in Carthage*, 63. Frend, "Blandina and Perpetua," 92,

observed that a comparison with Hermas' sea-monster, raising a cloud of dust, ties the Egyptian to the dragon of the first vision.

110. Amat, *Songes et Visions*, 81, identified these attendants as angels.

111. The Montanists cited this verse in support of their ordination of women. Epiphanius, *Haer.* 49.2.5.

112. Robeck, *Prophecy in Carthage*, 64. See also Scholer, 12.

113. *The Gospel of Mary*, trans. W. W. Isenberg, in *In Her Words: Women's Writings in the History of Christian Thought*, ed. Amy Oden (Nashville, Tenn.: Abingdon Press, 1994), 18.

114. *Gos. Thom.* Logion 22, trans. A. Guillaumont, et. al. (New York: Harper and Brothers, 1959), 17–19.

115. For a discussion of gender transformation in both the *Gospel of Thomas* and the *Passion*, see Elizabeth Castelli, "'I Will Make Mary Male': Pieties of the Body and Gender Transformation of Christian Women in Late Antiquity," in *Body Guards: The Cultural Politics of Gender Ambiguity*, ed. Julia Epstein and Kristina Straub (New York: Routledge, 1991), 29–49.

116. *Gos. Thom.* Logion 114, Guillaumont, 57.

117. Robeck, *Prophecy in Carthage*, 64–65, notes that "the *Gospel of Thomas* was found in Egypt prior to the third century. Its movement to Carthage would not have been difficult, and the esoteric nature of the gnosticism in this document *may* have had some early influence in Carthaginian Christianity." For other views about the influence of the *Gospel of Thomas* on the *Passion*, see Frend, "Blandina and Perpetua," 173; Trevett, *Montanism*, 179; and Scholer, 13.

118. Epiphanius, *Haer.* 49.2.1–3.3. See also Klawiter, "The Role of Martyrdom and Persecution," 259–60.

119. Epiphanius, *Haer.* 49.1.2–3.

120. Marie-Louise von Franz, *Passio Perpetuae: Das Schicksal einer Frau zwischen zwei Gottesbildern* (Zurich: Daimon Verlag, 1982), 91–92; and Epiphanius, *Haer.* 48.13.1. See also Bonwetsch, 59; and de Labriolle, *La Crise Montaniste*, 73–76.

121. Rader, "A Protest Account of Third-Century Christianity," 10.

122. *Passion* 10.8.

123. Louis Robert, "Une vision de Perpétue, martyre à Carthage en 203," *Comptes rendus de l'Academie des Inscriptions et Belles-Lettres* (1982), 263–64, preferred the Greek version to the Latin and concluded that Perpetua intended to identify the towering figure not as a trainer but as a judge, "in reality, the supreme Judge" (my translation). Ibid., 262 n. 148. Robert, 253–56, argued that the inferiority of the Latin version proved that Perpetua wrote her diary in Greek. Brent Shaw, 28 n. 63, however, correctly observed "simply that Perpetua was not conversant with the jargon of the arena or amphitheatre, whereas her Greek translator was."

124. Weinrich, 238–39, discussed the possibility that this divine person

represented Christ risen to judge the earth, dressed in a tunic striped with purple to symbolize his victory over a bloody death. For Weinrich, however, the imagery more closely recalled God the Father: "the figure generally performs the functions of an agonothete to which the Father is compared by Tertullian;" and, "when Perpetua takes the victor's prize from the figure's hand, he kisses her and calls her 'daughter.'" See also below, where Tertullian called the Holy Spirit the trainer of martyrs.

125. Tertullian, *Mart.* 3.3–4.

126. See also 1 Cor. 9.25; 2 Tim. 4.7–8; 1 Pet. 5.4.

127. *Herm. Sim.* 8.1–2. See also Robeck, *Prophecy in Carthage*, 67–68.

128. *Passion* 10.9.

129. Robert, 255–56, observed the hand-to-hand combat, the absence of gladiatorial equipment, Perpetua's nudity, and the application of oil to her body and concluded that this contest was a *pankration*, a contest in boxing and wrestling. Shaw, 28 n. 63, however, contended that the text included elements from both gladiatorial and athletic contests.

130. An early Montanist, Theodotus, reportedly "once was raised up and taken into heaven." Anonymous, cited in Eusebius, *Hist. Eccl.* 5.16.14. See also Amat, *Songes et Visions*, 84.

131. *Passion* 10.10–11.

132. Pettersen, 140. See Robeck, *Prophecy in Carthage*, 68. For other biblical parallels see Ps. 91.13 and the eschatological Ps. 110.1.

133. Dölger, "Der Kampf mit dem Ägypter in der Perpetua-Vision, 185–87. See also Rev. 2.10; *Mart. Pol.* 3; *Mart. Lyons* 16, 25; *The Martyrdom of Saints Carpus, Papylus, and Agathonicê*, 35; and Origen, *Mart.* 36.

134. Tertullian, *Mart.* 3.5.

135. Yet nowhere are found unambiguous reliance upon and exact quotations from his sources; Saturus shapes the material freely and independently. Habermehl, 171–72.

136. *Passion* 11.1–9.

137. The Greek phrase indicated a liturgical formula: "Go and rejoice." This benediction would appropriately follow the kiss of peace. The Latin phrase, however, repeated the idea present in the second vision of Dinocrates, where the child began " to play" (8.4). Robeck, *Prophecy in Carthage*, 80.

138. *Passion* 13.1–8.

139. Tertullian, *An.* 53.6.

140. This supposition is strengthened by the fact that Tertullian cites the *Passion* directly in *An.* 55.4.

141. Robeck, *Prophecy in Carthage*, 73–74.

142. Luke 16.22. Tertullian, *Cult. fem.* 2.13.6, likewise taught that "the stoles of martyrdom are (now) preparing: the angels who are to carry us are (now) being awaited!"

143. "And God planted a garden eastward (ἀνατολάς) in Edem" (Gen.

2.8, LXX). Again, Tertullian equated Paradise with the Garden of Eden. Tertullian, *Res.* 26.14; *Mon.* 5.4. See also Theophilus, *Autol.* 2.19, where Paradise is "a domain in the eastern regions, excellent for light, radiant in its very brilliant atmosphere, and with very beautiful gardens."

144. R. Petraglio, "Des influences de l'Apocalypse dans la '*Passio Perpetuae*' 11–13," in *L'Apocalypse de Jean*, ed. R. Petraglio (Geneva: Librairie Droz, 1979), 28. See, for example, 1.12–16, the vision of the Son of Man in the middle, clothed in a robe, and with hair white like snow; 4.1–8, the seer ascending through a door to see the throne of God surrounded by elders and four living creatures, who ceaselessly sing, "Holy! Holy! Holy!"; 6.11, the martyrs given white robes; 7.9–17, the multitude of white-robed martyrs, angels, elders, and the four living creatures gathered around the throne, and 21.23, the New Jerusalem, which is illuminated by the Lord God and the Lamb.

145. *Passion* 11.2. See also Rev. 4.6–8, 5.8–14.

146. *Passion* 12.4. See also Rev. 4.4, Vulgate, 586.

147. Jan N. Bremmer, *The Rise and Fall of the Afterlife* (New York: Routledge, 2002), 61, noted that "the Greek form of the words may well point to its use in contemporary liturgy."

148. See also Rev. 4.2, 8; 1.14; and Isa. 6.3. Christopher Rowland, 401, based on the youthful aspect of the divine figure, posited a Christophany in this vision.

149. Robinson, 27.

150. Amat, *Passio sanctarum Perpetuae et Felicitatis*, 233, followed Robinson in her edition of the Latin text.

151. *Passion* 11.6.

152. See also Rev. 22.2: "On either side of the river is the tree of life with its twelve kinds of fruit, producing its fruit each month; and the leaves of the tree are for the healing of the nations" (NRSV).

153. See also Ps. 96.12; Isa. 44.23, 55.12. Robinson, 38–39.

154. See *T. Abr.* 3. Robinson, 38, also cited *The History of Barlaam and Josaphat*, in which "the leaves of the trees made a tuneful sound."

155. *T. Abr.* 20.

156. *1 Enoch* 32.2–4. This translation of *1 Enoch* is mine based upon a Greek fragment. Saturus' referred to the fragrance of heaven in the second act of his vision.

157. *The Book of Enoch (I Enoch)* 40.10, 46.1, 108.12, trans. R. H. Charles, with an introduction by W. O. E. Oesterley (London: Society for Promoting Christian Knowledge, 1929), 60, 63, 154. These sections of *1 Enoch* are extant only in Ethiopic.

158. *Passion* 11.2; *Herm. Vis.* 1.4.

159. *Herm. Vis.* 3.10. Compare with *Passion* 12.3. See also Robinson, 32–34 for other, less remarkable parallels.

160. Robinson, 42, found influence of the Petrine apocalypse upon the

Apocalypse of Esdras, the *Apocalypse of Paul,* and the *History of Barlaam and Jos-aphat.* See also Montague Rhodes James, "The Revelation of Peter: A Lecture on the Newly Recovered Fragment," in J. Armitage Robinson and Montague Rhodes James, eds., *The Gospel According to Peter, and The Revelation of Peter: Two Lectures on the Newly Recovered Fragments Together with the Greek Texts,* 2d ed. (London: C. J. Clay and Sons, 1892), 61.

161. *Apoc. Pet.* 5.

162. Saturus did not comment specifically on the towering stature of God, but he did state that four angels lifted them up to kiss him and that they could not see his feet. *Passion* 12.3, 5.

163. See Serapion, cited in Eusebius, *Hist. Eccl.* 5.19.1–4: the Montanists resisted the bishops, who, in turn, denounced the movement. See also Barnes, *Tertullian,* 78.

164. De Soyres, 141. See also Klawiter, "The Role of Martyrdom and Persecution," 259.

165. Weinrich, 227.

166. Frend, *The Donatist Church,* 117.

167. Klawiter, "The Role of Martyrdom and Persecution," 259.

168. "Ye Servants of God, . . . seek well to understand the condition of faith, the reasons of the Truth, the laws of Christian Discipline, which forbid among other sins of the world, the pleasures of the public shows," including games in the circus *(circenses).* Tertullian, *Spect.* 1.1, 7.1–2, 8.1–7; *Pud.* 7.5. John Kaye, *The Ecclesiastical History of the Second and Third Centuries Illustrated from the Writings of Tertullian* (London: Griffith Farran and Co., 1824), xvi, included this treatise in Tertullian's Montanist period.

169. De Soyres, 45.

170. Ibid., 141.

171. Robeck, *Prophecy in Carthage,* 85.

172. *Passion* 16.1.

173. Trevett, *Montanism,* 181–82, saw in this pericope a "momentary glimpse into the lives of other Montanist women in times of stress." The bonds of the Spirit were more important to Felicitas and the unnamed woman who adopted her baby than blood ties. Furthermore, Felicitas' natural family had been replaced by the spiritual family consisting of her co-confessors.

174. Tertullian, *Fug.* 9.4.

175. *Passion* 16.4. Puden's conversion illustrated Tertullian's earlier words: "The oftener we are mown down by you, the more in number we grow; the blood of Christians is seed." Tertullian, *Apol.* 50.13.

176. Allard, 140–41.

177. Tertullian, *Jejun.* 12.2.

178. Allard, 105–6.

179. My translation. Throughout the Old and New Testaments, the day was used as a metaphor for the final time of judgment for both the righteous

and the wicked, hence references to "the day of judgment" (Matt. 10.15. 12.36; Mark 6.11; 2 Pet. 2.9, 3.7; 1 John 4.17): "the day of wrath" (Job 21.30; Prov. 11.4; Zeph. 1.15; Rom. 2.5); and "the day of the Lord" (Isa. 2.12, 13.6–9; Jer. 46.10; Joel 1.15; Amos 5.18; Acts 2.20; 1 Thess. 5.2; 2 Pet. 3.10). Often the biblical writers shortened the reference, as did Saturus, simply to "that day" (Matt. 7.22; Luke 10.12; 2 Thess. 1.10; 2 Tim. 4.8).

180. Secundulus was executed in prison (14.2). See also Barnes, *Tertullian*, 75.

181. Tertullian, *Spect.* 30.3.

182. After a Roman bath, *"Saluum lotum!"* was a greeting of good omen, used ironically here by the mob. Musurillo, 131 n. 21. See also the second baptism of blood in Tertullian, *Bapt.* 16.

183. In Perpetua's first vision (4.5), Saturus ascended the ladder first.

184. Barnes, *Tertullian*, 78, saw in Perpetua's act a near-suicidal act of Montanist rigor.

185. See Pelikan, *The Emergence of the Catholic Tradition*, 105, where Montanist emphasis on the Spirit influenced Tertullian's Trinitarian doctrine.

186. Both husbands were included in the narrative of the shorter Latin *Acts*, which sought to expunge Montanistic elements from the *Passion. Acts* 5.1–6.6. For a further comparison of the *Passion* and the *Acts*, see chapter four.

187. Robeck, *Prophecy in Carthage*, 84.

188. For Catholic attitudes toward women during this period see Irenaeus, *Frag.* 32; Clement of Alexandria, *Strom.* 4.8. The difference between Catholics and Montanists is delineated clearly by comparing Tertullian's attitudes before and after his conversion to Montanism: Catholic Tertullian, *Cult. fem.* 1.1.1–2; *Bapt.* 17.4–5; and Montanist Tertullian, *Marc.* 5.8.12; *Res.* 11.2; *Exh. cast.* 10.5.

189. Ruth A. Tucker and Walter Liefeld, *Daughters of the Church* (Grand Rapids: Zondervan, 1987), 114–15.

190. Weinrich, 226, listed the *Martyrdom of Polycarp*, the *Passion of Marian and James*, and the *Passion of Montanus and Lucius.*

191. De Nie, 116; Dodds, 47–53; Dronke, 1–16; Lefkowitz, 418; Salisbury, 98; von Franz, *The Passion of Perpetua*, 10.

192. Von Campenhausen, *Ecclesiastical Authority and Spiritual Power in the Church of the First Three Centuries*, 181–82; Pelikan, *The Emergence of the Catholic Tradition*, 106.

193. Pelikan, *The Emergence of the Catholic Tradition*, 98–99, 106.

194. D'Alès, "L'Auteur de la *Passio Perpetuae*," 16; Shewring, introduction to *The Passion of Perpetua and Felicity*, xxii.

195. Tertullian, *Pud.* 20.2.

196. Ibid., 10.1–14.

197. *Herm. Mand.* 4.3.1–7. See also Quasten, 97–99.

198. Trevett, *Montanism*, 67, 117.

199. Tabbernee, "To Pardon or Not to Pardon?" 382–84.

200. Tertullian, *Or.* 16.1.

201. Ritschl, 538.

202. Tertullian, *Jejun.* 1. See also Trevett, *Montanism*, 109.

203. Schepelern, 162. See also Pelikan, *The Emergence of the Catholic Tradition*, 98.

204. Barnes, *Tertullian*, 78.

205. Trevett, *Montanism*, 71. See also Barnes, *Tertullian*, 46–47.

206. Powell, 47.

207. The redactor of the *Acts* mistakenly dated the martyrdom of Perpetua and her companions during the persecution under Valerian and Gallienus in 257. *Acts* 1.1.

208. *Acts* 3.6. The relationship of the *Acts* to the *Passion* and its bearing on the evidence of Montanism is discussed in chapter four.

209. Tilley, 834.

210. Tilley, 835–36, assumed that those who identify Perpetua as a Montanist do so in order to marginalize her as a heretical woman and to devalue the *Passion* by its association with her: "The whole question of the orthodoxy of the *Passion* is nothing but a covert attack on women's wisdom." Her insinuation about the motives of other scholars, however, is neither necessary nor appropriate. As she herself admitted later, recognition of Perpetua as a Montanist should not impede the study of the *Passion*, invalidate Perpetua's martyrdom, or minimize the value this work for the history of these martyrs, both women and men, and for an "appropriation of that history for contemporary spirituality."

211. Ibid., 832.

212. Ibid., 844–85, 851.

213. Frend, *Saints and Sinners in the Early Church*, 70–72.

Notes to Chapter 4

1. Freppel, *Tertullien*, vol. 1 (Paris: Ambroise Bray, 1864), 348–49; Adhemar d'Alès, "L'Auteur de la *Passio Perpetuae*," 14; Shewring, introduction to *The Passion of Perpetua and Felicity*, xxii; van Beek (1938), 4; Campos, 377; Delehaye, *Les Passions des Martyrs*, 54–55; Weinrich, 228; Robeck, *Prophecy in Carthage*, 15; Tabbernee, *Montanist Inscriptions and Testimonia*, 58.

2. See Tabbernee, *Montanist Inscriptions and Testimonia*, 105–16, for inscriptions, mosaics, and murals that commemorate Perpetua and the others.

3. De Labriolle, *La Crise Montaniste*, 341–42; d'Alès, "L'Auteur de la *Passio Perpetuae*," 15–16; Weinrich, 226; Robeck, *Prophecy in Carthage*, 16.

4. Robinson, 51. See also Amat, introduction to *Passion*, 85; and Owen, introduction to *The Passion of SS. Perpetua and Felicitas*, 76. The shorter Latin *Acts of Perpetua and Felicitas* hereafter is cited as *Acts*; *The Passion of Perpetua*,

as *Passion*. Quotations of the *Passion* will be cited parenthetically. Unless indicated otherwise, all translations of Greek texts are mine, and all translations of the *Passion* are from *The Martyrdom of Saints Perpetua and Felicitas*, in *The Acts of the Christian Martyrs*, trans. with an introduction by Herbert Musurillo. Latin and Greek texts are from the edition edited by Amat. Other Latin translations are acknowledged in the footnotes.

5. Literally "on the fourth (day) before the *nones* of February." (See the preface, Amat's introduction to *Passion*, 98; see also Robinson, 61). The *nones* of the month fell on the fifth day, except during March, May, July, and October, when it occurred on the seventh day. The designation derived from the ninth day, counting inclusively, before the *Ides*, or the fifteenth day, of the month. *Cassell's Latin Dictionary*, ed. D. P. Simpson (New York: Macmillan, 1959), s.v. "nonae." See also Harris and Gifford, 12. By a mistake of a later copyist, who conflated the Latin *nonis Martiis* with the Greek Φευρουαρίαις, the Greek *Passion* ascribed the martyrdom to the *nones* of February in the second line. Robinson, 17.

6. The Basilian Commemoration set aside February 2 to honor the martyrs; the remaining eastern commemorations reserved that date for the Feast of Purification and moved the martyrs' day to February 1. March 7, however, was the unvarying date in the West. Robinson, 17 n. 1.

7. This detail, however, was debated by Harris and Gifford, 2–4, who supported it, and Robinson, 22–26, who denied it.

8. See also Robinson, 6.

9. De Labriolle, *La Crise Montaniste* 348.

10. *Passion* 16.1. See also Robinson, 6.

11. Robinson, 6.

12. Actually, two editions of the *Acts* exist, and text B appears to be a later abridgement of text A. Cornelius Johannes Maria Joseph van Beek, ed., *Passio sanctarum Perpetuae et Felicitatis* (Nijmegen, Holland: Dekker and Van de Vegt, 1936), 106*. Unless noted otherwise, references in this paper, are to text A. All translations of the *Acts* are mine based on the texts in *Acta sanctarum Perpetuae et Felicitatis* in *Passion de Perpétue et de Félicité suivi de Actes*, ed. Jacqueline Amat, Sources Chrétiennes, vol. 417 (Paris: Les Éditions du Cerf, 1996), 278–302.

13. The verbal coincidences between the *Acts* and Codex Casinensis indicate that the redactor was familiar with the traditional Latin *Passion*. At the same time, the similarities with the Greek *Passion* suggest that the redactor and the translator utilized the same Latin manuscript from which Codices Compendiensis and Salisburgensis derived. Robinson, 15–16. See also van Beek (1936), 104*.

14. Adolf Harnack, *Die Chronologie der Altchristlichen Litteratur bis Eusebius*, 2:321. See also Aubé, 517.

15. Paul Monceaux, *Histoire Littéraire de l'Afrique Chrétienne depuis les*

Origines jusqu'a l'Invasion Arabe, vol. 1, *Tertullien et les Origines* (Paris: n.p., 1901; reprint, Brussels: Culture et Civilisation, 1963), 81. Delehaye, *Les Passions des Martyrs*, 52, agreed that the *Acts* was a Catholic version, as opposed to the Montanist *Passion*, but contended that the abridgements were motivated by liturgical, not orthodox, concerns.

16. *Acts*, 1.1. Amat, introduction to *Passion*, 266, stated that the relationship between Revocatus and Felicitas was possible but that Saturus and Saturninus were connected only through their homophonic names.

17. *Mart. Scill.* 1–30. See also Halporn, 227. Delehaye, *Les Passions des Martyrs*, 53, insisted that the redactor's account of the interrogation only developed an already trivial theme, but Amat, introduction to *Passion*, 266, conjectured that the redactor accessed oral traditions and/or court minutes for this section.

18. See also "the fruits of the flock" *(fructibus gregis)* in *Acts* (Text B) 3.6.

19. The dating of the *Acts* is debatable: Monceaux, 82, contended that the redactor was nearly contemporary with the martyrdom, an impossible idea considering the citation of the wrong persecution; Frend, *The Donatist Church*, 126 n. 3, dated it not later than the mid-third century; Delehaye, *Les Passions des Martyrs*, 54, placed the *Acts* in the fourth century, and van Beek (1936), 103* n. 1, concurred; Shaw, 34, suggested that the redactor's carelessness regarding the period of persecution was typical of the mid-fourth century; and Amat, introduction to *Passion*, 269–71, posited the fifth century. The word play on the martyrs' names, a tendency shared with Augustine's sermons, suggests a late fourth- to early fifth-century date.

20. Shaw, 35, provided a translation of this interrogation of Felicitas and Perpetua.

21. *Acts* 6.1.

22. Shaw, 36.

23. Salisbury, 5–8.

24. *Acts* 7.2–3.

25. *Acts* 8.1–2.

26. *Acts* 9.5.

27. *Acts* 9.5.

28. Shewring, introduction to *The Passion of Perpetua and Felicity*, xxii.

29. Weinrich, 228.

30. Adolf Harnack, "Montanism," specified that, during the early third century, Carthaginian Montanists strove to remain within the orthodox church but eventually formed their own congregations over the issue of veiling virgins. See also Powell, 38; and Tabbernee, "Remnants of the New Prophecy," 195–97.

31. The *Metamorphoses* by Apuleius of Madauros, written about two decades earlier, included a fictitious satire of a supposedly Christian woman. For this story and the account of the Scillitans, see Barnes, *Tertullian*, 60.

32. For a discussion of the similarities between the Christianity of the *Passion* and that of Donatism, see Frend, *The Donatist Church*, 116–18.

33. Trevett, *Montanism*, 70. See also W. H. C. Frend, "The North African Cult of Martyrs: From Apocalyptic to Hero-Worship," in *Jenseitsvorstellungen in antike und Christentum: gedenkschrift für Alfred Stuiber* (Münster Westfalen: Aschendorffshe Verlagsbuchhandlung, 1982), 154.

34. Robeck, *Prophecy in Carthage*, 97, 149.

35. Justo González, *A History of Christian Thought*, vol. 1, *From the Beginnings to the Council of Chalcedon* (New York: Abingdon Press, 1970), 245, saw Tertullian's direct influence in Cyprian's *On the Dress of Virgins, On the Lord's Prayer, On the Vanity of Idols,* and *On the Advantage of Patience.*

36. Powell, 38. Against similar argumentation, de Labriolle, *La Crise Montaniste,* 471, observed that, despite Tertullian's obvious influence on Cyprian, the Catholic bishop never mentioned the Montanist's name. Powell, 38, responded, "This would be significant did Cyprian ever name, quote or refer directly to any writer at all."

37. Pontius, *Vita Cyp.* 1.2. All translations are from *The Life of Cyprian,* trans. Mary Madeleine Müller and Roy Joseph Deferrari, in FOTC, vol. 15, *Early Christian Biographies,* ed. Roy Joseph Deferrari (n.p.: Fathers of the Church, 1952).

38. Frend, *The Donatist Church,* 126 n. 3.

39. By 354, the names of Perpetua and Felicitas were entered in the Philocalian calendar of martyrs venerated publicly at Rome. J. P. Kirsch, "Felicitas and Perpetua," *The Catholic Encyclopedia,* vol. 6, ed. Charles G. Herbermann and others (New York: The Encyclopedia Press, 1913).

40. Barnes, *Tertullian,* 79; Musurillo, xxvi.

41. Freppel, 349; Campos, 377; Weinrich, 228; Tabbernee, *Montanist Inscriptions and Testimonia,* 58.

42. Steinhauser, 245.

43. Victor's opinions circulated in Mauretania among the bishop Optatus, the priest Peter, and the monk Renatus. Augustine became involved when Renatus forwarded to him Victor's two books refuting Augustine's statements about the origin of the soul included in a letter to Optatus. Roland J. Teske, introduction to Augustine, *The Nature and Origin of the Soul,* trans. Roland J. Teske, in WSA, part 1, vol. 23, *Answer to the Pelagians,* ed. John E. Rotelle (Hyde Park, N.Y.: New City Press, 1995), 467–69.

44. On the contrary, Augustine, *Nat. orig.* 3.13.19, contrasted Victor's view with Pelagianism. Steinhauser, 246.

45. Besides these two references cited in Steinhauser, Victor utilized *Adversus Marcionem, Adversus Praxean,* and *De resurrectione carnis.* Teske, 530 n. 8; 560 n. 20; 560 n. 51.

46. Steinhauser, 247–49.

47. Augustine, *Nat. orig.* 3.15.23. All translations of this work are from

Roland J. Teske, in WSA, part 1, vol. 23, *Answer to the Pelagians*, ed. John E. Rotelle (Hyde Park, N.Y.: New City Press, 1995). See also Steinhauser, 249.

48. Augustine, *Nat. orig.* 1.10.12, 4.18.26–27.

49. Steinhauser, 249, pointed out that Augustine "had taken a similar stance in his controversy with the Donatists, who constantly called upon the authority of Cyprian, bishop but above all martyr. Nowhere in his anti-Donatist writings did Augustine attempt to refute Cyprian. Instead, he accused the Donatists of misunderstanding and even deforming the teaching of Cyprian."

50. W. H. Shewring, introduction to *The Passion of Perpetua and Felicity*, xxix, included the fourth sermon in his collection without evaluating its genuineness, but he did regard it as interesting and worthy of consideration. See also Augustine, *Serm.* 280–82, in *Sermons on the Saints*, trans. Edmund Hill, in WSA, part 3, vol. 8, ed. John E. Rotelle (Hyde Park, N.Y.: New City Press, 1994). Shewring's translations are cited hereafter as Shewring; Hill's translations, as WSA.

51. Augustine, *Serm.* 280.2, WSA.

52. Augustine, *Serm.* 282.1, WSA.

53. Augustine, *Serm.* 282.3, WSA. See also Augustine, *Serm.* 281.3, WSA: "You see, the names of both women were the same as the reward of all the martyrs. I mean to say, why do martyrs endure all that they do, if not in order to revel in perpetual felicity? So these women were called what everyone is called to. And that's why, although there was a very large team engaged in that contest, it is by the names of these two that the eternal bliss of them all is signified, and the annual festival of them all is notified." See also Shaw, 41.

54. Augustine, *Serm.* 280.1. As Shaw, 38, pointed out, Augustine's only explanation for the women's "manliness" was an appeal to Pauline doctrine, "where, in the millennial scheme of things, actual gender differences are to be abolished." Indeed, in Augustine's commentary on Gal. 3.28, he taught that, "[i]n this faith, there is no differentiation between . . . male and female" but that the distinction between the sexes "is removed now in the unity of the faith but remains in this mortal life." Furthermore, Augustine applied the rules regulating how Christians should live together with regard to differences of gender only to husbands and wives, ignoring the application of Gal. 3.28 to relations of men and women in the church. Augustine, *Exp. Gal.* (my translation).

55. Augustine, *Serm.* 281.1, WSA.

56. Augustine, *Serm.* 281.2, WSA.

57. Augustine, *Serm.* 281.3, WSA.

58. Augustine, *Serm.* 280.1, WSA.

59. Augustine, *Serm.* 281.1, WSA. See also Salisbury, 175; and Shaw, 38–39.

60. Augustine, *Serm.* 280.1, Shewring.

61. Augustine, *Serm.* 394, Shewring.

62. Salisbury, 175.

63. Augustine, *Serm.* 394.

64. Augustine, *Haer.* 28.

65. Quodvultdeus, *Sermo de tempore barbarico* 1.5.1–9. All translations of Quodvultdeus' sermon are mine. See also Shaw, 41–43.

66. Quodvultdeus also echoed Augustine's oft-repeated pun on the martyrs' names.

67. *Cassell's Latin Dictionary*, ed. D. P. Simpson (New York: Macmillan, 1968).

68. De Labriolle, *La Crise Montaniste*, 341–42. See also Weinrich, 226.

69. *Mart. Pol.* preface.

70. *Mart. Pol.* 5.2.

71. *Mart. Pol.* 11.2.

72. *Mart. Pol.* 4.

73. Bigg, 186; W. M. Calder, "Philadelphia and Montanism," *BJRL* 7 (1923): 332–36; H. Grégoire and P. Orgels, "La véritable date du martyre de S. Polycarpe (23 février 177) et le *Corpus Polycarpianum*," *Analecta Bollandistes* 69 (1951): 21–22; M. Simonetti, "Alcune osservazioni sul martirio di S. Policarpo," *Giornale italiano di filologia* 9 (1956): 338–40; Hans von Campenhausen, "Bearbeitungen und Interpolationen des Polykarpmartyriums," in *Aus der Frühzeit des Christentums: Studien zur Kirchengeschichte des ersten und zweiten Jahrhunderts* (Tübingen: J. C. B. Mohr [Paul Siebeck], 1963), 270–71; Frend, *Martyrdom and Persecution in the Early Church*, 217; Gerd Buschmann, *Das Martyrium des Polykarp übersetzt und erklärt*, Kommentar zu den Apostolischen Vätern, vol. 6, ed. N. Brox, G. Kretschmar, and K. Niederwimmer (Göttingen: Vandenhoeck and Ruprecht, 1998), 128–29; idem., "*Martyrium Polycarpi* 4 und der Montanismus," *Vig. Chr.* 49 (1995): 110–12; Weinrich, 179 n. 17.

74. For history of research on the date of Polycarp's martyrdom, see J. B. Lightfoot, 646–722; and W. H. C. Frend, "Note on the Chronology of the Martyrdom of Polycarp and the Outbreak of Montanism," in *Oikoumene; studi paleocristiani publicati in onore del Concilio Ecumenico Vatican*, ed. Jeanne Courcelle (Catania: Università de Catania, 1964), 500–501. For the dating of the origins of Montanism, see chapter one above.

75. Barnes, "Pre-Decian *Acta Martyrum*," 512; Musurillo, xiii; B. Dehandschutter, "The Martyrdom of Polycarp and the Outbreak of Montanism," *Ephemerides Theologicae Lovaniensis* 75 (1999): 430.

76. Von Campenhausen, "Bearbeitungen und Interpolationen des Polykarpmartyriums," 254.

77. Ibid., 291–92.

78. Mart. *Pol.* 4.

79. Grégoire and Orgels, 24.

80. M. Simonetti, 338–40.

81. Lightfoot, 619–20, 677; Barnes, "Pre-Decian *Acta Martyrum*," 512; Tabbernee, *Montanist Inscriptions and Testimonia*, 139; Dehandschutter, 434–35.

82. Trevett, *Montanism*, 41.

83. Dehandschutter, 434.

84. Tabbernee, *Montanist Inscriptions and Testimonia*, 217 n. 12; idem., "Early Montanism and Voluntary Martyrdom," 41. Compare Quintus with "Eutychian from the heresy of the Phrygians" in *The Martyrdom of Pionius the Presbyter and His Companions*, 11.2, in *The Acts of the Christian Martyrs*, trans. with an introduction by Herbert Musurillo (Oxford: At the Clarendon Press, 1972), 151.

85. *Mart. Pol.* 5, 19.1.

86. *Mart. Pol.* 14.3, 22.1.

87. Besides the Trinitarian expressions, see *Mart. Pol.* 14.2.

88. *Mart. Pol.* 19.2.

89. Barnes, "Pre-Decian *Acta Martyrum*," 518, admitted nearly universal acceptance of this date but pointed out that Eusebius' *Ecclesiastical History*, upon which the date depends, conflicted with his *Chronicon*, which dated the persecution a decade earlier.

90. Eusebius, *Hist. Eccl.* 5.3.4.

91. De Labriolle, *La Crise Montaniste*, 215.

92. Monceaux, 403; Tabbernee, "Early Montanism and Voluntary Martyrdom," 39. See also de Soyres, 39 n. 2.

93. Eusebius, *Hist. Eccl.* 5.4.2.

94. De Soyres, 39.

95. Schwegler, 253; Adolf Harnack, *History of Dogma*, vol. 2, trans. Neil Buchanan (Boston: Roberts Brothers, 1897), 97; de Soyres, 38–40; T. Barns, "The Catholic Epistles of Themison: A Study in 1 and 2 Peter," *The Expositor*, 6th Series, 8 (1903): 44; Louis Duchesne, *The Churches Separated from Rome*, trans. Arnold Harris Matthew (New York: Benziger Brothers, 1907), 93; idem., *Early History of the Christian Church*, vol. 1, *From Its Foundation to the End of the Third Century*, trans. Claude Jenkins (New York: Longmans, Green and Company, 1913), 201–2; Frend, *Martyrdom and Persecution*, 16–17; Kraft, 266.

96. In fact, Schwegler, 223 n. 6, claimed that Irenaeus' relationship to Montanism was unmistakable ("*Irenäus: lassen seine Verwandtschaft mit dem montanistischen System nicht verkennen. . . .*"). See also de Soyres, 7.

97. Irenaeus, *Haer.* 3.11.9. Alexander Roberts and James Donaldson, translators of *Adversus Haereses* in ANF, vol. 1, ed. Alexander Roberts and James Donaldson (Edinburgh: T. and T. Clark, 1873; reprint, Grand Rapids: Eerdmans, 1978), 429, understood Irenaeus to be writing these words against the Montanists. The language, however, clearly must have been aimed at their opponents instead. De Soyres, 111, inferred from 3.11.9 a diatribe against the

Alogoi. See also Grant, *Augustus to Constantine,* 136; idem., *Irenaeus of Lyons,* The Early Church Fathers, ed. Carol Harrison (New York: Routledge, 1997), 6; and Eric Osborn, *Irenaeus of Lyons* (Cambridge: University Press, 2001), 6.

98. Irenaeus, *Haer.* 4.33.7. See also de Soyres, 111. Cecil M. Robeck, Jr., "Irenaeus and 'Prophetic Gifts'," in *Essays on Apostolic Themes,* ed. Paul Elbert (Peabody, Mass.: Hendrickson Publishers, 1985), 108, however, suggests that Irenaeus referred to the false prophecy of the Gnostic magician Marcus.

99. *Mart. Lyons* cited in Eusebius, *Hist. Eccl.* 5.1.3.

100. Frend, *Martyrdom and Persecution,* 2–3; de Soyres, 38–39.

101. *Mart. Lyons,* cited in Eusebius, *Hist. Eccl.* 5.1.9–10.

102. De Soyres, 39–40. See also Barns, 44. Judging from his Latin translation of Eusebius' *Ecclesiastical History,* Rufinus, *Eusebii Ecclesiasticae Historiae,* 5.1.10, considered the statement Montanistic and modified the phrase so that it referred to Jesus: "having in himself the advocate on our behalf, Jesus" (my translation).

103. De Labriolle, *La Crise Montanist,* 225–27. See also Tabbernee, "Early Montanism and Voluntary Martyrdom," 39.

104. *Mart. Lyons,* cited in Eusebius, *Hist. Eccl.* 5.1.49.

105. Barns, 44. See also Bigg, 186; Carrington, 244.

106. Tabbernee, "Early Montanism and Voluntary Martyrdom," 40.

107. *Mart. Lyons,* cited in Eusebius, *Hist. Eccl.* 5.1.25–26.

108. Frend, "Blandina and Perpetua," 169.

109. *Mart. Lyons,* cited in Eusebius, *Hist. Eccl.* 5.1.41.

110. *Mart. Lyons,* cited in Eusebius, *Hist. Eccl.* 5.1.55.

111. *Mart. Lyons,* cited in Eusebius, *Hist. Eccl.* 5.3.1–3.

112. Barns, 44; Bigg, 186. Carrington, 248, tentatively equated the Gallic Alcibiades with the Montanist Alcibiades mentioned by Eusebius in the next paragraph.

113. Possibly Attalus was concerned more about Gnosticism, with its doctrine that matter was evil, than about Montanism. See G. A. Williamson, ed., *The History of the Church from Christ to Constantine,* trans. with an introduction by G. A. Williamson (New York: Dorset Press, 1965), 205 n. 4.

114. Frend, *Martyrdom and Persecution,* 16; de Labriolle, *La Crise Montanist,* 228–29.

115. *Mart. Lyons,* cited in Eusebius, *Hist. Eccl.* 5.2.3.

116. Anonymous, cited in Eusebius, *Hist. Eccl.* 5.18.5–7. This anti-Montanist source accused Themiso of obtaining release through bribery and Alexander of being imprisoned for robbery, but such libels have been dismissed by scholars, including Barns, 54, and Trevett, *Montanism,* 48.

117. *Mart. Lyons,* cited in Eusebius, *Hist. Eccl.* 5.2.5.

118. Tertullian, *Pud.* 21.7. See also Klawiter, "The Role of Martyrdom and Persecution," 255–56.

119. Kraft, 266.

120. Eusebius, *Hist. Eccl.* 5.2.8.

121. De Labriolle, *La Crise Montanist*, 230. See also Williamson, 205 n. 3.

122. Kraft, 266.

123. Frend, "Blandina and Perpetua," 173–74, suggested that the two acts had in common "a movement within Christianity in the last quarter of the second century based on a profound conviction of the approaching end of the existing age and the glorification of the role of confessor and martyr as vehicles of the Holy Spirit in bringing that about."

124. "In the *Passio Perpetuae* the eschatological theme is even more prominent;" "There is, however, a more developed theology of the Spirit [in the *Passio Perpetuae*] than is discernable in the Acta of the Lyon martyrs;" and "[a]t Lyon, . . . they die without visions of Paradise." Ibid., 171, 174. See also idem, *Martyrdom and Persecution*, 16.

125. Saturninus is mentioned by Tertullian, *Scap.* 3.4, as one who suffered after persecuting Christians: "Vigellius Saturninus, who first here used the sword against us, lost his eyesight." See also Musurillo, 87 n. 2.

126. For a discussion of the date of the *Acts of the Scillitan Martyrs*, see J. Armitage Robinson, introduction to *The Acts of the Scillitan Martyrs*, appendix to *The Passion of S. Perpetua*, in *Texts and Studies: Contributions to Biblical and Patristic Literature* 1:2 (Cambridge: At the University Press, 1891; reprint, Nendeln/Liechtenstein: Kraus Reprint, 1967), 106–7.

127. Monceaux, 63; Musurillo, xxii; E. C. E. Owen, introduction to *The Acts of the Scillitan Martyrs*, in *Some Authentic Acts of the Early Martyrs*, trans. E. C. E. Owen (London: Society for Promoting Christian Knowledge, 1927), 71.

128. *Mart. Scill.* 12 also recorded the first reference to a Latin collection of sacred writings.

129. Delehaye, *Les Passions des Martyrs*, 278–79; 283. See also Monceaux, 68: "One understands also that there is forgery in many apocryphal narratives, where the furious invectives of magistrates were echoed by the blustering of the martyrs. This did not speak well at all of either proconsuls or the apostles of a peaceful religion" (my translation).

130. Hippolyte Delehaye, *The Legends of the Saints*, trans. Donald Attwater (New York: Fordham University Press, 1962), 89–90. See also Musurillo, lii.

131. *Mart. Scill.* 2, 6, 7.

132. "I do not recognize the empire of this world. Rather, I serve that God whom no man has seen, nor can see, with these eyes." *Mart. Scill.* 6. Unless indicated otherwise all translations are from *The Acts of the Scillitan Martyrs*, in *The Acts of the Christian Martyrs*, trans. with an introduction by Herbert Musurillo (Oxford: At the Clarendon Press, 1972).

133. *Mart. Scill.* 17.

134. My translation from *The Acts of the Scillitan Martyrs*, ed. J. Armitage Robinson, in *Texts and Studies: Contributions to Biblical and Patristic Literature*, vol. 1, part 2 (Cambridge: At the University Press, 1891; reprint, Nendeln/Liechtenstein: Kraus Reprint, 1967).

135. Roy J. Deferrari, ed., introduction to Pontius, *The Life of Cyprian*, FOTC 15:3; Monceaux, 179.

136. Delehaye, *Les Passions des Martyrs*, 62; Musurillo, xxx.

137. Pontius, *Vita Cyp.* 1.2.

138. *Acts Cyp.* 1.5. All translations taken from *The Acts of Cyprian*, in *The Acts of Christian Martyrs*, trans. with an introduction by Herbert Musurillo (Oxford: At the Clarendon Press, 1972).

139. Robeck, *Prophecy in Carthage*, 149, noted that "Cyprian's term as bishop of Carthage was punctuated with visionary revelations from beginning to end."

140. Pontius, *Vita Cyp.* 12. *The Acts of Cyprian* 2.1 alluded to this vision but provided no details.

141. Pontius, *Vita Cyp.* 13, FOTC 15:18–19.

142. *Passion* 10.8.

143. Pontius, *Vita Cyp.* 1, 19. See also Richard Reitzenstein, *Die Nachrichten über den Tod Cyprians: Ein philologischer Beitrag zur Geschichte Märtyrerliteratur*, Sitzungsberichte der Heidelberger Akademie der Wissenschaften (Heidelberg: Carl Winters Universitätsbuchhandlung, 1913), 51.

144. All translations of these two documents are from *The Acts of the Christian Martyrs*, trans. with an introduction by Herbert Musurillo.

145. *Mart. Mont. & Luc.* 23.7.

146. *Mart. Mar. & Jam.* 1.1.

147. *Mart. Mar. & Jam.* 6.10–14; *Mart. Mont. & Luc.* 13.1, 21.3–4.

148. *Mart. Mar. & Jam.* 13.1; *Mart. Mont. & Luc.*, 16.4. See also 2 Macc. 7:20–23.

149. Musurillo, xxxiii. Adhemar d'Alès, *Recherches de science religieuse* 9 (1918): 319–78, cited in Musurillo, lxvii n. 36, suggested that Pontius composed, at least, *The Martyrdom of Montanus and Lucius*. Pio Franchi de' Cavalieri, *Gli Atti dei SS. Montano, Lucio e compagni: Recensione del testo ed introduzione sulle sui relazioni con la Passio S. Perpetuae* (Rome: Buchhandlung Spithöver, 1898), 55, determined that *The Martyrdom of Montanus and Lucius* was written by an imitator of Cyprian. Indeed, the exaltation of Cyprian, the episcopacy, and such themes as Catholic unity indicated involvement of a Cyprianic school of thought.

150. *Mart. Mar. & Jam.* 6.5–15. The paradise, complete with cypress trees, recalled Saturus' vision in the *Passion* 11.6; Marian's arousal after drinking and speaking, Perpetua's vision in the *Passion* 4.9–10.

151. *Mart. Mar. & Jam.* 7. The young man of indescribable height resembled the towering figure, dressed in a purple-striped tunic, that supervised Perpetua's contest with the Egyptian. *Passion* 10.8.

152. *Mart. Mont. & Luc.* 7. See also *Passion* 4.3; Robeck, *Prophecy in Carthage*, 243 n. 52.

153. *Mart. Mont. & Luc.* 8. The never-empty cups recalled Dinocrates'

golden bowl in the *Passion* 8.3, but Quartillosa's orthodox image of milk contrasted with Perpetua's Montanist cheese in the *Passion* 4.9. Saturus (*Passion* 11–12), also received a picture of heaven.

154. *Mart. Mont. & Luc.* 2.

155. *Mart. Mont. & Luc.* 4.2, Musurillo, 216–17.

156. Harris and Gifford, 27.

157. *Passion* 3.5–9.

158. *Mart. Mont. & Luc.* 6.1, Musurillo, 218–19.

159. *Passion* 6.1–3.

160. Harris and Gifford, 27. For an opposing view, see Monceaux, 170, who pointed out that, at the conclusion of the *Acts of Cyprian*, the proconsul Galerius Maximus died.

161. Agapius and Secundius (*Mart. Mar. & Jam.* 3.1) were bishops; James was a deacon, and Marian, a lector (*Mart. Mar. & Jam.* 5.2–3). Victor was a presbyter (*Mart. Mont. & Luc.* 7.2); Herennianus, a subdeacon (*Mart. Mont. & Luc.* 9.2); and Flavian, a deacon (*Mart. Mont. & Luc.* 20.2). Flavian's eulogy of Lucian, a priest, destined him for the bishopric (*Mart. Mont. & Luc.* 23.4).

162. *Mart. Mar. & Jam.* 6.6–14; *Mart. Mont. & Luc.*, 11.2. See also J. W. Trigg, "Martyrs and Churchmen in Third-Century North Africa," in *Stud. Pat.*, vol. 15:1, ed. Elizabeth A. Livingstone (Berlin: Akademie-Verlag, 1984), 244.

163. *Mart. Mar. & Jam.* 1.2: "common sharing in the mystery of our faith (*communem sacramenti religionem*);" *Mart. Mont. & Luc.* 23.3: "the peace of the Church (*ecclesiae pacem*)."

164. *Mart. Mar. & Jam.* 2.3.

165. Harris and Gifford, 26–27.

166. Reitzenstein, 51.

167. Karl Holl, "Die Vorstellung vom Märtyrer und die Märtyrerakte in ihrer geschichtlichen Entwicklung," in *Gesammelte Aufsätze zur Kirchengeschichte*, vol. 2, *Der Osten* (Tübingen: J. C. B. Mohr, 1928), 85. See also Frend, *The Donatist Church*, 128–29; and Rader, "A Protest Account of Third-Century Christianity," 14 n. 7.

168. Trigg, 244. See also Monceaux, 169; Delehaye, *Les Passions des Martyrs*, 55–62; and de' Cavalieri, 55.

169. Trigg, 246.

170. James L. Ash, Jr., "The Decline of Ecstatic Prophecy in the Early Church," *Theological Studies* 37 (June 1976): 250. See also Reitzenstein, 49.

171. Cyprian, *Ep.* 66.8.3. All translations of Cyprian's correspondence are by Rose Bernard Donna, in FOTC, vol. 51, *Saint Cyprian: Letters (1–81)*, ed. Roy Joseph Deferrari (Washington, D.C.: The Catholic University of America Press, 1964).

172. Firmilian to Cyprian, *Ep.* 75.7.4.

173. Reitzenstein, 50.

Notes to Conclusion

1. Musurillo, xxv.
2. Schepelern, 126.
3. Powell, 47.
4. Le Goff, 48–50.

Selected Bibliography

Primary Sources

Acta Martyrum. Edited by P. Theodoric Ruinart. Regensburg: G. Josephi Manz, 1859.

The Acts of the Martyrdom of Perpetua and Felicitas: The Original Greek Text. Edited by J. Rendel Harris and Seth K. Gifford. London: C. J. Clay and Sons, 1890.

The Acts of Paul and Thecla. Translated by R. McL. Wilson. In *New Testament Apocrypha*, vol. 2, ed. Edgar Hennecke and Wilhelm Schneelmelcher, 353–64. Philadelphia: The Westminster Press, 1964.

The Acts of the Scillitan Martyrs. Edited by J. Armitage Robinson. In *Texts and Studies: Contributions to Biblical and Patristic Literature* vol. 1, part 2, 106–21. Cambridge: At the University Press, 1891; reprint, Nendeln/ Liechtenstein: Kraus Reprint, 1967.

The Acts of the Scillitan Martyrs. In *The Acts of the Christian Martyrs.* Translated with an Introduction by Herbert Musurillo, xxii–xxiii, 86–89. Oxford: At the Clarendon Press, 1972.

The Acts of St. Cyprian. In *The Acts of the Christian Martyrs.* Translated with an Introduction by Herbert Musurillo, xxx–xxxi, 168–75. Oxford: At the Clarendon Press, 1972.

The Apocalypse of Peter. Translated by Andrew Rutherford. In *The Ante-Nicene Fathers*, vol. 10, ed. Alexander Roberts and James Donaldson, 145–47. Edinburgh: T. and T. Clark, 1873; reprint, Grand Rapids: Eerdmans, 1978.

Ascensio Isaiae: Textus. Corpus Christianorum Series Apocryphorum, vol. 7. Turnhout: Brepols, 1995.

The Ascension of Isaiah. Edited by R. H. Charles. London: Adam and Charles Black, 1900.

Augustine. *Augustine's Commentary on Galatians.* Translated with an Introduction by Eric Plumer. Oxford Early Christian Studies, ed. Gillian Clark and Andrew Louth. Oxford: Oxford University Press, 2003.

———. *De anima et ejus origine.* In *Sancti Aurelii Augustini, Hipponensis Episcopi, Opera Omnia*, vol. 44, 475–548, Patrologia Latina. Paris: J. P. Migne Successores, 1865.

————. *De haeresibus.* In *Aurelii Augustini Opera*, vol. 46, 263–345, Corpus Christianorum Series Latina. Turnholt: Brepols, 1969.

————. *Expositionis Epistolae ad Galatas.* In *Sancti Aurelii Augustini, Hipponensis Episcopi, Opera Omnia*, vol. 35, 2105–48, Patrologia Latina. Paris: J. P. Migne Successores, 1865.

————. *The Heresies.* Translated by Roland J. Teske. In *The Works of Saint Augustine: A Translation for the 21st Century*, part 1, vol. 18, *Arianism and Other Heresies*, ed. John E. Rotelle, 34–60. Hyde Park, N.Y.: New City Press, 1995.

————. *The Nature and Origin of the Soul.* Translated by Roland J. Teske. In *The Works of Saint Augustine: A Translation for the 21st Century*, part 1, vol. 23, *Answer to the Pelagians*, ed. John E. Rotelle, 473–559. Hyde Park, N.Y.: New City Press, 1995.

————. *Sermo 394.* In *Sancti Aurelii Augustini, Hipponensis Episcopi, Opera Omnia*, vol. 39, 1715–16, Patrologia Latina. Paris: J. P. Migne Successores, 1865.

————. *Sermones 280–82.* In *Sancti Aurelii Augustini, Hipponensis Episcopi, Opera Omnia*, vol. 38, 1280–86, Patrologia Latina. Paris: J. P. Migne Successores, 1865.

————. *Sermons on the Saints.* Translated by Edmund Hill. In *The Works of Saint Augustine: A Translation for the 21st Century*, part 3, vol. 8, ed. John E. Rotelle. Hyde Park, N.Y.: New City Press, 1994.

Basil. *Letters.* Vol. 2. Translated by Agnes Clare Way. In *The Fathers of the Church: A New Translation*, vol. 28, ed. Roy Joseph Deferrari. New York: Fathers of the Church, 1955.

————. *Saint Basil: The Letters.* Vol. 3. Loeb Classical Library, ed. T. E. Page. Cambridge, Mass.: Harvard University Press, 1962.

The Book of Enoch (1 Enoch). Translated by R. H. Charles. With an Introduction by W. O. E. Oesterley. London: Society for Promoting Christian Knowledge, 1929.

Das Buch Henoch. Edited by Johannes Flemming and Ludwig Radermacher. Die Griechischen Christlichen Schriftsteller der Ersten Drei Jahrhunderte. Leipzig: J. C. Hinrichs'sche Buchhandlung, 1901.

Clement of Alexandria. *The Stromata, or Miscellanies.* Translated by William Wilson. In *The Ante-Nicene Fathers*, vol. 2, ed. Alexander Roberts and James Donaldson, 299–567. Edinburgh: T. and T. Clark, 1873; reprint, Grand Rapids: Eerdmans, 1983.

Cyprian. *Saint Cyprian: Letters (1–81).* Translated by Rose Bernard Donna. In *The Fathers of the Church: A New Translation*, vol. 51, ed. Roy Joseph Deferrari. Washington, D.C.: The Catholic University of America Press, 1964.

Cyril of Jerusalem. *Catecheses.* Translated by Leo P. McCauley and Anthony A. Stephenson. In *The Fathers of the Church: A New Translation*, vol. 64, *The Works of Saint Cyril of Jerusalem*, vol. 2, ed. Bernard M. Peebles, 3–142. Washington, D.C.: The Catholic University of America Press, 1970.

———. *Opera quae exstant omnia: et ejus nomine circumferuntur, ad manuscriptos codices nec-non ad superiores editiones castigata, dissertationibus and notis illustrata, cum nova interpretatione and copiosis indicibus.* Edited by Antoine-Augustin Touttee. Paris: Jacob Vincent, 1720.

de Labriolle, Pierre, ed. *Les Sources de L'histoire du Montanisme: textes grecs, latins, syriaques.* Collecteanea Friburgensia 24. Paris: Ernest Leboux, 1913.

Didache. Translated by J. B. Lightfoot. In *The Apostolic Fathers: Greek Texts and English Translations.* Edited and revised by Michael W. Holmes, 246–69. Grand Rapids: Baker, 1999.

Epiphanius. *The Panarion of Epiphanius of Salamis: Books II and III.* Translated by Frank Williams. New York: E. J. Brill, 1994.

———. *Panarion haer. 34–64.* Edited by Karl Holl. Die Griechischen Christlichen Schriftsteller der Ersten Jahrhunderte. Berlin: Akademie-Verlag, 1980.

Epistle of Barnabas. Translated by J. B. Lightfoot. In *The Apostolic Fathers: Greek Texts and English Translations.* Edited and revised by Michael W. Holmes, 270–321. Grand Rapids: Baker, 1999.

Eusebius. *Eusebius Werke.* Vol. 2, part 1, *Ecclesiasticae Historiae,* books 1–5, ed. Eduard Schwartz. Die Griechischen Christlichen Schriftsteller der Ersten Drei Jahrhunderte. Leipzig: J. C. Hinrichs'sche Buchhandlung, 1903.

———. *The History of the Church from Christ to Constantine.* Edited and translated with an Introduction by G. A. Williamson. New York: Dorset Press, 1965.

The Ezra-Apocalypse. Translated by G. H. Box. London: Sir Isaac Pitman and Sons, 1912.

The Fourth Book of Ezra. Edited by Robert L. Bensly. With an Introduction by Montague Rhodes James. Cambridge: 1895.

The Gospel According to Thomas. Translated by A. Guillaumont, H.-Ch. Puech, G. Quispel, W. Till, and Yassah 'Abd Al Masih. New York: Harper and Brothers, 1959.

The Gospel of Mary. Translated by W. W. Isenberg. In *In Her Words: Women's Writings in the History of Christian Thought.* Edited by Amy Oden, 17–20. Nashville, Tenn.: Abingdon Press, 1994.

Grant, Robert M., ed. *Second-Century Christianity: A Collection of Fragments.* London: Society for Promoting Christian Knowledge, 1957.

Hermae Pastor Graece: Addita Versione Latina Recentiore e Codice Palatineo. Edited by Oscar de Gabhardt and Adolfus Harnack. Lipsiae: J. C. Hinrichs, 1877.

Heine, Ronald E., ed. *The Montanist Oracles and Testimonia.* Patristic Monograph Series, no. 14, North American Patristic Society. Macon, Ga.: Mercer University Press, 1989.

Hippolytus. *The Apostolic Tradition.* Edited by Gregory Dix. London: Society for Promoting Christian Knowledge, 1937.

————. *La Tradition Apostolique*. Edited by Bernard Botte. Sources Chrétiennes. Paris: Les Éditions du Cerf, 1984.

————. *The Refutation of All Heresies*. Translated by J. H. MacMahon. In *The
Ante-Nicene Fathers*, vol. 5, ed. Alexander Roberts and James Donaldson,
9–162. Edinburgh: T. and T. Clark, 1873; reprint, Grand Rapids: Eerdmans, 1978.

————. *Refutatio Omnium Haeresium*. Edited by Miroslav Marcovich. Patris-
tische Texte und Studien, vol. 25, ed. K. Aland and E. Muhlenberg. Berlin:
Walter De Gruyter, 1986.

Ignatius. *Epistles*. Translated by Alexander Roberts and James Donaldson. In
The Ante-Nicene Fathers, vol. 1, ed. Alexander Roberts and James Don-
aldson, 45–132. Edinburgh: T. and T. Clark, 1873; reprint, Grand Rapids:
Eerdmans, 1979.

Irenaeus. *Against Heresies*. Translated by Alexander Roberts and James Don-
aldson. In *The Ante-Nicene Fathers*, vol. 1, ed. Alexander Roberts and
James Donaldson, 315–567. Edinburgh: T. and T. Clark, 1873; reprint,
Grand Rapids: Eerdmans, 1979.

————. *Fragments from the Lost Writings of Irenaeus*. Translated by Alexander
Roberts and James Donaldson. In *The Ante-Nicene Fathers*, vol. 1, ed.
Alexander Roberts and James Donaldson, 568–78. Edinburgh: T. and T.
Clark, 1873; reprint, Grand Rapids: Eerdmans, 1979.

————. *Sancti Irenaei, Episcopi Lugdunensis, Libros quinque adversus haereses*.
Edited by W. Wigan Harvey. 2 vols. Cambridge: Typis Academicis, 1857;
reprint, Ridgewood, N.J.: Gregg Press, 1965.

Jerome. *Letters and Select Works*. Translated by W. H. Fremantle. In *Nicene and
Post-Nicene Fathers*, 2d series, vol. 6, ed. Philip Schaff and Henry Wace.
Edinburgh: T. and T. Clark, 1892; reprint, Grand Rapids: Eerdmans,
1979.

————. *Lives of Illustrious Men*. Translated by Ernest Cushing Richardson. In
Nicene and Post-Nicene Fathers, 2d series, vol. 3, ed. Philip Schaff and Henry Wace. Edinburgh: T. and T. Clark, 1892; reprint, Grand Rapids: Eerdmans, 1979.

Lightfoot, J. B., ed. *The Apostolic Fathers*. Part 2, vol. 1, *Ignatius and Polycarp*. 2d
ed. n.p.: Macmillan, 1889; reprint, Peabody, Mass.: Hendrickson Publishers, 1989.

Lives of the Later Caesars. Translated by Anthony Birley. New York: Penguin
Books, 1976.

The Martyrdom of Marian and James. In *The Acts of the Christian Martyrs*.
Translated with an Introduction by Herbert Musurillo, xxxiii–xxxiv,
194–213. Oxford: At the Clarendon Press, 1972.

The Martyrdom of Montanus and Lucius. In *The Acts of the Christian Martyrs*.
Translated with an Introduction by Herbert Musurillo, xxxiv–xxxvi,
214–39. Oxford: At the Clarendon Press, 1972.

The Martyrdom of Perpetua. Translated by W. H. Shewring. With an Introduction and Commentary by Sara Maitland. Visionary Women Series, ed. Monica Furlong. Evesham, England: Arthur James, 1996.

The Martyrdom of Perpetua. Translated by Rosemary Rader. In *A Lost Tradition: Women Writers of the Early Church.* Edited by Patricia Wilson-Kastner, G. Ronald Kastner, Ann Millin, Rosemary Rader, and Jeremiah Reedy, 19–32. Lanham, Md.: University Press of America, 1981.

The Martyrdom of Perpetua and Felicitas. In *The Acts of the Christian Martyrs.* Translated with an Introduction by Herbert Musurillo, xxv–xxvii, 106–31. Oxford: At the Clarendon Press, 1972.

The Martyrdom of Perpetua and Felicitas. Translated by R. E. Wallis. In *The Ante-Nicene Fathers,* vol. 3, ed. Alexander Roberts and James Donaldson, 697–706. Edinburgh: T. and T. Clark, 1873; reprint, Grand Rapids: Eerdmans, 1978.

The Martyrdom of Pionius the Presbyter and His Companions. In *The Acts of the Christian Martyrs.* Translated with an Introduction by Herbert Musurillo, xxviii–xxx, 136–67. Oxford: At the Clarendon Press, 1972.

The Martyrdom of Polycarp. In *The Acts of the Christian Martyrs.* Translated with an Introduction by Herbert Musurillo, xiii–xv, 2–21. Oxford: At the Clarendon Press, 1972.

The Martyrdom of Saints Carpus, Papylus, and Agathonicê. In *The Acts of the Christian Martyrs.* Translated with an Introduction by Herbert Musurillo, xv–xvi, 22–37. Oxford: At the Clarendon Press, 1972.

The Martyrs of Lyons. In *The Acts of the Christian Martyrs.* Translated with an Introduction by Herbert Musurillo, xx–xxii, 62–85. Oxford: At the Clarendon Press, 1972.

Nouum Testamentum Latine. Translated by Jerome. Edited by Johannes Wordsworth and Henricus Iulianus White. 2d ed. Oxford: Oxford University Press, 1911.

Origen. *Liber denique de Oratione.* In *Origenis Opera Omnia quae Graece vel Latine Tantum Exstant,* vol. 17, ed. Henric Eduard Lommatsch, 79–297. Berlin: S. J. Joseephy, 1844.

————. *Prayer/Exhortation to Martyrdom.* Translated by John J. O'Meara. In *Ancient Christian Writers: The Works of the Fathers in Translation,* vol. 19, ed. Johannes Quasten and Joseph C. Plumpe, 15–140. New York: Newman Press, 1954.

Passio sanctarum Perpetuae et Felicitatis. Edited by Cornelius Johannes Maria Joseph van Beek. Nijmegen, Holland: Dekker and Van de Vegt, 1936.

Passio sanctarum Perpetuae et Felicitatis. Edited by Cornelius Johannes Maria Joseph van Beek. Bonn: Peter Hanstein, 1938.

Passion de Perpétue et de Félicité suivi de Actes. Edited by Jacqueline Amat. Sources Chrétiennes, vol. 417. Paris: Les Éditions du Cerf, 1996.

The Passion of Perpetua and Felicity: A New Edition and Translation of the Latin

Text together with the Sermons of S. Augustine upon These Saints. Translated by W. H. Shewring. London: Sheed and Ward, 1931.

Passion of SS. Perpetua and Felicitas. In *Some Authentic Acts of the Early Martyrs.* Translated by E. C. E. Owen, 74–92. London: Society for Promoting Christian Knowledge, 1927.

The Passion of S. Perpetua. Edited by J. Armitage Robinson. In *Texts and Studies: Contributions to Biblical and Patristic Literature,* vol. 1, part 2. Cambridge: At the University Press, 1891; reprint, Nendeln/Liechtenstein: Kraus Reprint, 1967.

Pontius. *The Life of Cyprian.* Translated by Mary Magdeleine Müller and Roy Joseph Deferrari. In *The Fathers of the Church: A New Translation,* vol. 15, *Early Christian Biographies,* ed. Roy Joseph Deferrari, 5–26. n.p.: Fathers of the Church, 1952.

———. *Vita Cypriani.* In *Vite dei santi,* vol. 3, *Vita di Cipriano/Vita di Ambrogio/Vita di Agostino,* ed. A. A. R. Bastiaensen, 4–48. Milano: Fondazione Lorenzo Valla, 1975.

Praedestinatus. *Praedestinatorum Haeresis.* Patrologia Latina, vol. 53, 587–672. Paris: J. P. Migne Successores, 1879.

Prudentius. *Discourse of the Martyr St. Romanus against the Pagans.* Translated by M. Clement Eagan. In *The Fathers of the Church: A New Translation,* vol. 43, *The Poems of Prudentius,* ed. Roy Joseph Deferrari, 240–59. Washington, D.C.: The Catholic University of America Press, 1962.

Pseudo-Tertullian. *Adversus omnes haereses.* Edited by Emil Kroymann. In *Quinti Septimi Florentis Tertulliani Opera,* vol. 2, 1399–1410. Corpus Christianorum Series Latina. Turnhout: Brepols, 1954.

———. *Against All Heresies.* Translated by S. Thelwall. In *Ante-Nicene Christian Library,* vol. 18, ed. Alexander Roberts and James Donaldson, 259–73. Edinburgh: T. and T. Clarke, 1870.

Quodvultdeus. *Sermo de tempore barbarico.* In *Opera Quodvultdeo Carthaginiensi episcopo tributa.* Corpus Christianorum Series Latina, vol. 60, ed. R. Braun. Turnhout: Brepols, 1976.

Robinson, J. Armitage, and Montague Rhodes James, eds. *The Gospel According to Peter, and The Revelation of Peter: Two Lectures on the Newly Recovered Fragments Together with the Greek Texts.* 2d ed. London: C. J. Clay and Sons, 1892.

The Scriptores Historiae Augustae. Translated by David Magie. Vol. 1. Cambridge, Mass.: Harvard University Press, 1921.

The Septuagint with Apocrypha: Greek and English, ed. Lancelot C. L. Brenton. London: Samuel Bagster and Sons, 1851; reprint, Peabody, Mass.: Hendrickson Publishers, 1999.

Shepherd of Hermas. Translated by J. B. Lightfoot. In *The Apostolic Fathers: Greek Texts and English Translations.* Edited and revised by Michael W. Holmes, 368–73. Grand Rapids: Baker, 1999.

Tabbernee, William, ed. *Montanist Inscriptions and Testimonia: Epigraphic Sources Illustrating the History of Montanism.* Patristic Monograph Series, no. 16, North American Patristic Society. Macon, Ga.: Mercer University Press, 1997.

Tertullian. *Ad Martyras.* Translated by S. Thelwall. In *The Ante-Nicene Fathers*, vol. 3, ed. Alexander Roberts and James Donaldson, 693–96. Edinburgh: T. and T. Clark, 1873; reprint, Grand Rapids: Eerdmans, 1978.

———. *Adversus Marcionem.* Edited and Translated by Ernest Evans. 2 vols. Oxford Early Christian Texts, ed. Henry Chadwick. Oxford: At the Clarendon Press, 1972.

———. *Against Marcion.* Translated by Peter Holmes. In *The Ante-Nicene Fathers*, vol. 3, ed. Alexander Roberts and James Donaldson, 269–474. Edinburgh: T. and T. Clark, 1873; reprint, Grand Rapids: Eerdmans, 1978.

———. *Against Praxeas.* Translated by Peter Holmes. In *The Ante-Nicene Fathers*, vol. 3, ed. Alexander Roberts and James Donaldson, 597–627. Edinburgh: T. and T. Clark, 1873; reprint, Grand Rapids: Eerdmans, 1978.

———. *Apology.* Translated by S. Thelwall. In *The Ante-Nicene Fathers*, vol. 3, ed. Alexander Roberts and James Donaldson, 17–55. Edinburgh: T. and T. Clark, 1873; reprint, Grand Rapids: Eerdmans, 1978.

———. *Apology.* Translated by Rudolph Arbesmann, Emily Joseph Daly, and Edwin A. Quain. In *Tertullian, Apologetical Works, and Minucius Felix, Octavius.* The Fathers of the Church: A New Translation, vol. 10, ed. Roy Joseph Deferrari, 7–128. New York: Fathers of the Church, 1950.

———. *The Apparel of Women.* Translated by Rudolph Arbesmann, Emily Joseph Daly, and Edwin A. Quain. In *Tertullian, Disciplinary, Moral, and Ascetic Works.* The Fathers of the Church: A New Translation, vol. 40, ed. Joseph Deferrari, 117–52. New York: Fathers of the Church, 1959.

———. *The Chaplet.* Translated by Rudolph Arbesmann, Emily Joseph Daly, and Edwin A. Quain. In *Tertullian, Disciplinary, Moral, and Ascetic Works.* The Fathers of the Church: A New Translation, vol. 40, ed. Joseph Deferrari, 231–70. New York: Fathers of the Church, 1959.

———. *The Chaplet, or De Corona.* Translated by S. Thelwall. In *The Ante-Nicene Fathers*, vol. 3, ed. Alexander Roberts and James Donaldson, 93–104. Edinburgh: T. and T. Clark, 1873; reprint, Grand Rapids: Eerdmans, 1978.

———. *De Fuga in Persecutione.* Translated by S. Thelwall. In *The Ante-Nicene Fathers*, vol. 4, ed. Alexander Roberts and James Donaldson, 116–25. Edinburgh: T. and T. Clark, 1873; reprint, Grand Rapids: Eerdmans, 1982.

———. *Flight in Time of Persecution.* Translated by Rudolph Arbesmann, Emily Joseph Daly, and Edwin A. Quain. In *Tertullian, Disciplinary, Moral, and Ascetic Works.* The Fathers of the Church: A New Translation, vol. 40, ed. Joseph Deferrari, 275–310. New York: Fathers of the Church, 1959.

———. *Of Patience.* Translated by S. Thelwall. In *The Ante-Nicene Fathers*, vol.

3, ed. Alexander Roberts and James Donaldson, 707–17. Edinburgh: T. and T. Clark, 1873; reprint, Grand Rapids: Eerdmans, 1978.

———. *On the Apparel of Women*. Translated by S. Thelwall. In *The Ante-Nicene Fathers*, vol. 4, ed. Alexander Roberts and James Donaldson, 14–26. Edinburgh: T. and T. Clark, 1873; reprint, Grand Rapids: Eerdmans, 1982.

———. *On Baptism*. Translated by S. Thelwall. In *The Ante-Nicene Fathers*, vol. 3, ed. Alexander Roberts and James Donaldson, 669–80. Edinburgh: T. and T. Clark, 1873; reprint, Grand Rapids: Eerdmans, 1978.

———. *On Exhortation to Chastity*. Translated by S. Thelwall. In *The Ante-Nicene Fathers*, vol. 4, ed. Alexander Roberts and James Donaldson, 50–58. Edinburgh: T. and T. Clark, 1873; reprint, Grand Rapids: Eerdmans, 1982.

———. *On Fasting*. Translated by S. Thelwall. In *The Ante-Nicene Fathers*, vol. 4, ed. Alexander Roberts and James Donaldson, 102–15. Edinburgh: T. and T. Clark, 1873; reprint, Grand Rapids: Eerdmans, 1982.

———. *On Modesty*. Translated by S. Thelwall. In *The Ante-Nicene Fathers*, vol. 4, ed. Alexander Roberts and James Donaldson, 74–101. Edinburgh: T. and T. Clark, 1873; reprint, Grand Rapids: Eerdmans, 1982.

———. *On Monogamy*. Translated by S. Thelwall. In *The Ante-Nicene Fathers*, vol. 4, ed. Alexander Roberts and James Donaldson, 59–72. Edinburgh: T. and T. Clark, 1873; reprint, Grand Rapids: Eerdmans, 1982.

———. *On Repentance*. Translated by S. Thelwall. In *The Ante-Nicene Fathers*, vol. 3, ed. Alexander Roberts and James Donaldson, 657–66. Edinburgh: T. and T. Clark, 1873; reprint, Grand Rapids: Eerdmans, 1978.

———. *On the Resurrection of the Flesh*. Translated by Peter Holmes. In *The Ante-Nicene Fathers*, vol. 3, ed. Alexander Roberts and James Donaldson, 545–96. Edinburgh: T. and T. Clark, 1873; reprint, Grand Rapids: Eerdmans, 1978.

———. *On the Soul*. Translated by Rudolph Arbesmann, Emily Joseph Daly, and Edwin A. Quain. In *Tertullian, Apologetical Works, and Minucius Felix, Octavius*. The Fathers of the Church: A New Translation, vol. 10, ed. Joseph Deferrari, 179–312. New York: Fathers of the Church, 1950.

———. *On the Veiling of Virgins*. Translated by S. Thelwall. In *The Ante-Nicene Fathers*, vol. 4, ed. Alexander Roberts and James Donaldson, 27–37. Edinburgh: T. and T. Clark, 1873; reprint, Grand Rapids: Eerdmans, 1982.

———. *Patience*. Translated by Rudolph Arbesmann, Emily Joseph Daly, and Edwin A. Quain. In *Tertullian, Disciplinary, Moral, and Ascetic Works*. The Fathers of the Church: A New Translation, vol. 40, ed. Joseph Deferrari, 193–224. New York: Fathers of the Church, 1959.

———. *Prayer*. Translated by Rudolph Arbesmann, Emily Joseph Daly, and Edwin A. Quain. In *Tertullian, Disciplinary, Moral, and Ascetic Works*. The

Fathers of the Church: A New Translation, vol. 40, ed. Joseph Deferrari, 157–90. New York: Fathers of the Church, 1959.

———. *Scorpiace.* Translated by S. Thelwall. In *The Ante-Nicene Fathers*, vol. 3, ed. Alexander Roberts and James Donaldson, 545–96. Edinburgh: T. and T. Clark, 1873; reprint, Grand Rapids: Eerdmans, 1978.

———. *The Shows, or De Spectaculis.* Translated by S. Thelwall. In *The Ante-Nicene Fathers*, vol. 3, ed. Alexander Roberts and James Donaldson, 79–92. Edinburgh: T. and T. Clark, 1873; reprint, Grand Rapids: Eerdmans, 1978.

———. *Spectacles.* Translated by Rudolph Arbesmann, Emily Joseph Daly, and Edwin A. Quain. In *Tertullian, Disciplinary, Moral, and Ascetic Works.* The Fathers of the Church: A New Translation, vol. 40, ed. Joseph Deferrari, 47–110. New York: Fathers of the Church, 1959.

———. *Tertullian's Homily on Baptism.* Edited and Translated with an Introduction and Commentary by Ernest Evans. London: S.P.C.K., 1964.

———. *To His Wife.* Translated by S. Thelwall. In *The Ante-Nicene Fathers*, vol. 4, ed. Alexander Roberts and James Donaldson, 39–49. Edinburgh: T. and T. Clark, 1873; reprint, Grand Rapids: Eerdmans, 1982.

———. *To the Martyrs.* Translated by Rudolph Arbesmann, Emily Joseph Daly, and Edwin A. Quain. In *Tertullian, Disciplinary, Moral, and Ascetic Works.* The Fathers of the Church: A New Translation, vol. 40, ed. Joseph Deferrari, 17–32. New York: Fathers of the Church, 1959.

———. *To Scapula.* Translated by S. Thelwall. In *The Ante-Nicene Fathers*, vol. 3, ed. Alexander Roberts and James Donaldson, 105–8. Edinburgh: T. and T. Clark, 1873; reprint, Grand Rapids: Eerdmans, 1978.

———. *A Treatise on the Soul.* Translated by Peter Holmes. In *The Ante-Nicene Fathers*, vol. 3, ed. Alexander Roberts and James Donaldson, 181–235. Edinburgh: T. and T. Clark, 1873; reprint, Grand Rapids: Eerdmans, 1978.

———. *Treatises on Penance: On Penitence and On Purity.* Translated and Annotated by William P. Le Saint. Ancient Christian Writers: The Works of the Fathers in Translation, vol. 28, ed. Johannes Quasten and Walter J. Burghardt. New York: Newman Press, 1959.

Quinti Septimi Florentis Tertulliani Opera. 2 vols. Corpus Christianorum Series Latina. Turnhout: Brepols, 1954.

Testament of Abraham. Translated by Michael E. Stone. Missoula, Mont.: Society of Biblical Literature, 1972.

Theophilus of Antioch. *Ad Autolycum.* Edited by Robert M. Grant. Oxford: Oxford University Press, 1970.

———. *To Autolycus.* Translated by Marcus Dods. In *The Ante-Nicene Fathers*, vol. 2, ed. Alexander Roberts and James Donaldson, 89–121. Edinburgh: T. and T. Clark, 1873; reprint, Grand Rapids: Eerdmans, 1983.

Secondary Sources

Allard, Paul. *Histoire des persécutions.* Vol. 2. Paris: Librairie Victor Lecoffre, 1919.

Alzog, John. *History of the Church.* Vol. 1. Translated by F. J. Pabisch and Thomas S. Byrne. New York: Benziger Brothers, 1874.

Amat, Jacqueline. *Songes et Visions: L'au-delà dans la littérature latine tardive.* Paris: Études Augustiniennes, 1985.

Amat, Jacqueline, ed. Introduction to *Passion de Perpétue et de Félicité suivi de Actes.* Edited by Jacqueline Amat. Sources Chrétiennes, vol. 417. Paris: Les Éditions du Cerf, 1996.

Ash, James L., Jr. "The Decline of Ecstatic Prophecy in the Early Church." *Theological Studies* 37 (June 1976): 227–52.

Aubé, Benjamin. *Les chrétiens dans l'Empire romain.* Studia Historica, vol. 103. Paris: Ristampa Anastatica Invariata dell'Edizione, 1881; reprint, Roma: "L'Erma" di Bretschneider, 1972.

Aune, David E. *Prophecy in Early Christianity and the Ancient Mediterranean World.* Grand Rapids: Eerdmans, 1983.

Ayer, Joseph Cullen, Jr. *A Source Book for Ancient Church History from the Apostolic Age to the Close of the Conciliar Period.* New York: Charles Scribner's Sons, 1913.

Balling, Jakob. "Martyrdom as Apocalypse." In *In the Last Days: On Jewish and Christian Apocalyptic and Its Period.* Edited by Knud Jepperson, Kirsten Nielsen, and Bent Rosendal, 41–48. Aarhus C, Denmark: Aarhus University Press, 1994.

Barnes, Timothy David. "Legislation Against the Christians." *Journal of Roman Studies* 58 (1968): 32–50.

———. "Pre-Decian *Acta Martyrum.*" *Journal of Theological Studies* 19 (1968): 509–31.

———. *Tertullian: A Historical and Literary Study.* Oxford: Clarendon Press, 1971; rev. ed. 1985.

———. "The Chronology of Montanism," *JTS* 21 (1970): 403–4.

Barnett, Maurice. *The Living Flame: Being a Study of the Gift of the Spirit in the New Testament with Special Reference to Prophecy, Glossolalia, Montanism, and Perfection.* London: The Epworth Press, 1953.

Barns, T. "The Catholic Epistles of Themison: A Study in 1 and 2 Peter." *The Expositor.* 6th Series, 8 (1903): 40–62.

Bastiaensen, A. A. R. "Tertullian's Reference to the *Passio Perpetuae* in *De Anima* 55, 4." In *Studia Patristica,* vol. 17:2, ed. by Elizabeth A. Livingstone, 790–96. Oxford: Pergamon Press, 1982.

Baumeister, Theofried. "Martyrium als Thema Frühchristlicher Apologetischer Literatur." In *Martyrium in Multidisciplinary Perspective.* Edited by M. Lamberigts and P. Van Deun, 323–32. Leuven, Belgium: Leuven University Press, 1995.

Baur, Frederick Christian. *The Church History of the First Three Centuries.* Vol. 1. 3d ed. Translated by Allan Menzies. London: Williams and Norgate, 1878.

Bigg, Charles. *The Origins of Christianity.* Edited by T. B. Strong. Oxford: At the Clarendon Press, 1909.

Bonwetsch, G. Nathanael. *Die Geschichte des Montanismus.* Erlangen: Verlag von Andreas Deichert, 1881.

Braun, René. "Nouvelles Observations Linguistiques sur le Rédacteur de la 'Passio Perpetuae.'" *Vigiliae Christianae* 33 (1979): 105–17.

———. "Séance du 26 Mars 1955." *Revue des études latines* 33 (1955): 78–81.

Bremmer, Jan N. *The Rise and Fall of the Afterlife.* New York: Routledge, 2002.

Bruce, F. F. *The Spreading Flame.* The Advance of Christianity through the Centuries, vol. 1, ed. F. F. Bruce. Grand Rapids: Eerdmans, 1958.

Buschmann, Gerd. *Das Martyrium des Polykarp übersetzt und erklärt.* Kommentar zu den Apostolischen Vätern, vol. 6, ed. N. Brox, G. Kretschmar, and K. Niederwimmer. Göttingen: Vandenhoeck & Ruprecht, 1998.

———. "*Martyrium Polycarpi* 4 und der Montanismus." *Vigiliae Christianae* 49 (1995): 105–45.

Calder, W. M. "Philadelphia and Montanism." *Bulletin of John Rylands Library* 7 (1923): 309–53.

Campos, Julio. "El autor de la *Passio SS Perpetuae et Felicitatis.*" *Helmantica* 10 (1959): 357–81.

Cardman, Francine. "Acts of the Women Martyrs." *Anglican Theological Review* 70 (1988): 144–50.

Carrington, Philip. *The Early Christian Church.* Vol. 2, *The Second Christian Century.* Cambridge: At the University Press, 1957.

Castelli, Elizabeth. "'I Will Make Mary Male': Pieties of the Body and Gender Transformation of Christian Women in Late Antiquity." In *Body Guards: The Cultural Politics of Gender Ambiguity,* ed. Julia Epstein and Kristina Straub, 29–49. New York: Routledge, 1991.

Cloke, Gillian. "*Mater* or Martyr: Christianity and the Alienation of Women within the Family in the Later Roman Empire." *Theology and Sexuality* 5 (1996): 37–57.

Cooper, Kate. "The Voice of the Victim: Gender, Representation and Early Christian Martyrdom." *Bulletin of the John Rylands University Library of Manchester* 80 (1998): 147–57.

Coxe, A. Cleveland. Introduction to *The Martyrdom of Perpetua and Felicitas.* Translated by R. E. Wallis. In The Ante-Nicene Fathers, vol. 3, ed. Alexander Roberts and James Donaldson. Edinburgh: T. and T. Clark, 1873; reprint, Grand Rapids: Eerdmans, 1978.

d'Alès, Adhemar. "L'Auteur de la passio Perpetuae." *Revue d'histoire ecclesiastique* 8 (1907): 5–18.

———. *La Théologie de Tertullien.* 3d ed. Paris: Gabriel Beauchesne and Company, 1905.

Daniélou, Jean. *A History of Early Christian Doctrine Before the Council of Nicæa.* Vol. 3, *The Origins of Latin Christianity.* Translated by David Smith and John Austin Baker. Edited with a Postscript by John Austin Baker. Philadelphia: The Westminster Press, 1977.

Davies, J. G. *The Early Christian Church: A History of Its First Five Centuries.* Grand Rapids: Baker, 1965.

———. "Tertullian, *De Resurrectione Carnis LXIII:* A Note on the Origins of Montanism." *Journal of Theological Studies* 6 (1955): 90–94.

———. "Was the Devotion of Septimius Severus to Serapis the Cause of the Persecution of 202–3?" *Journal of Theological Studies* 5 (1954): 73–76.

de' Cavalieri, Pio Franchi. *Gli Atti dei SS. Montano, Lucio e compagni: Recensione del testo ed introduzione sulle sui relazioni con la Passio S. Perpetuae.* Rome: Buchhandlung Spithöver, 1898.

Deferrari, Roy Joseph, ed. Introduction to Pontius, *The Life of Cyprian.* Translated by Mary Magdeleine Müller and Roy Joseph Defeffari. In *The Fathers of the Church: A New Translation,* vol. 15, *Early Christian Biographies.* n.p.: Fathers of the Church, 1952.

de Labriolle, Pierre. *La Crise Montaniste.* Paris: Ernest Leroux, 1913.

———. *History and Literature of Christianity from Tertullian to Boethius.* Translated by Herbert Wilson. With an Introduction by Aidan Gasquet. New York: Alfred A. Knopf, 1925.

Delehaye, Hippolyte. *The Legends of the Saints.* Translated by Donald Attwater. New York: Fordham University Press, 1962.

———. *Les Passions des Martyrs et les Genres Littéraires.* Bruxelles: Société des Bollandistes, 1966.

de Nie, Giselle. "'Consciousness Fecund through God': From Male Fighter to Spiritual Bride-Mother in Late Antique Female Sanctity." In *Sanctity and Motherhood: Essays on Holy Mothers in the Middle Ages.* Edited by Anneke B. Mulder-Bakker. Garland Medieval Casebooks, ed. Joyce E. Salisbury and Christopher Kleinhenz, 101–61. New York: Garland Publishing, 1995.

de Soyres, John. *Montanism and the Primitive Church: A Study in the Ecclesiastical History of the Second Century.* Cambridge: Deighton, Bell, and Co., 1878; reprint, Lexington, Ky.: The American Theological Library Association, 1965.

Dehandschutter, B. "The Martyrdom of Polycarp and the Outbreak of Montanism." *Ephemerides Theologicae Lovaniensis* 75 (1999): 430–37.

den Boeft, Jan, and Jan Bremmer. "Notiunculae Martyrologiae II." *Vigiliae Christianae* 36 (1982): 383–402.

de Tillemont, M. Lenain. *Memoires pour Servir a L'Histoire Ecclesiastique.* 2d ed. Paris: Charles Robustel, 1701.

Dodds, E. R. *Pagan and Christian in an Age of Anxiety: Some Aspects of Religious Experience from Marcus Aurelius to Constantine.* Cambridge: At the University Press, 1965.

Dölger, F. J. "Antike Parallelen zum leidenden Dinocrates in der Passio Perpetuae." *Antike und Christentum* 2 (1930): 1–40.

———. "Der Kampf mit dem Ägypter in der Perpetua-Vision: Das Martyrium als Kampf mit dem Teufel." *Antike und Christentum* 3 (1932): 177–88.

Donaldson, James. "Shepherd of Hermas." *Theological Review* 14 (1877): 504–19.

Donaldson, Stuart A. *Church Life and Thought in North Africa A.D. 200.* Cambridge: University Press, 1909.

Dronke, Peter. *Women Writers of the Middle Ages: A Critical Study of Texts from Perpetua (203) to Marguerite Porete (1310).* Cambridge: Cambridge University Press, 1984.

Duchesne, Louis. *The Churches Separated from Rome.* Translated by Arnold Harris Matthew. New York: Benziger Brothers, 1907.

———. *Early History of the Christian Church.* Vol. 1, *From Its Foundation to the End of the Third Century.* Translated by Claude Jenkins. New York: Longmans, Green and Company, 1913.

Elm, Susanna. "Montanist Oracles." In *Searching the Scriptures*, vol. 2, *A Feminist Commentary*. Edited by Elisabeth Schüssler Fiorenza, 131–38. New York: Crossroad Publishing Company, 1994.

Engelsen, Nils Ivar Johan. "Glossolalia and Other Forms of Inspired Speech According to 1 Corinthians 12–14." Ph.D. Diss., Yale University, 1970.

Enslin, Morton S. "Puritan of Carthage." *The Journal of Religion* 27 (1947): 197–212.

Fee, Gordon D. *God's Empowering Presence: The Holy Spirit in the Letters of Paul.* Peabody, Mass.: Hendrickson Publishers, 1994.

Fliche, Augustin, and Victor Martin, eds. *Histoire de L'Église.* Vol. 2, *De la fin du 2e siècle à la paix constantinienne*, by Jules Lebreton and Jacques Zeiller. Paris: Bloud and Gay, 1978.

Fontaine, Jacques. *Aspects et problémes de la prose d'art Latine au IIIe siècle: La genèse des styles Latins chrétiens.* Torino: Bottega d'Erasmo, 1968.

Forbes, Christopher. *Prophecy and Inspired Speech in Early Christianity and Its Hellenistic Environment.* Peabody, Mass.: Hendrickson, 1997.

Fox, Robin Lane. *Pagans and Christians.* New York: Alfred A. Knopf, 1989.

Freeman, Greville. "Montanism and the Pagan Cults." *Dominican Studies* 3 (1950): 297–316.

Frend, W. H. C. "Blandina and Perpetua: Two Early Christian Heroines." In *Women in Early Christianity.* Edited by David M. Scholer. Studies in Early Christianity: A Collection of Scholarly Essays, vol. 14, ed. Everett Ferguson, 87–97. New York: Garland Publishing, 1993.

———. *The Donatist Church: A Movement of Protest in Roman North Africa.* Oxford: At the Clarendon Press, 1952.

———. *Martyrdom and Persecution in the Early Church: A Study of a Conflict from the Maccabees to Donatus.* Garden City, N.Y.: Doubleday and Company, 1967.

―――. "Montanism: A Movement of Prophecy and Regional Identity in the Early Church." *Bulletin of John Rylands Library of Manchester* 70 (1988): 25–34.

―――. "The North African Cult of Martyrs: From Apocalyptic to Hero-Worship." In *Jenseitsvorstellungen in antike und Christentum: gedenkschrift für Alfred Stuiber*, 154–67. Münster Westfalen: Aschendorffshe Verlagsbuchhandlung, 1982.

―――. "Note on the Chronology of the Martyrdom of Polycarp and the Outbreak of Montanism." In *Oikoumene; studi paleocristiani publicati in onore del Concilio Ecumenico Vatican*, ed. Jeanne Courcelle, 499–506. Catania: Università de Catania, 1964.

―――. "Open Questions Concerning the Christians and the Roman Empire in the Age of the Severi." *Journal of Theological Studies* 25 (1974): 333–51.

―――. *The Rise of Christianity*. Philadelphia: Fortress Press, 1984.

―――. *Saints and Sinners in the Early Church: Differing and Conflicting Traditions in the First Six Centuries*. Theology and Life Series, vol. 11. Wilmington, Del.: Michael Glazier, 1985.

Freppel, C. E. *Tertullien*. Vol. 1. Paris: Ambroise Bray, 1864.

Fridh, Åke. *Le problème de la Passion des Saintes Perpétue et Félicité*. Studia Graeca et Latina Gothoburgensia, 26. Göteborg: Acta Universitatis Gothoburgensis, 1968.

Fuller, J. M. "Tertullian." *Dictionary of Christian Biography*, vol. 4, ed. William Smith and Henry Wace. London: John Murray, 1887.

Gieseler, John C. L. *A Compendium of Ecclesiastical History*. Vol. 1. Rev. from 4th ed. Translated by Samuel Davidson. New York: Harper and Brothers, 1849.

González, Justo L. *A History of Christian Thought*. Vol. 1, *From the Beginnings to the Council of Chalcedon*. New York: Abingdon Press, 1970.

―――. *The Story of Christianity*. Vol. 1, *The Early Church to the Dawn of the Reformation*. San Francisco: HarperSanFrancisco, 1984.

Goree, Balfour William, Jr. "The Cultural Bases of Montanism." Ph.D. Diss., Baylor University, 1980.

Grant, Robert M. *Augustus to Constantine: The Emergence of Christianity in the Roman World*. San Francisco: HarperSanFrancisco, 1970; reprint, New York: Barnes and Noble Books, 1996.

―――. *Irenaeus of Lyons*. The Early Church Fathers, ed. Carol Harrison. New York: Routledge, 1997.

Groh, Dennis E. "Utterance and Exegesis: Biblical Interpretation in the Montanist Crisis." In *The Living Text: Essays in Honor of Ernest W. Saunders*. Edited by Dennis E. Groh and Robert Jewett, 73–95. Lanham, Md.: University Press of America, 1985.

Gwatkin, Henry Melvill. *Early Church History to A.D. 313*. Vol. 2. London: MacMillan and Co., Limited, 1909.

Habermehl, Peter. *Perpetua und der Ägypter oder Bilder des Bösen im Frühen Afrikanischen Christentum.* Berlin: Akademie Verlag, 1992.

Halporn, J. W. "Literary History and Generic Expectations in the *Passio* and *Acta Perpetuae.*" *Vigiliae Christianae* 45 (1991): 223–41.

Hamilton, Edith. *Mythology.* New York: New American Library, 1942.

Harris, J. Rendel and Seth K. Gifford, ed. Introduction to *The Acts of the Martyrdom of Perpetua and Felicitas: The Original Greek Text.* London: C. J. Clay and Sons, 1890.

Harnack, Adolf. *Die Chronologie der Altchristlichen Litteratur bis Eusebius.* 2 vols. Leipzig: J. C. Hinrichs'sche Buchhandlung, 1904.

———. *History of Dogma.* Vol. 2. Translated by Neil Buchanan. Boston: Roberts Brothers, 1897.

———. "Montanism." *Encyclopaedia Britannica,* 11th ed.

Hart, Mattie Elizabeth. "Speaking in Tongues and Prophecy as Understood by Paul and at Corinth, with Reference to Early Christian Usage." Ph.D. Diss., University of Durham, 1975.

Heffernan, Thomas J. "History Becomes *Heilgeschichte:* The Principle of the Paradigm in the Early Christian *Passio sanctarum Perpetuae et Felicitatis.*" In *Interpreting Texts from the Middle Ages: The Ring of Words in Medieval Literature,* ed. Ulrich Goebel and David Lee, 119–38. Studies in Russian and German, ed. Ulrich Goebel and Peter I. Barta. Lewiston, N.Y.: Edwin Mellen Press, 1994.

———. "The Passion of Saints Perpetua and Felicitas and the *Imitatio Christi.*" In *Sacred Biography: Saints and Their Biographers in the Middle Ages,* 185–230. New York: Oxford University Press, 1988.

———. "Philology and Authorship in the *Passio Sanctarum Perpetuae et Felicitatis.*" *Traditio* 50 (1995): 315–25.

Heine, Ronald E. "The Role of the Gospel of John in the Montanist Controversy." *The Second Century* 6 (1987): 1–19.

———. "John and the Montanist Debate in Rome." In *Studia Patristica,* vol. 21, ed. Elizabeth A. Livingstone, 95–100. Leuven: Peeters Press, 1989.

Holl, Karl. "Die Vorstellung vom Märtyrer und die Märtyrerakte in ihrer geschichtlichen Entwicklung." In *Gesammelte Aufsätze zur Kirchengeschichte.* Vol. 2, *Der Osten,* 68–102. Tübingen: J. C. B. Mohr, 1928.

Huber, Elaine C. *Women and the Authority of Inspiration: A Reexamination of Two Prophetic Movements from Contemporary Feminist Perspective.* Lanham, Md.: University Press of America, 1985.

———. "Women and the Authority of Inspiration: A Reexamination of Two Prophetic Movements from a Christian Feminist Perspective." Ph.D. Diss., Graduate Theological Union, 1984.

Ide, Arthur Frederick. *Martyrdom of Women: A Study of Death Psychology in the Early Christian Church to 301 CE.* Garland, Tex.: Tangelwüld, 1985.

James, Montague Rhodes. Introduction to *The Fourth Book of Ezra.* Edited by Robert L. Bensly. Cambridge: 1895.

Jedin, Hubert, and John Dolan, eds. *History of the Church.* Vol. 1, *From the Apostolic Community to Constantine,* by Karl Baus. With an Introduction by Hubert Jedin. New York: The Seabury Press, 1980.

Jensen, Anne. *God's Self-Confident Daughters: Early Christianity and the Liberation of Women.* Translated by O. C. Dean, Jr. Louisville, Ky.: Westminster John Knox Press, 1996.

Kaye, John. *The Ecclesiastical History of the Second and Third Centuries Illustrated from the Writings of Tertullian.* London: Griffith Farran and Co., 1824.

Kelly, J. N. D. *Early Christian Doctrines.* Rev. ed. San Francisco: Harper and Row, 1978.

————. *Jerome: His Life, Writings and Controversies.* London: Gerald Duckworth and Co., 1975; reprint, Peabody, Mass.: Hendrickson, 1998.

Kidd, B. J. *A History of the Church to A.D. 461.* Vol. 1, *To A.D. 313.* Oxford: At the Clarendon Press, 1922.

Kirsch, J. P. "Felicitas and Perpetua." *The Catholic Encyclopedia,* vol. 6, ed. Charles G. Herbermann, Edward A. Pace, Condé B. Pallen, Thomas J. Shahan, John J. Wynne. New York: The Encyclopedia Press, 1913).

Klawiter, Frederick C. "The New Prophecy in Early Christianity: The Origin, Nature and Development of Montanism AD 165–220." Ph.D. Diss., University of Chicago, 1975.

————. "The Role of Martyrdom and Persecution in Developing the Priestly Authority of Women in Early Christianity: A Case Study of Montanism." *Church History* 49 (1980): 251–61.

Knox, R. A. *Enthusiasm: A Chapter in the History of Religion.* Oxford: At the Clarendon Press, 1950.

Kraemer, Ross Shepard. *Her Share of the Blessings: Women's Religions among Pagans, Jews, and Christians in the Greco-Roman World.* New York: Oxford University Press, 1992.

Kraft, Heinrich. "Die Lyoner Märtyrer und der Montanismus." In *Pietas: Festschrift für Bernhard Kötting,* ed. Ernst Dassmann and K. Suso Frank, 250–66. *Jahrbuch für Antike und Christentum,* vol. 8, ed. Franz Joseph Dölger. Münster Westfalen: Aschendorffsche Verlagsbuchhandlung, 1980.

Kurtz, Johann Heinrich. *Church History.* Translated by John MacPherson. In *The Foreign Biblical Library,* vol. 1., ed. W. Robertson Nicoll. New York: Funk and Wagnalls Company, 1888.

Lardner, Nathaniel. *The Credibility of the Gospel History.* In *The Works of Nathaniel Lardner,* vol. 2. London: William Ball, 1838.

Le Clercq, Henri. *Les Martyrs.* Vol. 1, *Les Temps Neroniens et le Deuxième Siècle.* Paris: H. Oudin, 1902.

Lefkowitz, Mary R. "Motivations for St. Perpetua's Martyrdom." *Journal of the American Academy of Religion* 44 (1976): 417–21.

Lefkowitz, Mary R., and Maureen B. Fant, eds. *Women's Life in Greece and Rome.* Baltimore: The Johns Hopkins University Press, 1982.

Le Goff, Jacques. *The Birth of Purgatory*. Translated by Arthur Goldhammer. Chicago: The University of Chicago Press, 1984.

Lietzmann, Hans. *Geschichte der alten Kirche*. Vol. 2, *Ecclesia catholica*. Berlin: Verlag Walter de Gruyter & Co., 1953.

Lyman, Rebecca. "Perpetua: A Christian Quest for Self." *Journal of Women and Religion* 8 (1989): 26–33.

Maldonado-Pérez, Zaida. "The Subversive Dimensions of the Visions of the Martyrs of the Roman Empire of the Second through Early Fourth Centuries." Ph.D. Diss., Saint Louis University, 1999.

Massingberd Ford, Josephine. "Was Montanism a Jewish-Christian Heresy?" *Journal of Ecclesiastical History* 17 (1966): 145–58.

Matthews, J. R. Review of *Tertullian: A Historical and Literary Study*, by Timothy David Barnes. *Journal of Theological Studies* 24 (1973): 245–49.

McDonnell, Kilian. "Communion Ecclesiology and Baptism in the Spirit: Tertullian and the Early Church." *Theological Studies* 49 (1988): 671–93.

McGinn-Moorer, Sheila Elizabeth. "The New Prophecy of Asia Minor and the Rise of Ecclesiastical Patriarchy in Second Century Pauline Traditions." Ph.D. Diss., Northwestern University, 1989.

McGowan, Andrew. *Ascetic Eucharists: Food and Drink in Early Christian Ritual Meals*. Oxford Early Christian Studies, ed. Gillian Clark and Andrew Louth. Oxford: Clarendon Press, 1999.

McKechnie, Paul. *The First Christian Centuries: Perspectives on the Early Church*. Downers Grove, Ill.: InterVarsity Press, 2001.

———. "'Women's Religion' and Second-Century Christianity." *Journal of Ecclesiastical History* 47 (1996): 409–31.

Meeks, Wayne A. "The Image of the Androgyne: Some Uses of a Symbol in Earliest Christianity." *History of Religions* 13 (1974): 165–208.

Miller, Patricia Cox. "Dreams in Patristic Literature: Divine Sense or Pagan Nonsense?" In *Studia Patristica*, vol. 18:2, ed. Elizabeth A. Livingstone, 185–90. Kalamazoo, Mich.: Cistercian Publications, 1989.

———. "'A Dubious Twilight': Reflections on Dreams in Patristic Literature." *Church History* 55 (1986): 153–64.

Milman, Henry Hart. *The History of Christianity*. Vol. 2. New and rev. ed. New York: W. J. Widdleton, Publisher, 1866.

Monceaux, Paul. *Histoire Littéraire de l'Afrique Chrétienne depuis les Origines jusqu'a l'Invasion Arabe*. Vol. 1, *Tertullien et les Origines*. Paris: n.p., 1901; reprint, Brussels: Culture et Civilisation, 1963.

Moriarty, Rachel. "The Claims of the Past: Attitudes to Antiquity in the Introduction to *Passio Perpetuae*." In *Studia Patristica*, vol. 31, ed. Elizabeth A. Livingstone, 307–13. Leuven, Belgium: Peeters, 1997.

Mourret, Fernand. *A History of the Catholic Church*. Vol. 1, *Period of Early Expansion*. Translated by Newton Thompson. St. Louis: B. Herder Book Co., 1931.

Musurillo, Herbert, ed. Introduction to *The Acts of the Christian Martyrs*. Translated by Herbert Musurillo. Oxford: At the Clarendon Press, 1972.

Neander, Augustus. *General History of the Christian Religion and Church*. Vol. 1. 11th American ed. New York: Hurd and Houghton, 1871.

Newman, Albert Henry. *A Manual of Church History*. Vol. 1, *Ancient and Mediæval Church History (To A.D. 1517)*. Philadelphia; American Baptist Publication Society, 1899.

Orbán, A. P. "The Afterlife in the Visions of the *Passio SS. Perpetuae et Felicitatis*." In *Fructus centesimus: mélanges offerts á Gerard J. M. Bartelink á l'occasion de son soixante-cinquiéme anniversaire*, ed. A. A. R. Bastiaensen, A. Hilhorst, and C. H. Kneepkens, 269–77. Instrumenta patristica 19. Dordrecht: Kluwer, 1989.

Osborn, Eric. *Irenaeus of Lyons*. Cambridge: Cambridge University Press, 2001.

———. *Tertullian, First Theologian of the West*. Cambridge: Cambridge University Press, 1997.

Osiek, Carolyn. "Perpetua's Husband." Journal of Early Christian Studies 10 (2002): 287–90.

Owen, E. C. E. Introduction to *Passion of SS. Perpetua and Felicitas*. In *Some Authentic Acts of the Early Martyrs*. Translated by E. C. E. Owen. London: Society for Promoting Christian Knowledge, 1927.

Parke, H. W. *Greek Oracles*. London: Hutchinson University Library, 1967.

Pelikan, Jaroslav. *The Christian Tradition: A History of the Development of Doctrine*. Vol. 1, *The Emergence of the Catholic Tradition (100–600)*. Chicago: The University of Chicago Press, 1971.

———. "Montanism and Its Trinitarian Significance." Church History 25 (1956): 99–109.

Petraglio, R. "Des influences de l'Apocalypse dans la 'Passio Perpetuae' 11–13." In L'Apocalypse de Jean, ed. R. Petraglio, 15–29. Geneva: Librairie Droz, 1979.

Petroff, Elizabeth Alvilda. *Medieval Women's Visionary Literature*. New York: Oxford University Press, 1986.

Pettersen, Alvyn. "Perpetua-Prisoner of Conscience." Vigiliae Christianae 41 (1987): 139–53.

Poirier, John C. "Montanist Pepuza-Jerusalem and the Dwelling Place of Wisdom." Journal of Early Christian Studies 7 (1999): 491–507.

Powell, Douglas. "Tertullianists and Cataphrygians." Vigiliae Christianae 29 (1975): 33–54.

Quasten, Johannes. *Patrology*. Vol. 1, *The Beginnings of Patristic Literature*. Westminster, Md.: Christian Classics, 1986.

Rader, Rosemary. "The Martyrdom of Perpetua: A Protest Account of Third-Century Christianity." In *A Lost Tradition: Women Writers of the Early Church*, ed. Patricia Wilson-Kastner, G. Ronald Kastner, Ann Millin, Rosemary Rader, and Jeremiah Reedy, 1–17. Lanham, Md.: University Press of America, 1981.

Ramsay, W. M. *The Church in the Roman Empire before A.D. 170.* New York: G. P. Putnam's Sons, 1893.

Reitzenstein, Richard. *Die Nachrichten über den Tod Cyprians: Ein philologischer Beitrag zur Geschichte Märtyrerliteratur.* Sitzungsberichte der Heidelberger Akademie der Wissenschaften. Heidelberg: Carl Winters Universitätsbuchhandlung, 1913.

Renan, Ernest. *The History of the Origins of Christianity.* Book 7, *Marcus-Aurelius.* London: Mathieson and Company, n.d.

Ritschl, Albrecht. *Die Entstehung der altkatholischen Kirche: Eine kirchen- und dogmengeschichtliche Monographie.* Bonn: Adolph Marcus, 1857.

Rives, James. "The Piety of a Persecutor." *Journal of Early Christian Studies* 4:1 (1996): 1–25.

Robeck, Cecil Melvin, Jr. "Irenaeus and 'Prophetic Gifts'." In *Essays on Apostolic Themes,* ed. Paul Elbert, 104–14. Peabody, Mass.: Hendrickson Publishers, 1985.

————. *Prophecy in Carthage: Perpetua, Tertullian, and Cyprian.* Cleveland, Ohio: The Pilgrim Press, 1992.

————. "The Role and Function of Prophetic Gifts for the Church at Carthage, AD 202–258." Ph.D. Diss., Fuller Theological Seminary, 1985.

Robert, Louis. "Une vision de Perpétue, martyre à Carthage en 203." *Comptes rendus de l'Academie des Inscriptions et Belles-Lettres* (1982), 228–76.

Robertson, James C. *History of the Christian Church from the Apostolic Age to the Reformation: A.D. 64–1517.* Vol. 1. New and rev. ed. London: John Murray, 1876.

Robinson, J. Armitage, ed. Introduction to *The Passion of S. Perpetua.* In *Texts and Studies: Contributions to Biblical and Patristic Literature,* vol. 1, part 2. Cambridge: At the University Press, 1891; reprint, Nendeln/Liechtenstein: Kraus Reprint, 1967.

Rogier, Louis J., ed. *The Christian Centuries.* Vol. 1, *The First Six Hundred Years,* by Jean Daniélou and Henri Marrou. Translated by Vincent Cronin. New York: McGraw-Hill Book Company, 1964.

Rossi, Mary Ann. "The Passion of Perpetua, Everywoman of Late Antiquity." In *Pagan And Christian Anxiety: A Response to E. R. Dodds,* ed. Robert C. Smith and John Lounibos, 53–86. Lanham, Md.: University Press of America, 1984.

Rowland, Christopher. *The Open Heaven: A Study of Apocalyptic in Judaism and Early Christianity.* New York: Crossroad, 1982.

Rupprecht, Ernst. "Bemerkungen zur *Passion SS. Perpetuae et Felicitatis.*" *Rheinisches Museum für Philologie* 90 (1941): 177–92.

Salisbury, Joyce E. *Perpetua's Passion: The Death and Memory of a Young Roman Woman.* New York: Routledge, 1997.

Salonius, A. H. *Passio S. Perpetuae: Kritische Bemerkungen mit besonderer Berücksichtigung der griechisch-lateinischen Überlieferung des Textes*. Helsingfors: Helsingfors Centraltryckeri Och Bokbinderi Aktiebolag, 1921.

Schaff, Philip. *History of the Christian Church*. Vol. 2, *Ante-Nicene Christianity A.D. 100–325*. New York: Charles Scribner's Sons, 1910; reprint, Grand Rapids: Eerdmans, 1963.

Schepelern, Wilhelm. *Der Montanismus und die phrygischen Kulte: Eine religionsgeschichtlich Untersuchung*. Translated by W. Baur. Tübingen: Verlag von J. C. B. Mohr. 1929.

Scholer, David M. "'And I Was a Man': The Power and Problem of Perpetua." *Daughters of Sarah* 15 (1989): 10–14.

Schwegler, F. C. A. *Der Montanismus und die Christiliche Kirche des Zweiten Jahrhunderts*. Tübingen: Ludwig Friedrich Fues, 1841.

Shaw, Brent D. "The Passion of Perpetua." *Past and Present* 139 (1993): 3–45.

Shewring, W. H. "Prose Rhythm in the *Passio S. Perpetuae*." *Journal of Theological Studies* 30 (1928): 56–57.

Shewring, W. H., ed. Introduction to *The Passion of Perpetua and Felicity: A New Edition and Translation of the Latin Text together with the Sermons of S. Augustine upon These Saints*. London: Sheed and Ward, 1931.

Sider, Robert D. "Approaches to Tertullian: A Study of Recent Scholarship." *Second Century* 2 (1982): 228–60.

Simonetti, M. "Alcune osservazioni sul martirio di S. Policarpo," *Giornale italiano di filologia* 9 (1956): 328–44.

Starks Kierstead, Melanie. "The Socio-Historical Development of the New Prophecy: An Historical Inquiry to the Foundations of Montanism." Ph. D. Diss., Drew University, 1996.

Steinhauser, Kenneth B. "Augustine's Reading of the *Passio sanctarum Perpetuae et Felicitatis*." In *Studia Patristica*, vol. 33, ed. Elizabeth A. Livingstone, 244–49. Leuven, Belgium: Peeters, 1997.

Sullivan, Lisa M. "'I Responded, "I Will Not . . .': Christianity as Catalyst for Resistance in the *Passio Perpetuae et Felicitatis*." *Semeia* 79 (1997): 63–74.

Sweetman, Robert. "Christianity, Women, and the Medieval Family." In *Religion, Feminism, and the Family*, ed. Anne Carr and Mary Stewart Van Leeuwen, 127–48. The Family, Religion, and Culture Series, ed. Don S. Browning and Ian S. Evison. Louisville, Ky.: Westminster John Knox Press, 1996.

Syme, Ronald. *Emperors and Biography: Studies in the Historia Augusta*. Oxford: At the Clarendon Press, 1971.

Tabbernee, William, ed. "Early Montanism and Voluntary Martyrdom." *Colloquium: The Australian and New Zealand Theological Review* 17 (1985): 33–44.

———. "Montanist Regional Bishops: New Evidence from Ancient Inscriptions." *Journal of Early Christian Studies* 1 (1993): 249–80.

————. "The Opposition to Montanism from Church and State." Ph.D. Diss., University of Melbourne, 1978.

————. "'Our Trophies Are Better Than Your Trophies': The Appeal to Tombs and Reliquaries in Montanist-Orthodox Relations." In *Studia Patristica*, vol. 31, ed. Elizabeth A. Livingstone, 206–17. Leuven: Peeters Press, 1997.

————. "Perpetua, Optatus, and Friends: Christian Ministry in Carthage c. 203 C.E.," <http://divinity.library.vanderbilt.edu/burns/chroma/clergy/Tabborders.html#N_8_> (September 2003).

————. "Portals of the Montanist New Jerusalem: The Discovery of Pepouza and Tymion." *Journal of Early Christian Studies* 11 (2003): 87–93.

————. "Remnants of the New Prophecy: Literary and Epigraphical Sources of the Montanist Movement." In *Studia Patristica*, vol. 21, ed. Elizabeth A. Livingstone, 193–201. Leuven: Peeters Press, 1989.

————. "Revelation 21 and the Montanist 'New Jerusalem.'" *Australian Biblical Review* 37 (1989): 52–60.

————. "To Pardon or Not to Pardon?: North African Montanism and the Forgiveness of Sins." In *Studia Patristica*, vol. 36, ed. M. F. Wiles and E. J. Yarnold, 375–86. Leuven: Peeters Press, 2001.

————. "'Will the Real Paraclete Please Speak Forth!': The Catholic-Montanist Conflict over Pneumatology." In *Advents of the Spirit: An Introduction to the Current Study of Pneumatology*, ed. Bradford E. Hinze and D. Lyle Dabney, 97–115. Marquette Studies in Theology, vol. 30, ed. Andrew Tallon. Milwaukee, Wis.: Marquette University Press, 2001

Telfer, W. "The Date of the Martyrdom of Polycarp." *Journal of Theological Studies* 3(1952): 79–83.

Teske, Roland. Introduction to Augustine, *The Nature and Origin of the Soul.* Translated by Roland J. Teske. In *The Works of Saint Augustine: A Translation for the 21ˢᵗ Century*, part 1, vol. 23, *Answer to the Pelagians*, ed. John E. Rotelle. Hyde Park, N.Y.: New City Press, 1995.

Tilley, Maureen. "The Passion of Perpetua and Felicity." In *Searching the Scriptures*, vol. 2, *A Feminist Commentary*, ed. Elisabeth Schüssler Fiorenza, 829–58. London: SCM Press Ltd., 1995.

Trevett, Christine. "Fingers up Noses and Pricking with Needles: Possible Reminiscences of Revelation in Later Montanism." *Vigiliae Christianae* 49 (1995): 258–69.

————. *Montanism: Gender, Authority, and the New Prophecy.* Cambridge: Cambridge University Press, 1996.

Trigg, J. W. "Martyrs and Churchmen in Third-Century North Africa." In *Studia Patristica*, vol. 15:1, ed. Elizabeth A. Livingstone, 242–46. Berlin: Akademie-Verlag, 1984.

Tucker, Ruth A., and Walter Liefeld. *Daughters of the Church.* Grand Rapids: Zondervan, 1987.

van Beek, Cornelius Johannes Maria Joseph, ed. Introduction to *Passio sanctarum Perpetuae et Felicitatis*. Nijmegen, Holland: Dekker and Van de Vegt, 1936.

———. Introduction to *Passio sanctarum Perpetuae et Felicitatis*. Bonn: Peter Hanstein, 1938.

von Campenhausen, Hans. "Bearbeitungen und Interpolationen des Polykarpmartyriums." In *Aus der Frühzeit des Christentums: Studien zur Kirchengeschichte des ersten und zweiten Jahrhunderts.* Tübingen: J. C. B. Mohr [Paul Siebeck], 1963.

———. *Ecclesiastical Authority and Spiritual Power in the Church of the First Three Centuries.* Translated by J. A. Baker. London: A. and C. Black, 1969; reprint, Peabody, Mass.: Hendrickson Publishers, 1997.

———. *The Fathers of the Latin Church.* Translated by Mandred Hoffman. London: Adam and Charles Black, 1964.

von Franz, Marie-Louise. *Passio Perpetuae: Das Schicksal einer Frau zwischen zwei Gottesbildern.* Zurich: Daimon Verlag, 1982.

———. *The Passion of Perpetua.* Translated by Elizabeth Welsh. Jungian Classics Series, vol. 3. Irving, Tex.: Spring Publications, 1980.

Waszink, J. H., ed. *Quinti Septimi Florentis Tertulliani De Anima.* Amsterdam: J. M. Meulenhoff, 1947.

Weinrich, William C. *Spirit and Martyrdom: A Study of the Works of the Holy Spirit in Contexts of Persecution and Martyrdoms in the New Testament and Early Christian Literature.* Washington, D.C.: University Press of America, 1981.

Wypustek, Andrzej. "Magic, Montanism, Perpetua, and the Severan Persecution." *Vigiliae Christianae* 51 (1997): 276–97.

Index of Modern Authors

Subject Index

The New Prophecy & "New Visions" was designed and composed in Bell MT by Kachergis Book Design of Pittsboro, North Carolina. It was printed on 60# Natures Natural paper and bound by Thomson-Shore, Dexter, Michigan.